People and Places
Lost estates of Highgate, Hornsey and Wood Green

Dedicated to the memory of
Cecil Harris
Reginald Aldir
Donald Fishlock
George Halse
Molly Land
Frederick Mitchell
Ralph B. Pugh
M. Ruth Rogers
Jack Solley
Reginald W.A. Smith
and to all those who have helped
the *Hornsey Historical Society*
in its first twenty-five years

People and Places
Lost estates of Highgate, Hornsey and Wood Green

researched and
written by ten contributors and
edited by Joan Schwitzer

HORNSEY HISTORICAL SOCIETY

Cover picture: (1) A Georgian mansion in the northern environs of London: The Priory, Hornsey, as shown in John Hassell's *Picturesque Rides and Walks . . . 30 miles round the British Metropolis* (1817)

Published 1996
by Hornsey Historical Society
    The Old Schoolhouse
    136 Tottenham Lane
    London N8 7EL

ISBN 0 905794 17 6

Designed and typeset by Mike Hazeldine (0181-340 5446)
Printed by J.G. Bryson (Printer) Ltd., 156-162 High Road, London N2 9AS

List of subscribers

Peter Barber
Neil Barnes
A.R.J. Batterbury
Shirley Baxter
Pat and Gerry Brazier
Alan Champion
H.K.R. Clarke
Barbara Connell
Peter Curtis
John Davis
Matthew Day
The Dell Family
Stephen Dodgson
R.F. Doe
Tom and Ann Doig
Brian Don
Alan Dumayne
Colin Edwards
E.H.J. Edwards
Joan Elmey
Sylvia Fenton
Mrs. Muriel Fielder
Richard Fleet
Mrs Edna C.M. Ford, MBE
Vivienne Forrest
Bob Fowler
Prof. Frederick A. Fryer
Mrs. Ada Gang-Devi
Hugh Garnsworthy
Albert H. George
Mrs. Beryl Gollance
Mrs. Beryl Gore
Brenda Griffith-Williams
Mrs. Mary I. Groves
Roy Hidson
Muriel Hills
Mr. and Mrs. D.L. Hoy
Elizabeth Israel
Hilda Johnston
Prof. Hugh K. King
Peter Land
A.W.A. Leigh

Pauline P. Lewis
John Lynch
Mr. W.H. McBryde
Rachael Macdonald
Ludovic A. McRae
Alison Maddock
Mr. and Mrs. J.M. Marley
Stanley Marsden
Arthur Newstead
John Newstead
Derek and Jo Owen
Janet Owen (Mrs.)
Mrs. M.P. Page
Jeanne Parker (née Willats)
John C. Peach
George W.C. Peacock
Christine Perelman
Ruth Phillips
Albert Pinching
Diane Pink
W.T. Rees
Anthony Richardson
Eileen Ring
Kathy Roberts
Herbert Robins
Paul Rogers
Dr. M.J. Rowe
Dr. A. Eleri Rowlands
Jill Salmon
M.B. Smith (Edinburgh)
Winifred Stewart
D.A. Stokes
Isobel and Malcolm Stokes
R.H. Thompson
Joy Tomkins
Roy Tremlett
Eric Vogel
Anne M. Watson
Joyce Webster
Freda Wilson
Hilda and Don Wright

Abbreviations

BCM	Bruce Castle Museum (Haringey archives), Tottenham
BNL	British Newspaper Library, Colindale
BL	British Library, London WC1
BM	British Museum (Department of Prints & Drawings)
DNB	*Dictionary of National Biography*
FHL	Friends' House Library, Euston Road, London NW1
Gdl.	Guildhall Library, Aldermanbury, London EC2
GLRO	Greater London Record Office, Northampton Road, London EC1
HLSI	Highgate Literary & Scientific Institution, London N6
HUDC	Hornsey Urban District Council
H & FPJ	*Hornsey & Finsbury Park Journal* (later, *Hornsey Journal*)
HHS	Hornsey Historical Society, Tottenham Lane, London N8
HJ	*Hornsey Journal*
H. Lib.	Hornsey (Central) Library, Haringey Park, London N8
HSB	Hornsey School Board
ILN	*Illustrated London News*
LMAS	London & Middlesex Archaeological Society, Museum of London, EC2
Marcham	*Court Rolls of the Bishop of London's Manor of Hornsey 1603-1701* (1929), ed. by W. McBeath Marcham & Frank Marcham
MDR	Middlesex Deeds Register (at GLRO)
NPG	National Portrait Gallery
OED	*Oxford English Dictionary*
O.S.	Ordnance Survey
PRO	Public Record Office
RCHME	Royal Commission on the Historical Monuments of England, Blandford Street, London W1
RIBA	Royal Institute of British Architects (Drawings Collection), Portman Square, London W1
SH	Somerset House (Wills), Strand, London WC2
TMCR	Tottenham Manor Court Rolls (at BCM)
VCH	*Victoria History of the County of Middlesex*, University of London

Contents

List of illustrations

31. Winchester Hall and its environs to the north, 1864 (O.S. 1:2500, 1st ed.)
32. Winchester Hall from the south (print of drawing by W.W. West, HLSI)
33. The garden side of Winchester Hall (HLSI)
34. John William Jeakes (1817-74) (HLSI)
35. The entrance hall of Winchester Hall (BM Potter Collection, VII,38)
36. The garden of Winchester Hall, 1873 (BM Potter Coll., VII, 36)
37. Park House and its environs, 1864 (O.S. 1:2500, 1st ed.)
38. Former property adjacent to Park House, 1861 (MS12385, Gdl.)
39. Park House as an asylum c.1849 (contemporary print, HLSL)
40. Dr Andrew Reed (1787-1862), founder of the Asylum for Idiots
      (engraving by J. Thomson from painting by Wildman, 1829; NPG)
41. Christina Rossetti (1830-94) (copy of drawing in BM Dept. of Prints &
                                                       Drawings, NPG)
42. Southwood House estate in 1870 (O.S. 1:2500, 1st ed.)
43. General George Wade (1673-1748) (HLSI)
44. Section through Southwood House
                  (RIBA drawing for London Society, RCHME)
45. Southwood House c.1940 (*Saturday Book*, 1944)
46. The Limes and other Muswell Hill mansions in 1894 (O.S. 1:2500, 2nd ed.)
47. Bath House, Muswell Hill (GLRO, F47)
48. The Limes c.1888 (North Middlesex Photographic Society collection,
                                                       No.632)
49. Richard Marshall (1780-1863) (BCM, F.W. Draper slide collection)
50. The Elms in 1880 (BL Map Room, 137.a.ll.vol.2, no.3)
51. Fortismere c.1890 (RCHME)
52. Charles Edward Mudie (1818-1890) (contemporary line drawing)
53. Sales plan of Woodlands, 1890 (BCM)
54. Woodlands in the early 1860s, from John F. Lehmann, *Ancestors and
                  Friends* (Eyre &Spottiswoode, 1962)
55. Nina and Frederick Lehmann, c. 1852 (from R.C. Lehmann, *Memories of
                  half a century*, 1908)
56. Woodlands from the road, c.1888 (BCM)
57. Stapleton Hall and the farmland, 1870 (O.S. 1:2500, 1st ed.)
58. Enamel badge of 1773 for a member of the 'Corporation of Stroud
                  Green' (Victoria & Albert Museum)
59. Stapleton Hall and farmhouse c. 1820 (painting in BCM)
60. Stapleton Hall in club use, 1911 (N. Middlesex Photo. Society Coll.)

Acknowledgements

The contributors would like to thank the staff of the various libraries and archives in which they have worked for their help and understanding over the project, especially Rita Read of Bruce Castle Museum, Isobel Stokes of Hornsey Library, Gwynnedd Gosling of the Highgate Literary & Scientific Institution and Joseph Keith and Tabitha Driver at Friends' House Library. They are also very grateful to Peter Curtis for his advice and encouragement at all stages of production, and to Mike Hazeldine and Ruth Phillips for their unstinting help.

They acknowledge with thanks permission from the Trustees of the following institutions to reproduce illustrations from their collections:

Cornwall Record Office	(3)
Jewish Museum London	(4)
British Museum, Department of Prints & Drawings	(5, 8, 35, 36)
British Library, Department of Printed Books	(7)
British Library, Map Room	(50)
London Borough of Haringey	(1, 9, 14, 15, 16, 17, 24, 25, 28, 30, 48, 49, 53, 56, 59, 60)
Greater London Record Office	(12, 47)
Guildhall Library, London EC2	(6, 38)
Guildhall Library (Dean and Chapter of St. Paul's Cathedral Archive)	(22)
Library Committee of Britain Yearly Meeting of the Religious Society	(27)
Royal Horticultural Society, Lindley Library	(29)
Highgate Literary & Scientific Institution	(32, 33, 34, 39, 43)
National Portrait Gallery	(40, 41)
Royal Commission on the Historical Monuments of England	(44, 51)
Royal Institute of British Architects	(44)
Victoria & Albert Museum	(58)
David Higham Associates	(54)
Hutchinson (Publisher)	(45)

Introduction

In *An open elite?*[1] Lawrence Stone makes a distinction between the country houses or 'seats' of the aristocracy (the 'elite') in the period 1540-1880 and the houses in the country owned by professional men and merchants at that time. He was concerned solely with the first group in trying to answer the question which he afterwards took as the title of his book. He enquired into the family history of a representative sample of the landed gentry who had 'seats' to determine whether 'the elite' wished or were able to fend off would-be aspirants to their ranks from the monied middle classes. His conclusion was that on the whole the landed gentry kept their exclusiveness, thus challenging the widespread and long-standing belief that the aristocracy was always open to wealthy outsiders.[2] Properties not owned by 'the elite', with houses as splendid if not usually as large as aristocratic seats, often built within commuting distance of large towns[3], were left deliberately on one side.

Stone draws a distinction between the 'county nobility' and what he terms the 'parish gentry', *i.e.* leading figures in their own neighbourhood but not beyond. Very little research has hitherto been done into this section of society and the phrase 'parish gentry' may not be altogether appropriate. Not much thought has been given to the owners of mansions in the environs of the metropolis and other conurbations. This book, primarily a local history study, is an attempt to shed light on a few of the estates near to London where 'gentlemen's residences' stood, and which helped to shape subsequent urban development. These large family homes were called villas in the eighteenth century, but this would now be a misleading term since being debased by Victorian builders of small terraced houses. We have concentrated on 'lost' houses and vanished estates, on the principle that knowing what once existed but is no more is as important as tracing the story of survivors. 'Success' stories, as seen from a modern standpoint, are no criterion of special significance in the past. To neglect the vanished and forgotten is to distort history.

Twelve estates have been studied, all within the modern borough of Haringey, but before 1965 part of the old boroughs of Hornsey and Wood Green, which last named was itself once part of the Parish of Tottenham. This northern side of London, formerly rural Middlesex, was a favourite location for those whose professional or commercial interests lay in the City. Largely still forest in medieval times and used as hunting grounds by the lords of the manors, by the fifteenth century copyhold land was being acquired by non-resident purchasers in some of the burgeoning settlements. One of these and probably the earliest to attract this kind of attention was

Tottenham, reached by the Roman high road from London bridge, with its ancient parish church and manor house (Bruce Castle) and its manifold opportunities for wildfowling by the River Lea. Another was Hornsey, renowned for its peaceful pastoral landscape by the Moselle, and after 1613 by the New River, also with a village and parish church but near main roads to and from the City. The movement to acquire land outside London gathered pace from the mid sixteenth century, when law and order had been established in the countryside by a strong central government. In Muswell Hill, which offered spectacular views, manorial holdings and conventual land (after the dissolution of religious houses) had been parcelled out for 'suburban retreats' by Stuart times. Highgate on the south-east extremity of the Parish of Hornsey was prized for its lofty 'healthfull'[4] situation and the convenience of the main North road from the City running through it (since the fourteenth century). Here the Earl of Dorchester, Lord Cornwallis, and Sir Roger Cholmeley and other wealthy and titled professional men and merchants built a series of splendid houses round the central plateau. A few remain to this day: Lauderdale House built for an Elizabethan Master of the Mint, Cromwell House erected 1638, and, of a later era, Fairseat (now Channing Junior school) built for a Victorian Lord Mayor.

The twelve chapters examine houses similar to these, with large gardens and several acres attached so that the household could be virtually self-supporting. These were not mere imitations on a smaller scale of the seats of the aristocracy with their home farms, undertaken for purely social reasons. One of the motives for investment in property, apart from personal inclination, was a combination of financial security and political advantage. For centuries land was the obvious choice for the secure reposal of money and the prospect of future gain, and before 1832 any claim to political power or public office depended upon its possession. In the seventeenth and eighteenth centuries most of the houses in this study, having outlived their initial usefulness, were not lived in by their owners but were let. Many owners had land and houses elsewhere and suburban property changed hands frequently.

In the late eighteenth century, with increasing national prosperity, new purchasers came forward who were largely self-made men, with no private incomes or family estates to draw on, to whom life in a rural setting was a goal in itself, provided it was within reach of their office or workshop. The urge to remove the family from the confines of the city, with its unclean water and pervasive smells, was overpowering. Owner-occupiers in Victorian times were to create for themselves and their families a retreat from the harsh realities of an industrialising Britain, a rural idyll with elaborate gardens and buttercup meadows sustained by plentiful and cheap labour.

The idyll was not to last, no more than for the aristocracy. The 1880s were the beginning of the end. In the Victorian era new avenues of investment had opened up, notably railways, that largely replaced land and houses. Moreover land lost its function as a voting qualification. Land near the rapidly expanding metropolis was especially vulnerable. Tempting offers from developers were made and with improved communications it was possible for those who wished to continue to live in the country to buy a mansion further afield – in Hertfordshire or Surrey, for example. Eight of the twelve houses in this study disappeared between 1882 and 1902. One went nearly two hundred years before, but by accident. Two survived, one by institutional use, until after World War Two. Only one has remained, shorn of its land and in another guise.

The march of bricks and mortar was too strong to resist, except in rare cases, as at Muswell Hill where urbanisation was delayed for several decades. The impression left is of the weakness of the infant conservation movement in the late nineteenth century and of the impotent fury with which the destruction of trees, greensward, and ancient landmarks was witnessed when the mansions came down, not to mention the passing of a way of life.

References

1. *An open elite? England 1540-1880* by Lawrence Stone and Jeanne C. Fawtier Stone (OUP, 1st ed. 1984, abridged ed. 1986)

2. W.D. Rubinstein on "Businessmen into landowners: the question revisited" in *Land and society in Britain, 1700-1914. Essays in honour of F.M.L. Thompson*, ed. by Negley Harte and Roland Quinault (Manchester U.P., 1996) queries details of the Stones's methodology but largely endorses the conclusions of *An open elite?*

3. For further references to this phenomenon see Roy Porter, *English Society in the eighteenth century* (Penguin 1982) and F.M.L. Thompson, *The rise of respectable society. A social history of Victorian Britain 1830-1900* (Fontana, 1988).

4. So called by John Norden, the Elizabethan map-maker, in his *Speculum Britanniae*

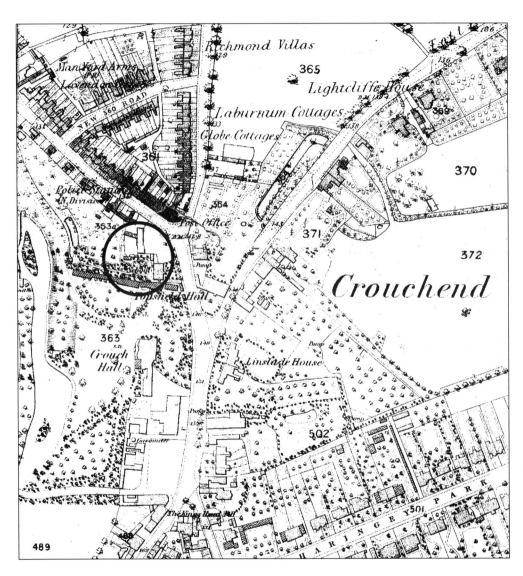

2. Crouch End in 1864. The Academy ("School" on the map, circled) was centrally located by the point where the Broadway forked west to Muswell Hill and north to Tottenham.

14

From Grene Lettyce to Academy: A Crouch End house 1613-1882

The context: Early Crouch End

When trying to make one's way through the traffic, shops and general bustle of modern Crouch End Broadway on a Saturday, it is difficult to believe that it once formed part of a sparsely populated rural manor of thickly wooded hills, scrubby wasteland and broad, often waterlogged valleys.[1] Among the very few signs of the hand of man was an extensive cultivated area lying at the foot of the hills in the south-west of the district, occupied by a handful of families. The open fields there were dissected by a minor track that branched at this point to run south, by two routes, to London, and north and northeast by two further routes towards Muswell Hill and Hornsey village respectively. By the beginning of the fourteenth century the track marked the boundary between two agricultural estates. The farm to the west (on the left coming from London), called Rowledge, was directly owned by the Bishop of London, who was lord of the manor of Hornsey. It extended westwards and uphill from the track all the way to what is now Queen's Wood and was bordered by other, smaller estates roughly following the line of Crescent, Avenue and Claremont Roads to the south and Cranley Gardens to the north. A sizeable portion of the farm still survives as the Crouch End Playing Fields. The estate, called Topsfield, that faced Rowledge Farm on the other, eastern, side of the track (on the right coming from London) may have existed as early as 1066. It then covered about 300 acres and extended from what is now Middle Lane southwards and uphill (hence, presumably the name Topsfield) to the boundary with Islington and eastwards to what is now Ferme Park Road. By 1374 it had gained a considerable degree of autonomy from the manor of Hornsey and had evolved into the sub-manor of Topsfield or Broadgates[2] with its own lord of the (sub-) manor.[3] As such it had its own mini-judicial system for controlling land tenure and dealing with minor legal infringements and its own form of medieval dues.

The marking of the precise, agreed boundaries between the Rowledge and Topsfield estates was accordingly of considerable importance. It was presumably for this purpose[4] that a cross was erected almost certainly on the triangular site of the present-day Clock Tower, perhaps at the turn of the fourteenth and fifteenth centuries. The cross ultimately gave its name to 'Crouche End', which is first recorded in 1465.[5] It probably never had any particular religious significance,[6] nor could it ever have served as a market cross, since the district had no market. In an age of almost general illiteracy it is inconceivable that it could have been a signpost. Boundary crosses, which often stood at crossroads, were however relatively commonplace in the later middle ages and particularly in the fifteenth century.[7] The existence round the corner from the Clock Tower of Freeze Lane, the earlier name for Middle Lane, strengthens the case for the cross having been a boundary cross: 'freeze' may be a corruption of the word 'frith', which can mean a hedge strengthened by wattle, marking an estate boundary[8].

The discovery of sculptured fragments, apparently from its base, during the excavation of the public lavatories in Crouch End in 1925 suggests that the original cross was elaborately carved.[9] If so, it would have resembled the handsome boundary crosses to be seen in two of the Limbourg brothers' illustrations in the well-known early fifteenth-century prayerbook, the *Tres Riches Heures* of the duc de Berry.[10] Eventually, however, the cross crumbled away and was probably replaced by a humble wooden boundary cross resembling that to be seen on a mid-sixteenth century Cornish estate plan.[11]

3. A medieval boundary cross of the type likely to have been used near the the manor house in Crouch End

From the start the cross stood within sight of houses. By the late fourteenth-century, and perhaps earlier, the manor house of Topsfield manor lay possibly but by no means certainly (since the homes of the lords of the manor varied over time) on the land, immediately to the north of today's Clock Tower, that was later to be occupied by Topsfield Hall. That building, which was probably the one 'juxta [or near] Highgate' destroyed by rebels during the Peasants Revolt of 1381,[12] belonged to the Maynard family. They were the London merchants, and lords of Topsfield Manor, who gave their name to Maynard Street, now Park

Road: a name which only just survives as the original, now second name of a public house on the corner of Lynton Road. The other buildings in Crouch End were humble, probably including Rowledge farmhouse (approximately on the site of Budgens on the Broadway) and a few cottages that served ale to passing travellers.

Since the late thirteenth-century, when the new road up Highgate Hill and through the Bishop of London's park had taken the bulk of the City of London's northbound traffic, Crouch End had been no more than a sleepy satellite or 'end' of Hornsey Village and lagged far behind Highgate and Hornsey Village (or 'Church End')[13] in population. Crouch End, like Muswell Hill but unlike Hornsey or Highgate, is missing from the first detailed printed map of south-east England, published by Christopher Saxton in the 1570s. It is, however, indicated on John Norden's map of Middlesex of 1594.

This was not only because the map was more detailed. In the years around 1600 several houses were built or rebuilt in Crouch End as fairly substantial summer residences for the families of London merchants. One was certainly a predecessor of Topsfield Hall, which is referred to as a 'newe house' in 1608 in the will of the then owner, William Ive.[14] Others were almost certainly Old Crouch Hall which stood on the Broadway on the site of Bank Buildings[15] and the building that is the subject of this chapter. Despite these signs of increasing popularity, throughout the seventeenth and eighteenth centuries Crouch End remained a quiet, though reputedly a healthy and picturesque, spot. Only after about 1725, when its layout is shown for the first time on a printed map,[16] is there any evidence of Crouch End being taken serious notice of by the wider world.

The house as a private residence 1578-1712
The building that was to become the Crouch End Academy occupied a little more than an acre of land lying approximately between what are now Crouch Hall Road and Shanklin Road along Park Road. Its predecessor, described in 1578 as a cottage, the 'Grene Lettyce at Crowchende', with a barn, stables, orchard 'and a small close or backside adjacent to the same containing one acre' which was used as pasture,[17] could well have been an unlicensed, part-time alehouse. It was owned and run by rather humble local people: Thomas Marshall and William Birkett, a husbandman, until 1578, then by the somewhat wealthier Richard Borne, a Hornsey yeoman or farmer, who also owned what was probably the predecessor of Old Crouch Hall across the road.[18] Borne's widow, Anne, who inherited the land in 1581, had married a certain William Osborne by 1584 and the house and its estate then passed to Thomas Osborne (possibly her son or stepson) and, just before his death in 1612/3 to his son, another William Osborne. The Hornsey court rolls show that the Osbornes were a leading local farming family with extensive landholdings throughout Crouch End and Muswell Hill. Though William

Osborne junior was described as a warden of the Tower of London,[19] he was not in the same class as the prosperous city merchants who were showing an increasing interest in the neighbourhood.

It is possible that the Osbornes may have rebuilt the cottage[20] shortly before William Osborne surrendered it to Richard Chambers in March 1613. Chambers was a wealthy city merchant and a member of the Girdlers' Company. The 8s 8d 'fine', or tax payable to the lord of manor for registration of the transfer of ownership, was as high as any that was subsequently to be paid suggesting that he had acquired more than a simple cottage. Since a basement room of the house had a shield with the arms and initials ('RcS')[21] of Chambers and his wife, and, beneath, the date '1613', the workmen employed by Chambers would also have had to work extremely quickly to complete the house within a year of purchase. It is more likely that the shield was part of the fitting out of an existing but newly-built house. Local legend on the subject of its construction does not help to date it more specifically since it referred cryptically to gossips who 'used to speak of the house as having been built by a kinsman of one of the old Bishops of Ely'.[22] With 11 hearths as of 1674, it counted as one of the larger houses in Hornsey. If overshadowed by the enormous mansion of the Marquess of Dorchester on the site of the Grove in Highgate Village, which had 33 hearths, Lauderdale House with 26, Cromwell House with 25 or the predecessor of Kenwood House with 24, it was about the same size as most of the spacious houses lining Highgate High Street, and the three other large houses facing onto Crouch End Broadway. Even Hornsey rectory only had six hearths and the Crouch End house had more hearths than any house in Hornsey Village apart from Brick Place which had 22. It was much larger than the cottages that predominated in the area and which had four or fewer fireplaces.[23]

Surviving photos of the early 1880s show a substantial timber-framed dwelling of three storeys with 'a warm-toned', tiled roof and three bays of large casement windows with elaborate frames which overhang the ground floor. It may originally have had small gables surmounting the windows.[24] In contrast to the street frontage, the sides and back of the house had few windows.[25] The closest surviving local parallel, though one storey lower, is Lauderdale House in Highgate which was built a few decades earlier also for a wealthy City merchant.[26] As was the case with Lauderdale House, the Crouch End house's timber and wattle frame may originally have been exposed. The gables would have been removed and weatherboarding that is so noticeable on surviving photographs installed in the middle of the eighteenth century, with the Ionic-pillared Georgian doorway and the three pillars supporting the overhang.

We have a good idea of the interior layout even though no detailed plan seems to have survived. The front door, which originally faced directly onto the 'waste' and the street, led into a small passage, with a small parlour on the right and a large room, which served as the hall and principal dining room, on the left.[27] At the end of the passage lay 'a noble carved staircase'[28] of rather massive proportions perhaps similar in type to the one that can still be seen in Cromwell House. Further back still were the kitchen, scullery and the small, secondary staircase leading to the servants' quarters in the attic. Accounts of the house shortly before its demolition speak of 'deep bay windows . . . and numerous airy and well-lighted chambers'. These lay on the first and second floors, both of which had six good sized rooms.[29] The outhouses lay behind and by the side – a little coach house in this position survived to the end. A comparison of the plan on the 1816 Enclosure Plan and the large scale Ordnance Survey maps of the 1860s suggests that a wing, containing most of the other outhouses, was demolished in the first half of the last century. The fact that the house was not more radically altered in the eighteenth and nineteenth-centuries probably reflects its later institutional use as a school. Had it been a private residence its owners might well have felt the urge to modernise – if they had had the money. The acre of pastureland stretched northwards along Maynard Street, which, thanks to neighbouring waste, was much wider than it is now. To the west there were 'picturesque views of trees, shrubs, hedges, uplands and haystacks' – of which echoes remain today in the views over the Crouch End Playing Fields from Shepherd's Hill and in the glimpses of Alexandra Palace and Park that can still be had from in front of the town hall lawn on Crouch End Broadway.

This probably accounted for the failure of the house to make good the social promise embodied in its size. Richard Chambers lived in the house –

Attractive though the house appeared, however, life there was frequently not as healthy as merchants in search of country air might have hoped. The house lay at the lowest point of Crouch End – itself one of the lowest points in Hornsey. After heavy rains water cascaded down towards the house from Crouch Hill and Crouch End Hill to the south and from Rowledge Farm to the west. Maynard Street was reduced to an impassable quagmire. Worse still, residents higher up the hill tried to divert the streams of water from their own premises, by 'makeing of dams to turn the water and all the filth and muck which comes down the highways into a ditch close by the dwelling house . . . whereby the foundacons of [the] said house is not only in dainger to rott and decay but alsoe the said mucke and filth which continually lyes there is very offensive to the health of [the residents]'.[30] It was a recurrent problem despite increasingly desperate efforts by the manorial court to force the occupants to do something about it: in April 1693, the house's then owner was being threatened with a £1 fine unless he personally scoured the 'several ditches against [his] lands at Crouchend and Maynards Street'.[31]

This probably accounted for the failure of the house to make good the social promise embodied in its size. Richard Chambers lived in the house –

presumably only during the summers – until his death in the closing months of 1632, when he left the house to his widow Susanna. She herself died in 1641, founding a charity, based on income from a cottage on the site of the present Linden Mansions on Hornsey Lane, to provide bread for the poor of Hornsey.[32] Their eldest son, the more famous Richard Chambers, inherited the house but did not occupy it, preferring to live in Brick Place in Hornsey Village which he had acquired shortly before his father's death in 1632.[33] The tenant through the political turmoil of the 1640s, 1650s and 1660s was Humphrey Holcombe, a London citizen whose principal home was in the parish of St Mary Aldermanbury. The parish register records the births and deaths of his numerous children between 1648 and 1664[34] and it was probably considerations of their precarious health that led him, rather unwisely, to rent the house in Crouch End. Presumably he did not have the money to rent a house of equal size in the healthier environs at the top of Highgate Hill.[35] Holcombe remained in occupation while ownership of the house passed, in 1653, from Richard Chambers junior to his nephew Abraham Chambers, a barrister who was son of another Abraham, a London alderman, and in 1665 to Abraham's brother, Monox. By the later 1660s Monox himself was occupying the house until it passed in 1669 to Richard Craddock, a City gentleman, who was married to Monox's cousin, Susanna, a daughter of Richard Chambers junior, who had died in 1658.[36] Craddock was a wealthy man with property in Bermondsey and manors in Durham,[37] but he seems to have lived in Crouch End, for all its discomforts, for most of his adult life. Craddock may have had an interest in education since in 1686 he was elected a governor of Highgate School (a privilege reserved to residents of Highgate and its vicinity) and in his will of 14 May 1712 he left a ring worth 20 shillings to each of his fellow-governors as well as £10 to the poor of Hornsey.[38]

Crouch End Academy 1714 (?)-1882
Most previous statements relating to the Crouch End Academy have implied that the school was founded in the 1680s – an impression fostered by its last principal.[39] It has been assumed that its founder was one John Yeo, a Hornsey resident since at least 1683 who died in 1711.[40] In May 1686, described as a school master licensed by the Bishop of London, he was excused from holding the office of a headman in Hornsey manor because 'he hath a considerable number of scholars the major part of whom are boarders in his house'.[41] There is no evidence to suggest that Yeo leased Craddock's house in Crouch End, however, and he appears in the Hornsey court rolls as owner (or, strictly speaking, copyhold tenant) of property in Hornsey village, quite distinct from Craddock's in Crouch End.[42] It could be that Yeo's eighteenth-century successors eventually leased the house and that in the now-lost records of the school, he was regarded as its founder. The founder

20

of the school might or, however, equally might not have been another teacher such as one George Spragg, who is also recorded as having kept a school in Hornsey in 1686.[43]

A little later the calligrapher and mathematician Humphry Johnson (1690-c.1724) had a boarding school at Hornsey, where he died.[44] He is a more likely candidate than the others as founder of what became the Crouch End Academy. His dates approximate more closely to those given in the earliest surviving references to the school's beginnings, particularly since as late as 1713, when he compiled a writing manual entitled *Youth's Recreation*, he was apparently still teaching at Old Bedlam Court without Bishopsgate in the City.[45] Moreover between 1714 and his death in 1742 across the road from the Craddocks' dwelling, in the house at the angle of what is now Park Road and Middle Lane,[46] lived precisely the sort of man who could well have known Johnson, and who would have had the influence to get him established in Crouch End. Though almost forgotten now, Samuel Buckley was the King's Printer, a publisher in his own right, and a correspondent of such leading literary lights as the essayist, Joseph Addison, and Alexander Pope. He was also on the fringes of government as editor of the government's official newspaper, *The London Gazette*.[47]

In 1722 Richard Craddock's son, William, sold his Crouch End house to Anthony da Costa (c. 1676-1747).[48] Da Costa had been partly brought up in Cromwell House in Highgate, which his father had acquired as a summer residence in 1675, and was to live there following his mother Leonore's death in 1727. Cromwell House had a 19 acre estate that extended eastwards down the hill as far as today's Claremont Road[49] and the house in Crouch End would have been clearly visible from there, so he may well have been aware of the house's existence long before he bought it. Anthony da Costa, a Jewish merchant with interests particularly in the East Indian, Spanish and Russian markets, was one of the richest men of his time.[50] In 1662, his father Alvaro had escaped persecution in Portugal by coming to England as a page in the suite of Charles II's bride, Catherine of Braganza, and the family had long enjoyed covert royal protection.[51] Despite lamenting in his Will that he had been 'a very great sufferer' from the South Sea Crash of 1720, Anthony still had £31,331 of East India stock and other investments four years later.[52] However it may have been more than the prospect of rents that led him to buy the house in Crouch End. That he had an interest in learning can be inferred from his election as a Fellow of the Royal Society in 1736.[53] His wife (and cousin) Catherine da Costa (1678-1756), who had been born in Somerset House and named after Catherine of Braganza, was something of a blue stocking. Voltaire himself recorded that she was more than able to hold her own in a theological conversation over dinner with him in London in 1726[54] and she was a painter of miniatures, a skill she had been taught by Bernard Lens II[55], a tutor to the royal family. It is likely that they both knew

4. Abraham da Costa, aged 10, painted by his mother, a noted miniaturist.
On his father's death in 1747 he became owner of the Crouch End Academy.

Samuel Buckley. The purchase and possible investment in the school may thus have been in part a reflection of the couple's scholarly and charitable interests since they are unlikely to have gained a substantial income from the house.[56]

On Anthony's death, his only son Abraham (1704-1760) succeeded as owner of the house. He continued as owner even after selling Cromwell House in 1749. Abraham was a rather tragic figure. Though healthy enough to go to university at Leiden as a youth (English universities were then closed to all but Anglicans), he became 'deprived of the use of his limbs by the palsy'[57] (possibly Parkinson's Disease?) and unable to look after himself, dying unmarried 'on Friday, 1st February 1760, about 1 o'clock at night of a lingering decay and the stone',[58] still owner of the Crouch End building.

It was in the period of the da Costas' ownership that we have the first firm evidence of the Crouch End house being used as a school. One Robert Lovell, who died intestate on 21 December 1734 in his seventy-eighth year was simply described on his tombstone in Hornsey churchyard as 'School Master of this Parish', but his wife, Jane, who is buried with him and who died in her seventy-fourth year on 7 October 1741 described herself in her Will as, more specifically 'of Crouchend in Hornsey, schoolmistress'.[59] Her heir and kinsman, John Lee (who paid for the Lovells' monument) had probably been helping to run the school from at least the mid-1720s, as apparently had his father of the same name before him. In 1760 Lee bought the premises from the executors of Abraham da Costa.[60] It must be likely that he and the Lovells had previously tenanted the house from the da Costas and, if so, it is they who, according to tradition, acted as involuntary hosts to Dick Turpin when he took refuge in their grounds during more than one of his escapades.[61] John Lee bequeathed the Crouch End building, with his East India stock, to his daughter Elizabeth Cooke, widow of John Cooke, a coffeeman of St Dunstans in the West, Fleet Street, on his death in 1769.

Her daughter, Elizabeth Plaskett and her son and grandchildren continued to own the school until 1808 as absentee landlords.[62]

A two-storeyed, five-bayed brick annexe was eventually built for the school. Its ground floor contained classrooms, and there was a refectory on the first floor, one end of which was partitioned to provide sleeping quarters for up to four full-time assistant teachers.[63] The building was aligned with but set back from, and to the north of, the main house, where the principal, his family and the pupils lived, and faced Maynard Street. It is difficult to say when it was built, except that it was 'of much later date'[64] than the main building. Its style, with its Dutch-style gables, was characteristic of the mid-seventeenth-century. It must, however, have been built after 1674, when the property was listed as having only eleven hearths (corresponding to the main house). There are no hints in the Hornsey court rolls of building activities between then and 1700. The cartographic evidence is uncertain before the early nineteenth century, when the wing is clearly to be seen in the Hornsey enclosure map of 1816 and, a trifle more ambiguously, in the Ordnance Surveyors' drawings of slightly earlier.[65] The eighteenth-century printed maps showing Crouch End in any detail, those by Warburton (1725) and Rocque (1746), are less clear.[66] Rocque's map does, however suggest that the wing existed by then. The school wing's casement windows, which went out of fashion from about 1700[67], would suggest that it was built very early in the eighteenth-century. It may be significant that the gateway extension that Anthony da Costa or his father Alvaro added to Cromwell House was also surmounted by a still-surviving, and equally archaic Dutch gable, albeit of a different design to those over the wing in the Crouch End house.[68]

The tenant and schoolmaster in 1780 was one John Davison.[69] He may be the same as the mathematician and schoolmaster John Davison who was active in London and its neighbourhood between about 1760 and 1790.[70] In 1784 Davison was succeeded by Nathaniel Norton (1738-1806).[71] He was evidently a kindly man of great ability, held in respect by his contemporaries and still remembered a century later. His portrait, showing 'a grave, pleasant-looking old English gentleman', hung in the school until it was sold for the last time.[72] Nothing more has been discovered about him.[73] In the 1790s, however, he employed two assistant teachers or 'ushers' who are better known.

The first was John Bewick (1760-1795), the younger brother and pupil of the wood engraver, Thomas Bewick.[74] Since 1786, John had worked as an engraver at Clerkenwell Green, but, with the onset of tuberculosis, he 'found he could not pursue . . . close confinement, on which account he engaged to teach drawing at the Hornsey Academy, then kept by Mr. Nathaniel Norton, which obliged him to keep a pony to ride backwards and forwards, thus dividing his time between his work office in London and the school for some years'.[75] In October 1793 he finally 'moved down to Crouch

5. Crouch End in 1800 – the earliest known view. A watercolour by John Bewick, younger brother of the wood engraver, Thomas Bewick. The pencilled coach and horses may have been intended as a tribute to the local coachmaster and his sister with whom the artist was friendly. The Academy is on the left, beyond the stack and barn, Topsfield Hall in the middle distance behind trees, and Broadway Chapel on the right.

End',[76] apparently to a house just a little to the north of the Academy. One of his watercolours, now held by the British Museum, seems to show the building, Bewick's pony and the back of the school, from across the little pond on the west side of the one-acre field.[77] Since John Bewick was a supernumerary teacher, he never actually lived in the teachers' quarters in the school. Drawing was an optional extra subject for the pupils and, as he himself wrote to his brother in December 1791, 'I attend twice a week to teach drawing'.[78] The supposedly healthy air of Hornsey and what John considered its 'most delightful charming and rural situation only one Hour's walk to London where you may one day unite all the Pleasures Conveniences & the Bustle of the Great City with the sweet retirement of the Rural Village'[79] were, however, and perhaps not surprisingly in view of what has been said above, of no avail. Having left for Northumberland in a vain attempt to recover his health in the early summer of 1795, he died there that December. Despite his great skill as a wood engraver, mainly for woodblock illustrations in children's books,[80] the surviving watercolours suggest he had little talent as a draughtsman of larger pictures. His allegories and watercolours of fish and animals are competent, but his views, including one of Hornsey village and another of Crouch End – the earliest view yet known – are clumsy though not without charm.[81]

The second teacher employed by Norton was a young English-born graduate of Aberdeen University – possibly the only graduate to have taught in the Academy. John Grant (1771-1846) must have started teaching in Crouch End by August 1792 when he witnessed Nathaniel Norton's Will.[82] He was eventually to make a name for himself as a literary critic and author of Latin and English grammars 'more than one of which proved popular and useful in collegiate establishments' – though there were accusations of plagiarism.[83] During the brief period (1808-1813) when the premises were owned by Norton's widow and children (Rachel Norton having purchased them), he is described as the tenant.[84] So he probably succeeded Norton as principal of the school on the latter's retirement in about 1802.[85]

Grant was evidently well-known in the neighbourhood. He struck up a particular friendship with a fellow philologist, Dr. Alexander Crombie (1762-1840). Crombie ran a school in Highgate (on the site of Holly Terrace, West Hill) for a few years after 1797[86] and Grant dedicated his *Institutes of Latin Grammar* (1808) to him. According to accounts written 36 years after his death, Grant 'possessed good powers as a conversationalist. [He] was intimate with Sir Richard Phillips,[87] who resided at Holloway and it is believed [Grant] contributed to some of Phillips's periodicals. The recreation of Grant lay in presiding over a knot of quidnuncs and literary gossips who used to meet of an evening at the Highgate Gatehouse. Among the company used to be John Ogden, a press corrector and Shakespearian scholar; John Baptiste Noel, George Spalding, a watercolour artist,[88] Clio Rickman, a small poet and miscellaneous journalist;[89] Kenny Meadows, the Shakespearean artist;[90] Greaves, who had been a land steward in the service of the Duchess of St Albans and occasionally John Nicholls, a kinsman of the antiquary. George Cruikshank used to speak of the Gatehouse gatherings at which Grant the Hornsey schoolmaster presided, describing the meetings as pleasant and intellectual. Grant as he grew old used to ride on a donkey from Crouch-end to the Highgate tavern'.[91] Indeed, according to some reports, 'when a very old man, the services of the animal were superseded on more than one occasion by the shoulders of a faithful friend, who finding that the donkey was disabled for the errand, volunteered to do duty for it rather than that the infirm schoolmaster should be deprived of his nocturnal glass and gossip'.[92]

It is tempting to regard these informal gatherings as an intellectual

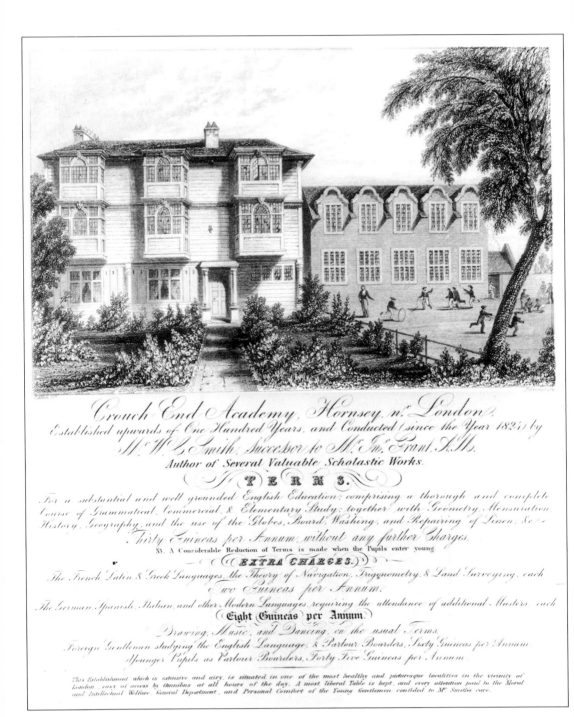

6. The prospectus of 1844, advertising a curriculum leading to a professional or commercial career

bridge between Coleridge and his coterie before 1832 and the Highgate Literary and Scientific Institution which was founded at a meeting held in the Gatehouse in 1839,[93] although Coleridge does not seem to have known Grant.[94] The discussions must certainly have been stimulating. Phillips and Rickman had been active republicans in the 1790s, and Rickman at least continued to venerate that revolutionary stormy petrel Tom Paine, whose biography he wrote. Grant, on the other hand, seems to have been a moderate Conservative, who lauded Crombie for being 'a hearty despiser of the cant of spurious liberalism'.[95]

Between about 1819 and 1824, Grant ran the Academy in association with a Suffolk man, William Smith.[96] If Grant provided intellectual input, Smith was evidently more adept as a businessman. It is thanks to an advert that he placed in the *Illustrated London News* of 13 July 1844 and a promotional leaflet which must have circulated at much the same time,[97] that we finally have detailed information about the school. It was a boarding school for boys. Both adverts have illustrations (one a woodcut, the other an aquatint) which show that the Academy altered little in the last forty years of its existence. It was described as 'spacious, the bedrooms airy, the playground large and dry and the walks in the fields most delightful', and was ' . . . situated in one of the most healthy and picturesque localities in the vicinity of London, easy of access by Omnibus at all hours of the day.[98] A most Liberal Table is kept and every attention paid to the Moral and Intellectual Welfare, General Deportment and Personal Comfort of the Young Gentlemen confided to Mr Smith's care'. 'The number of pupils generally averages between 40 and 50 and for the instruction of this limited number four tutors, besides the principal (exclusive of music) attend the house'.[99] Most of the boarders were accommodated in dormitories in the main house, but a few 'parlour boarders' who paid more, had their own rooms and dined with the principal and his family. It is said that the Academy was particularly favoured by officials of the East India Company, and the mention of John Lee's shares in the Company and the da Costas' links with it support this. The Academy also had a tradition of taking in 'Foreign Gentlemen studying the English language' – again at an extra charge – apparently mainly Frenchmen 'introduced originally, so it is said, by a Huguenot family at Stepney'.[100]

The Academy was of a very respectable size by the standards of the first half of the nineteenth century.[101] The census returns suggest that although the majority of the boys came from London, a sizeable proportion came from other parts of England. It was much bigger than the 'dame schools' and many of the other private and grammar schools of the time. Before its conversion into a public school after 1830, for instance, the Grammar School in Highgate only had 40 pupils. *The Hornsey Journal* was forced to admit in 1882 that 'it may not like Harrow, Eton and Winchester be able to put forth a roll of successful men as having been educated within its preciencts '(sic)[102], but it was no Dickensian institution. The school prided itself on its caring attitude to those in its charge. The advert in the *Illustrated London News* extolled the 'kind and parental treatment which [the boys] so liberally receive' with the staff making 'indefatigable exertions' to fulfil the parents' wishes 'under the mildest possible treatment'. Indeed it was emphasised that the school was 'most conveniently situated for parents desiring frequently to visit their children'.

The boys received a sound if not adventurous education which, as the last principal stated in an advert of about 1880, 'includes everything necessary for commercial or professional life.'[103] The boys were evidently not expected to continue to university. For 30 guineas a year (60 guineas for parlour boarders and foreign boys; 25 guineas for boys under ten), as well as 'Board, Washing, Repairing of Linen etc.', the boys received 'a substantial and well-grounded English Education comprising a thorough and complete Course of Grammatical, Commercial & Elementary Study together with Geometry, Mensuration, History, Geography and the use of the Globes'. Two guineas extra per subject brought them 'The French, Latin & Greek Languages, the Theory of Navigation, Trigonometry & Land Surveying' and an extra eight guineas for each language, 'The German, Spanish and Italian and other Modern Languages, requiring the Attendance of additional masters'.[104] In addition, instruction was available in drawing, music and dancing.

The presence of fifty or more boys and a small full-time staff must have made a considerable impact on the surrounding community. Washerwomen, gardeners, cobblers, a blacksmith (who was first recorded a short distance from the Academy, at the junction of Crouch and Crouch End Hills, in the late 1740s), handymen and casual domestic staff to cook and clean were certainly needed. The local hostelries would have found welcome custom among the staff and the visitors. A coachman, too, would have profited from the need of boys, teachers and parents (most of whom were probably not of the coach-keeping class) to go to and from town. It may be no coincidence that a girl to whom John Bewick formed a romantic attachment during his Crouch End years was the sister of the local coachmaster, Edward Vass, or (quite apart from Bewick's medical needs) that a close friend was Charles Brown, the local doctor. It is likely that the Academy gave considerable employment to the local physician and, one might guess, some even to local professional people who provided tuition in the additional subjects mentioned in the Academy's advertisements. It is probably no exaggeration to say that for much of the eighteenth and nineteenth centuries the Academy was the major source of employment (and, given the propensities of schoolboys) of life in the sleepy, largely residential hamlet of Crouch End.[105]

7. The Academy from the garden, 1882

For many decades the Academy was able to function seemingly unaltered even though by 1820 ownership of the Academy and its grounds had passed into the hands of builders. In 1813 the descendants of Nathaniel Norton had sold the site to George Henry Trimby who owned Samuel Buckley's former house at the corner of Middle Lane and Park Road. In 1816, as a result of the Hornsey Enclosure Act, Trimby acquired the strip of waste between the grounds of the Academy and Park Road. This brought the grounds of the Academy to their largest recorded extent, at nearly 2 acres. Three years later he sold out to a local bricklayer and plumber, John Proughton. Proughton lived in a large old house, Stone Cottage, which stood on former waste at right angles to the school block, and jutted out into Park Road.[106] The time was not yet ripe for sustained suburban development, however, despite the enthusiasm of other local builders, particularly of the Wright family, who had created a number of small houses and cottages throughout the hamlet from the 1780s.[107]

The Academy underwent few changes under William Smith's successors, Joseph Hatch (who was the principal between 1861-6), briefly William Vincent (1871), and in its final decade, Thomas Knight.[108] By the 1880s, however, the Academy was more commonly spoken of merely as

8. The Academy seen from Park Road in 1883

Crouch End School. There must also have been a sense that it was in decline. From 40 pupils aged 7 to 15 in 1841 and 43 in 1851, the censuses record that there were only 31 pupils in 1861, 32 in 1871 and 23 boarders in 1881.[109] In the same period the number of resident assistant teachers declined from 4 in 1841 (if Grant is included) and 1851 to 2 in 1861, 3 in 1871 and again 2 in 1881, while the number of servants (which always included a gardener) shrank from 5 to 2. In part this must have reflected the fact that at some point in the 1870s, the large one-acre field, one of the Academy's principal attractions, that had been attached to the house since its sixteenth-century beginnings, was sold off and added to the spacious gardens of 'Colonel' Bird, the occupant of the neighbouring Crouch Hall.[110]

Another index of decline can be detected in the age of the School's principals. The assistant teachers had always been young men in their twenties and thirties with careers elsewhere before them. By the 1860s, however, in contrast to earlier decades, the principals became alarmingly young, suggesting that, in face of competition from improving educational standards throughout the country, the school's reputation was no longer such as to attract mature headmasters. Where the Lovells had been well past middle age in the 1730s and 1740s and Norton 46 when he became principal, Joseph Hatch was 37 in 1861 and his successor William Vincent only 30 in 1871, though Thomas Knight (who had already been an assistant at the school in 1861) was 50 at the time that the school closed.

By the later 1870s the school was admitting day boys at prices from 4 guineas per term.[111] In part it may have been an attempt to keep up numbers in face of competition from free board schools and from the new, larger brand of public school, of which Highgate School was the most obvious example. In part it was also a response to the fact that Crouch End was at last becoming a built-up area and could provide a catchment area, even if in 1880 the Broadway looked much as it had decades earlier. The School's immediate setting to the north had begun to change. By the mid-1840s John Proughton's widow, Mary, and her three sons, the owners of the school, had built cottages on the former waste, immediately to the north of Stone Cottage. The street frontage of the Academy was reduced to 253 feet (just over 80 metres), though the building itself and the garden with its apple and pear trees and rural views were as pretty as ever and increasingly regarded as a relic of golden times past.[112] By the time Mrs Proughton died, aged 90, in November 1866, leaving her property to another builder, John Cowley, also of Stone Cottage, the existing buildings lining the east side of Park Road had been created. John Cowley bequeathed the site to his widow, to his builder son, another John Cowley and to his son-in-law James Davies of Bermondsey.

By 1880 it was obvious that the last relics of rural Crouch End and all the fields surrounding the former hamlet were on the brink of comprehensive urbanisation. Crouch Hall, the grand property next to the school, though still well-tended, was already lying empty and awaiting development.[113] Crouch End Board School, with accommodation for 604 pupils – and growing – had opened in 1877.[114] On 4 April 1882 Crouch End Academy and its grounds were sold for £2,500 to George Osborne Barratt of Japan House, Crouch Hill and within months they passed from him to the Imperial Property Investment Company, which was to become the major developer of the former Rowledge Farm area. The auctioneers had emphasised that the site was 'admirably suited for the creation of shops'. Detailed plans for the development of the Crouch Hall and Crouch End School estates, envisaging just this, were submitted to the Hornsey Local Board by the Cowleys acting with the Imperial Property Development Company early in November. The old building was demolished at the turn of the year.[115]

This was not quite the end of the story. Thomas Knight transferred with some of his pupils to Fairfield House on Tottenham Lane, where he remained until its demolition in 1894-5. From there he moved again to Norman House, on the Chestnuts estate just to the south of what is now

Priory Park. He continued to teach there until shortly after 1900, assisted by his son, Thomas Knight junior (b.1877), and his daughters Victoria (b.1866), Janette (b.1868) and Kate (b.1867) who 'acted as teachers and in various capacities'.[116] So insignificant was the scale of his activity by then, however, that the school is not listed with the other schools in the Hornsey directories.

The only physical reminder of the original Crouch End Academy today is an entrance at the end of an unnamed little passage which leads northwards from near the bottom of Crouch Hall Road. It stands on the former boundary between the Crouch Hall estate and the Academy. Beyond it, on what was once the orchard, there is a cobbled mews surrounded by garages and a path leading out onto the traffic jams of Park Road and the houses and shops that cover the Academy's once tree-lined street frontage.[117]

Peter Barber

References

1. The following paragraphs are based on the VCH, vol. vi, pp. 101, 105, 107.

2. 'Broadgates' may be linked to the Anglo-Saxon word 'gate' signifying road or way, in which case Broadgate could be the first reference to the Crouch End Broadway.

3. William McB. Marcham, 'The Village of Crouch End, Hornsey', *Transactions of the LMAS*. New Series, vii/3 (1937), pp.393-4; VCH, vol. vi, pp. 142-3. The [sub-] manor's size varied and by the late eighteenth century it had declined to a mere 50 acres in the immediate vicinity of Crouch End Broadway.

4. *cf.* Ben Travers, *The Book of Crouch End* (Buckingham: Barracuda Books, 1990), p.15.

5. Travers, p. 16. 'Crouch' can be compared to 'Crutched' as in 'Crutched Friars' in the City of London which also refers to a cross.

6. There was no chapel or church in the vicinity until late in the eighteenth century, when the Broadway Chapel (demolished 1925) is first recorded in a drawing by John Bewick (see p. 24) Though the cross lay by the side of a track which also led past the chapel of our Lady of Muswell/Mousewell (first mentioned in 1159), there is no evidence that the Crouch End cross was ever used as a wayside shrine by pilgrims. The Mousewell was never economically significant (*VCH*, vol. vi,

p. 108), suggesting that despite occasional visits by prominent figures such as a king of Scots, it was not much frequented.

7. Martin Warnke, *Political Landscape. The Art History of Nature* (London: Reaktion Books, 1995), pp. 9-12, 21-25.

8. *OED* and William Ravenhill & Oliver Padel, 'A Sixteenth-century map of West Down in Cardinham Parish, Cornwall', *Journal of the Royal Institution of Cornwall*, 1995, p.29. The southern part of Freeze (Middle) Lane marked the part of the western boundary of Topsfield Manor: see the plan of the Bishop of London's manor of Hornsey in William McB. Marcham & Frank Marcham (eds.), *Court Rolls of the Manor of Hornsey* 1603 -1701 (London: Grafton & Co., 1929) [henceforth referred to as 'Marcham'].

9. A diary entry in *The Muswell Hill Record* of 20 March 1925 recorded that during the construction of the public lavatories at Crouch End (presumably those beneath the Clock Tower), the workmen discovered 'a piece of carving in stone, with the figures of two people, one of whom is evidently a priest . . . at the back of it there is evidence that lead fillings had been used to keep it in position. It probably dates back to the 13th or 14th century'. I am most grateful to Ken Gay for bringing this newspaper reference to my attention.

10. Those illustrating the activities of March and the meeting of the Magi, reproduced e.g. in Franz Hattinger, *The Duc de Berry's Book of Hours* (Bern: Hallwag, 1962), plates III, XV.

11. Map of 'West Downe' (Cornwall Record Office, ARB 202/7) reproduced in Ravenhill & Padel, pp. 16-17.

12. I am grateful to my colleague Dr Andrew Prescott for this reference which derives from legal records in the Public Record Office utilised in his doctoral thesis, 'Judicial Records of the Rising of 1381' [Ph.D. thesis, University of London, 1984].

13. 'Church Ends', still known as such, are also to be found in Finchley and Hendon.

14 'Village of Crouch End', p. 400.

15. Though only firmly recorded from 1681, the architecture shown on early photos seems considerably older.

16. On John Warburton, 'A New and Correct Mapp of Middlesex, Essex and Hertfordshire with the Roads, Rivers, Sea Coasts Actually Surveyed'. The layout of Hampstead and Highgate had appeared on printed maps (by John Ogilby) all of 50 years earlier.

17. Marcham, 34 (1612), 159 (1669).

18. A messuage, garden, orchard and three acres of meadow in Topsfield manor ('Village of Crouch End', p. 421) and *cf.* 'Village of Crouch End', p.409.

19. Marcham, p. 34.

20. The court rolls refer to it as such and not as a tenement or messuage, even after its rebuilding.

21. *i.e.* 'Richard [and] Susanna Chambers': 'Village of Crouch End' , p.421. In accordance with standard seventeenth-century practice, as seen, for instance, on the private, token coinage, the letters almost certainly formed a pyramid, with the C at the top. Heraldic shields were common features in (particularly) the dining rooms of early seventeenth-century houses. Lauderdale House had some: Frederick Prickett, *History and Antiquities of Highgate* (Highgate, 1842), p.163; Peter Barber, Oliver Cox and Michael Curwen, *Lauderdale Revealed. A History of Lauderdale House, Highgate. The building, its owners and occupiers 1582-1993* (London: Lauderdale House Society, 1993), p. 64 citing inventory of 1685; and a couple, probably of the late 1630s, with the arms of the Sprignell family (the family of the younger Richard Chambers's first wife) survived in Cromwell House until a few years ago and are pictured in Philip Norman, *Cromwell House, Highgate*. Survey of London Monograph xii (London: LCC, 1926).

22. *H & FPJ* 23 April 1882. A check through the names of the bishops for the period 1550-1700 – which include Christopher Wren's father – has failed to disclose any link with names known to be associated with the house.

23. Percy W. Lovell & William McB. Marcham, *The Village of Highgate (The Parish of St. Pancras Part l)*, [Survey of London, volume xvii] (London: LCC, 1936), pp. 139-140; Marcham, pp. xiii-xiv.

24. I am grateful to Bridget Cherry for this suggestion.

25. Photographs of front and back are in the BM (Potter Collection, vol. 20, pp. 57-8); H.Lib. (North Middlesex Photographic Society collection); and in BCM.

26. *Lauderdale Revealed*, pp. 13-19.

27. *cf.* Lyndon F.Cave, *The Smaller English House. Its History and Development* (London: Hale, 1981), p.82. Prickett and Venables sale particulars, April 1882 (BM: Potter Collection, vol. 20, p. 53).

28. *H & FPJ* 23 April 1882. Also the source for the next quotation.

29. By 1882 the second floor also contained a bathroom and a WC and all the first and second-floor rooms were being used as bedrooms – with the second floor rooms being used presumably as dormitories for the boarders.

30. Hornsey Manor Court Rolls, April 1677 (Marcham, p. 178).

31. Marcham, p. 223.

32. Marcham, p. 99; Prickett, p. 92.

33. See pp. 44-47. Marcham, pp. 80-1.

34. 'Village of Crouch End', p. 422.

35. And see Peter Barber, 'Gambling in Wartime: the rise and fall of William Geere (1588/9-1652), *Camden History Review* 19 (1995), particularly p. 18.

36. Marcham, pp.122, 147,159; 'Village of Crouch End', p. 422.

37. 'Village of Crouch End', p. 423.

38. *Survey of London* xvii, p. 142; 'Village of Crouch End', p. 423. He died within the month and is buried in St Magnus Martyr Church in the City.

39. *VCH*, vol. vi, p. 196; 'Village of Crouch End', p. 426; *H & FPJ*, 23 April 1882; Thomas Knight's advert of about 1880 in BM Potter Collection. The advertising leaflet in the Guildhall Library (PR V HOR), probably of the 1840s, however, speaks more cautiously of 'upwards of One Hundred Years' and the 1844 advert in *the ILN* mentions that 'This establishment has now stood the test of public opinion and received the most liberal patronage for more than 130 years' – which would date its foundation as about 1712 – the year, we have seen, in which Richard Craddock died.

40. Marcham, p. 191; 'Village of Crouch End', p. 423.

41. Marcham, p. 201, n.l. 'Village of Crouch End', p. 423.

42. Marcham, p. 223. In an article in *the HJ* of 15 April 1932, Marcham suggested that Yeo' s establishment was on the site of what became the Nightingale Tavern.

43. *VCH*, vol. vi, p. 197.

44. Ambrose Heal, *English Writing-Masters, 1570-1800* (London, 1931), p. 66; VCH, vol. vi, p. 127. R.V.& P.S. Wallis, *Index of British Mathematicians 1700-1800* (Newcastle: Project for Historical Biobibliography, 1992).

45. One of the sentences that his pupils had to copy out was 'Writing, Arithmetick, Merchants Accounts are taught & youth Boarded by the Author'! There is a portrait of him as the frontispiece to his *New Treatise of Practical Arithmetick*.

46. 'Village of Crouch End', p. 433.

47. There are various letters and papers by him in the BL's Department of Manuscripts. Buckley was buried in St Mary's, Hornsey where his memorial inscription spoke of his 'having . . . discharged . . . offices of State . . . with Prudence, Fidelity and Gratitude to his Benefactors' until he 'Concluded his days in the Study of Letters and the enjoyment of Honest & Honorable Friendships'; Frederick Teague Cansick, *The Monumental Inscriptions of Middlesex with Biographical Notices and Description of Armorial Bearings* (London: Wertheimer, Lea & Co, 1875), p. 8.

48. 'Village of Hornsey', p. 423.

49. Norman, p. 62.

50. *Encyclopaedia Judaica*, vol. v, pp. 985-6.

51. Albert Hyamson, *The Sephardim of England. A History of the Spanish and Portuguese Community, 1492-1951* (London: Methuen, 1951), pp. 63-4; Anthony's Dutch brother-in-law, Francisco Lopes Suasso, second Baron Suasso (1657-1710), who was married to Rachel da Costa, played a large part in the financial arrangements for William III's invasion of England in 1688, reputedly lending him two million guilders (roughly £200,000) without security; Ole Peter Grell, Jonathan Israel, Nicholas Tyacke, *From Persecution to Toleration. The Glorious Revolution and Religion in England* (Oxford: Clarendon Press, 1991), pp. 141, 231; Daniel Swetschinski, Loeki Schonduve, *The Lopes Suasso family, bankers to William III* (Amsterdam: Amsterdam Jewish Museum, 1988), pp. 51-56.

52. Norman, p. 29; George Rudé, *Hanoverian London* (London: Secker & Warburg, 1971), p. 53.

53. *Encyclopaedia Judaica*, v, 986.

54. Information from Dr. Norma Perry who

came across this admiring reference to Catherine in Voltaire's notebooks.

55. Daphne Foskett, *A Dictionary of Miniature Painters* (1972); *Encyclopaedia Judaica*, xi, 1342-3; one of her most charming miniatures, now owned by the Jewish Museum in London, is the portrait of her son Abraham aged ten in 1714 on p. 22.

56. Even in 1882 the tenant was only paying £120 rent per year (Prickett & Venables sales particulars, 1882; BM: Potter Collection, vol. 20, p. 53).

57. Norman, p.29.

58. Family notes by Emanuel Mendes da Costa, BL Add. MS 29867, f.110.

59. Cansick, p. 25; 'Village of Crouch End', p.423.

60. 'Village of Crouch End', p.423.

61. *H & FPJ*, 23 April 1882. The story should not be taken too seriously!

62. 'Village of Crouch End', pp. 423-4.

63. Prickctt & Venables sales particulars, 1882; BM: Potter Collection, vol. 20, p.53.

64. *H & FPJ*, 23 April 1882.

65. Hornsey Enclosure map: GLRO MR/DE/ HOR. Yolande Hodson (ed.), *Ordnance Surveyors ' Drawings of the London Area 1799-1808*: London Topographical Society Publication no. 144 (1991).

66 John Warburton, Joseph Bland and Payler Smyth, 'a New and Correct Mapp of Middlesex, Essex and Hertfordshire with the Roads, Rivers, Sea Coasts Actually Surveyed', 1725: relevant section reproduced in Peter Barber & Christopher Board, *Tales from the Map Room* (London: BBC, p. 141)); John Rocque, 'An Exact Survey of the City' s of London, Westminster . . . and the Country Ten Miles Round' (1746).

67. Cave, pp. 194-5.

68. Norman, (1926); Pat Reed, "*Some Notes on Cromwell House, Highgate. The History and the Fabric*" (Typescript,

1980), particularly p. 19.

69. 'Village of Crouch End', p. 424.

70. *Index of Mathematicians*. However, as late as December 1779 the mathematician John Davison gave Exeter Court off the Strand as his address in the preface to his *A New System of Arithmetick* (1780).

71. 'Village of Crouch End', p.424.

72. *H & FPJ*, 23 April 1882.

73. Some letters from him to Thomas Bewick do survive in a private collection. They emphasise Norton's kindly nature and friendship and admiration for John Bewick. I am grateful to Nigel Tattersfield for informing me of their existence.

74. I am deeply indebted to Nigel Tattersfield, who has freely shared with me the fruits of his extended researches on John Bewick. For his preliminary account of the artist's life and work, see 'John Bewick 1760-1795', *Cherryburn Times. The Newsletter of The Bewick Society*, vol. 3/1 (Easter 1996), 1-6.

75. *Thomas Bewick, A Memoir of Thomas Bewick by Himself* (London: Cresset Press, 1961), p. 90 and more generally pp.89-91.

76. John Bewick's notebooks, quoted in Royal Commission on Historical Manuscripts, 15th Report, appendix III, p. 22.

77. 1882-3-11-1487 LB 1. The house where he lived may have been Stone Cottage, for which see note 106.

78. Letter to Thomas Bewick, 6 December 1791. Quoted in Montague Weekley, *Thomas Bewick* (London: OUP, 1953), p. 152.

79. Pencilled draft of a love letter now in Newcastle Public Library quoted in Weekley, p.153 (with misreadings)

80. Weekley (pp. 153-4) felt that while his work as an illustrator 'belongs far more to its period than his elder brother's . . . It has . . . a certain grave charm, and he possessed the gift of transmitting something of his winning disposition to his designs'.

81. BM 1882-3-11-1488 & 1489 LB 2&3. They are both unfinished. I am once again grateful to Nigel Tattersfield for pointing out that the stage coach in the Crouch End view may have been included to flatter John Bewick's friend Miss Vass whose brother, Edward Vass, was already running a service to London from Hornsey (for the company's later history see *VCH*, vol. vi, p. 106).

82. 'Village of Crouch End', p.425. He was ultimately buried in the same tomb in Hornsey churchyard as Norton and his family (Cansick, p.28).

83. *HJ*, 23 April 1882. This is the source for the next paragraph. Copies of two editions of his Latin grammars (1808,1823) and one copy of his English grammar (1813) are owned by the British Library. While admitting that there could be little originality in his Latin grammar he was adamant, in the introduction to his English grammar that 'he entertains no apprehension of being stigmatised as a servile copyist' .

84. 'Village of Crouch End', p.425.

85. John Lloyd, *The History, Topography and Antiquities of Highgate* (Highgate: HLSI, 1888), p. 385.

86. John Richardson, *Highgate. Its History since the fifteenth century* (London: Historical Publications, l983), p. 181; *Survey of London*, p.70; *DNB*.

87. 1769-1840, radical publisher and author (*DNB*).

88. fl. 1832-1875 (?) Huon Mallalieu, *The Dictionary of British Watercolour Artists up to 1920* (London: Antique Collectors' Club, 2nd ed., 1986), i, p. 318.

89 Thomas 'Clio' Rickman (1761-1834), radical bookseller and reformer (*DNB*).

90. Joseph Kenny Meadows (1790-1874), draughtsman (*DNB*).

91. *H & FPJ*, 23 April 1882.

92. Lloyd, p. 385, who also adds the names of George Daniel and William Upcott, sub-librarian of the London Institution, to Grant's circle.

93. Vera Crane (ed.), *Heart of a London Village. The Highgate Literary and Scientific Institution 1839-1990* (London: Historical Publications, 1991), p. 13. Grant, however, never joined the Institution (I am grateful to Gwynnedd Gosling for having searched the membership lists for his name).

94. There is no mention of Grant in *e.g. The Gillmans of Highgate* (1895).

95. In his obituary to Crombie in *The Times*. Quoted in the *DNB* article on Crombie.

96. 'Village of Crouch End', pp. 425-6 clarifies the rather murky evidence underlying this statement. Judging from Smith's age as given in the census of 1851, he was born in 1799 and would have been barely 20 when he became joint principal of the school. But it should be remembered that in 1783 William Pitt the Younger had become Prime Minister at the age of 24. The 1841 census shows that Grant, though classed as 'independent' and not as a teacher, was still living in the school and that Smith had been born in Suffolk.

97. The leaflet is to be found in the Gdl. (PR V HOR).

98. At the time an omnibus ran to town from the Hanley Arms on Hornsey Rise every ten minutes. See Dot Woodrow, 'Buses in the North London Suburbs 1829-1879', *HHS Bulletin* 21 (1980), p.19, and *cf. VCH*, vol. vi, p. 106.

99. In 1791, John Bewick had written of Norton's Academy having 'near 100 fine boys' [Weekley, p. 152], but he may have been exaggerating in order to impress his brother Thomas.

100. *HJ*, 23 April 1882. Why this should be so, when the Huguenots had several schools of their own, is not explained. Nevertheless the successive census returns do show a handful of French and French-Swiss boys (who were almost certainly Protestant) at the school.

101. John Bewick described it as a 'very large Academy' [Weekley, p. 152].

102. *H & FPJ*, 15 December 1882.

103. Cutting in BM: Potter Collection, vol. 20, p. 53.

104. One of the assistant teachers in 1871 was actually German (Census returns, 1871).

105. I am grateful to Nigel Tattersfield for reminding me of this important aspect of the Academy's existence and providing me with information about Bewick's circle (and see Weekley, pp. 153). For further details about taverns and trades in Crouch End, see 'Village of Crouch End', pp. 429-30; *VCH*, vol. vi, pp.143, 159, 162.

106. It stood on the site of 11 Park Road and was only demolished in 1964. There is a photograph in the Sidey Collection in Hornsey Library (*Notes on Hornsey Church and its District*), v, p.199. I am grateful to Alan Aris and Isobel Stokes for bringing this to my attention.

107. Middlesex Deeds Register, GLRO; 'Village of Crouch End', pp. 430- 1 ; *VCH*, vol. vi, pp. 110, 165; Travers,p. 17.

108. 'Village of Crouch End', p. 426; *H & FPJ*, 23 April 1882; census returns 1861, 1871.

109. This last figure, however, excludes day pupils.

110. Compare the First Edition O.S. 25" to one mile map of Crouch End surveyed in the late 1860s with the plan of 1882 accompanying the Venables and Prickett sales particulars (BM: Potter Collection, vol. 20, p. 52).

111. Advert in BM: Potter Collection, vol. 20, p. 53.

112. *Ibid.* See 'Plan of the Holborn & Finsbury Sewers 1846. North District'. BL. Crace Collection, portfolio xviii.6 (though this is not reliable in detail).

113. *HJ*, 23 April 1882.

114. *VCH*, vol. vi, p. 193.

115. 'Village of Crouch End', pp.426-7; *HJ*, 11 November, 15 December 1882. Sales details of Prickett & Venables; BM: Potter Collection, vol. 20, p. 53. The Potter Collection (vol. 20, pp. 57-8) also contains photos of the front and back of the building in the course of demolition in December 1882 (not *c.*1884 as in Travers, p. 21) .

116. *VCH*, vol. vi, p. 196; *HJ*, 3, 17 July 1953: letters of S.W. Kitchener and L.H. Cooper. The school, and Mr Knight, are last mentioned in *Kelly's Post Office Directory* for Hornsey of 1904-5.

117. See Marcham's plan 'Crouch End in 1862', illustrating his 'Village of Crouch End', reproduced in Travers, p. 28.

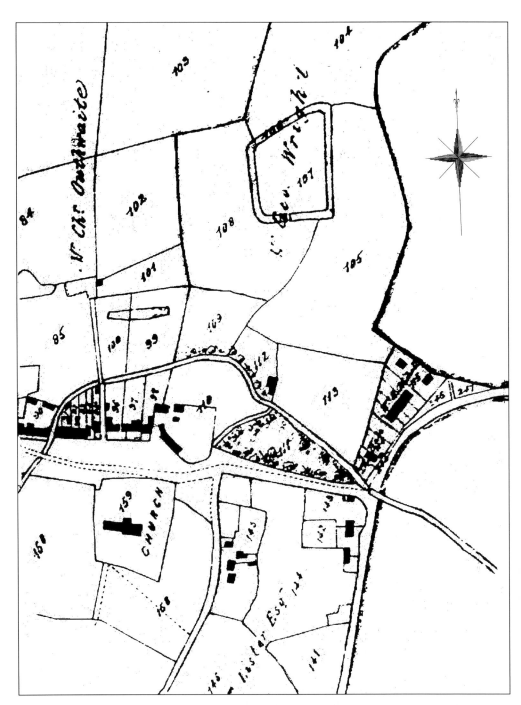

9. The Hornsey moat – shown on the *Enclosure Plan* accompanying the Hornsey Enclosure Award (1816). Not as accurate as the first large-scale Ordnance Survey map of Hornsey (1864) showing the railway when the moat had gone. Here the land inside the moat appears as field no. 107. After the railway was built, the New River was straightened to flow beside it.

A moated site c. 1556-1850:
Brick or Tower Place and its owners

When pursuing my interest in the parish boundaries of Hornsey, I looked carefully at the oldest detailed maps of the area: the map which accompanied the Enclosure Award in 1816, and the Ordnance Survey map of 1864. It was then that I noticed the distinct outline of a moat just north of the old parish church of St. Mary on the earlier map but missing from the later one. Although it was not labelled on the map, it was referred to as the 'Brick or Tower Place' in Edwin Monk's *Memories of Hornsey* and the transcription of the Hornsey Manor Rolls by the Marcham brothers. Both sources said Brick Place had been on the site of the pumping station of the water works in Hornsey High Street. I put this to the back of my mind until there was a suggestion that the area be developed, when I realised that it was a matter of some urgency to discover the history and exact location of the site. Little is known of Brick Place itself, so this is the story of those who owned and lived in it, with a few clues to its size and extent when it changed hands.

The origin of Brick or Tower Place is mysterious. Its end is clear. It was demolished in 1703 and its moat was covered by the embankment of the Great Northern Railway in 1847-50. Its position can be estimated only from maps made before the first Ordnance Survey of the area. The most detailed map was that accompanying the Enclosure Award in 1816, but it is not exact. It would appear that the centre of the moated enclosure was about 400 yards NNE of the tower of the parish church of St. Mary Hornsey, that is TQ 3075 8960. However, the Enclosure Award states that the platform within the moat covered an area of more than one acre, so it probably extended across the join between the 100 metre squares TQ 307896 and TQ 307895. The only features which were there during the existence of the moat and survive in the vicinity today, are the church tower and the parish boundary, which is still marked with boundary plates, along the edge of Alexandra Park which was then situated in Tottenham Parish and named Tottenham Wood.

At first sight, a moated site near the ancient Hornsey parish church would suggest a medieval manor house. The successive lords of the manor of Hornsey were the bishops of London who are not known to have resided in the parish after the hunting lodge at Highgate was abandoned before 1500. Nor is there any tradition of there being an ancient manor house. The site of Brick Place itself became so forgotten that more than a hundred years ago John Lloyd wrote in his *History of Highgate*[1] that it was uncertain where Brick Place stood.

The name of Brick Place probably provides a clue to its date, suggesting that it was built when brick was not widely used. Sutton House in Hackney was called *The Bryk Place* in 1525. Bricks were used for castles which were built to impress rather than withstand an army such as at Farnham and Herstmonceux in the previous century. The moated Hampton Court was an outstanding building in brick completed by 1529, with later additions and alterations.[2] Bricks were used locally in Hornsey church tower in about 1500.[3] The alternative name Tower Place implies that the structure was tall and calls to mind Canonbury Tower in a neighbouring parish. Moats were not uncommon and continued to be excavated even after the introduction of gunpowder made them less effective as defence against soldiers. They provided large houses with an open aspect to view from within and without, enhanced their visual impact, and provided security against intruders as well as a supply of water for fish and drainage of waste from the house. in the sixteenth century, when it is first documented, Highgate was becoming fashionable for out of town houses for City merchants and professional men of fortune, but its attractive lofty position did not provide the capability for a moated house set apart in a landscape of fields such as existed in Hornsey. Little is known of Brick Place itself, so this is the story of those who owned and lived in it, with a few clues to its size and extent when it changed hands.

Ranulph Cholmley (died 1563)
The site of Brick Place was owned by Ranulph (or Randle or Ralph) Cholmley from 1556. Ranulph was the third son of Sir Richard Cholmondeley (there are twenty three variations of the spelling) of Cholmondeley in Cheshire, and Elizabeth, daughter of Sir Randle Brereton, whose kinsmen, John and William Brereton, were associated with Duckett's manor in 1536. Ranulph's career is similar to that of the earlier years of Sir Roger Cholmley (founder of Highgate School) but about ten to fifteen years later. Their birth dates are difficult to determine. Ranulph's elder brother, Hugh, was born in 1513 and he died before reaching fifty. Sir Roger's birthdate is also unknown but it is recorded that he had been elected to the bench in 1524. Like Ranulph, Sir Roger did not inherit his father's estates. Sir Roger was the natural son of another Sir Richard Cholmley who had been Lieutenant Governor of Berwick, Governor of Hull and Lieutenant of the Tower of London. However, when this Sir Richard died in 1522 he made provision for his son, Roger, whom he placed at Lincoln's Inn. Foss in *Judges of England* states that "Sir Roger is confounded by Strype and others with his Cheshire kinsman Ranulph or Randle Cholmley, who like him was a reader at Lincoln's Inn, a serjeant at law, Recorder of London and Member of Parliament." Sir Roger was reader (i.e. tutor of law students) at Lincoln's Inn in 1524, 1529 and 1531; Ranulph was reader in the same place in 1552 and 1557. Sir Roger

was Recorder of London in 1536 and Ranulph followed in 1553. Sir Roger was Member of Parliament in 1537 and 1547, and Ranulph was recorded as M.P. on five occasions between 1554 and 1562. Sir Roger was Serjeant at Law in 1544 and Ranulph in 1558. Sir Roger bought land in Highgate in 1536[4] and Ranulph bought the site of Brick Place in 1556. It seems that Ranulph was following in Sir Roger's footsteps, some ten to twenty years later and it is inconceivable that they did not know each other. However, Ranulph did not achieve the eminence of Sir Roger who was knighted in 1537 and became Lord Chief Justice in 1552, though it is possible he may have done as well had he lived longer, but he died probably much younger two years before Sir Roger.

Like Sir Roger and other sons of landed gentry who led successful careers in London, Ranulph chose to purchase land locally, but it is not clear whether he was responsible for the building of Brick Place, but he seems the most likely person. The first record of the house by name was in 1578. As Recorder of London, Ranulph was the City's senior law officer and senior judge at the central criminal court and played an important part in City ceremonial particularly the election and swearing in of the Lord Mayor.[5] When Ranulph died without issue in 1563, his land in Hornsey passed to his elder brother, Sir Hugh Cholmley[6], who had inherited vast estates in Cheshire.

Sir Hugh Cholmley (1513 -1596)

Sir Hugh, owner of Brick Place, was knighted by Henry VIII at Leith for his conduct in the Duke of Norfolk's expedition to Scotland in 1544. He does not seem to have had his brother's close connection with the City, but he probably found the house convenient when visiting London. It was almost certainly used by his extended family. His grandson and eventual heir, Robert, was born 'at Crouchend near Highgate' on 26 June 1584.[7] It is not at all clear whether this could have been at Brick Place which was then owned by Thomas Aglionby, but the ownership of a house did not in any way imply that it was occupied by its owner.

Only eleven years after Sir Hugh inherited Brick Place, an event took place on 5th June 1574, at his property in Hornsey which was then occupied by Thomas Aglionby (see p.43).This was recorded in the court:[8]

"At the parish of St. Giles-without-Cripplegate, co. Midd. on the said day, William Tyler, late of London laborer, a lazy and cunning fellow, cosened Thomas Weare of the said parish out of two several sums of money, by representing that he was in possession of certain acres of wood growing near Tottenham, which he had bought of Lord Compton, who out of his good will to the deponent had himself measured and marked out the wood for him: that further, to get Thomas Weare's confidence, the same William Tyler represented himself, as staying and living in the house of Sir

Hugh Cholmondeley knt. at Harnsey *alias* Harryngay co. Midd.; that by these false representations the said William Tyler induced Thomas Weare to give him an order for a hundred cartloads of the said wood, to give him four pence "nomine finis *viz.* in Earnest" on the bargain for the wood, and yet further to give him twenty shillings in partial payment of the price agreed upon for the hundred loads of wood, whereas it appeared upon enquiry that William Tyler had no wood to sell, and was not living at Harnesey, but was a cheat. Having put himself 'Guilty', William Tyler was sentenced to the pillory at Fynnesbury. G.D.R., 26 April, 16 Eliz." [1574].

10. Sir Hugh Cholmley (1513-96), owner of Brick Place, and his second wife, Mary, appear in effigy on a fine alabaster altar tomb at Malpas in Cheshire where the family owned vast estates. Sir Hugh is dressed as a knight in armour with his head resting on a helm and an elaborate ruff round his neck. The stone was originally concealed beneath rich paintwork.

As William Tyler claimed to be living in Sir Hugh Cholmley's house, it seems likely that it was known that Sir Hugh owned it but was not himself resident at this time. He was very active in his native Cheshire where he was a justice, five times high sheriff, and deputy lieutenant of that county. He died in 1596, aged eighty-three, in Cheshire. His tomb is the centre piece of the Cholmondeley private chapel in Malpas church where the Cholmondeley screen dates from 1514. The sarcophagus has alabaster effigies of Sir Hugh and his second wife Mary (died 1588), and the kneeling figures of their children.[9]

Thomas Aglionby

In 1578, nearly twenty years before his death, Sir Hugh Cholmley surrendered Brick Place with ten houses and fifty-eight acres to Thomas Aglionby of Hornsey.[10] It seems that Aglionby had been living there for some years before he acquired the house and estate in 1578 as he is named as the occupant in 1572 when a serious case appears in the *Middlesex Sessions Rolls*[11]:

"1 April, 14 Elizabeth-Coroner's Inquisition post-mortem, taken at Hornesey co. Midd. on view of the body of Hugh Moreland late of Hornesey yoman, there lying dead: With Verdict that, on 29 March last past, between three and four p.m., the said Hugh Moreland and a certain Henry Yonge of the same place yoman were together in the yard of the house of Thomas Aglyonby of Hornesey aforesaid gentleman, when they quarelled and fought, the said Hugh Moreland having in his hands a shovel and the said Henry Yonge being armed with a 'shackforth' [pitchfork]; when in the affray had between them Henry Yonge with the said 'shackforth' gave Hugh Moreland in his left eye a blow, of which he died on the present first day of April. G.D.R., 22 May, 14 Eliz." [1572].

Thomas Aglionby left this property in his Will for life to his wife Cecily (who subsequently married again becoming Cecily Payne).[12] Cecily settled 14 acres on their son Ambrose Aglionby in 1603 and he expanded it to twenty-six acres by 1605[13], mortgaged it with 'his tenement called the Churchegates in which Francis Burton dwells' to Richard Deacon. Unlike the later Aglionbys, Richard Deacon was active in the locality and was elected constable the same year. Despite his office, Richard Deacon, with others was ordered to 'fill up the pitt in the highe waie which they have made by digging for gravell to the annoyance of his Majesty's people' in 1607. Brick Place was still occupied by Richard Deacon in 1622. Thomas Aglionby was away in Ireland from 1622 to 1629 with Henry Viscount Falkland who was Lord Deputy there.[14] When he returned, Aglionby sold the house with thirty-two acres to Richard Chambers the younger, alderman of London, and Catherine his wife in 1631.[15] In his absence, John Wetherley of Highgate had held the lease which he acquired at some time between 1622 and 1631.

John Wetherley

John Wetherley, father and son, were yeomen, that is free tenants and prominent farmers who were qualified to serve on juries. They were also brickmakers and builders. They lived in Swains Lane and owned a row of four cottages near the top, where the cemetery is now, opposite grounds which were the precursor of Waterlow Park. Here there was a strip of water known as 'the moat' which possibly had its conduit head on the site of the uppermost pond.[16] This four-foot-wide strip of water may have originated as a quarry for brick making or road repairs, and is fed by springs. It served as an ornamental feature separating the grounds of two houses, one on the site of Fairseat occupied by Sir Roger Cholmley, and the other Lauderdale House. It also served as a reservoir for a piped water supply to Lauderdale House[17], built in 1582. In his Will proved in 1631, John Wetherley junior left his Swains Lane cottages to his wife Margaret, subsequently to be passed to his son William. In 1657 it was already owned by Dr Elisha Coysh.

The Wetherleys' names (in a variety of spelling) appear frequently in the Court Rolls of the manors of Hornsey and Cantelowes (in St. Pancras parish), most often for digging pits in the common land.They were probably extracting clay for making bricks and may have created or enlarged the ponds and 'moats' in the vicinity. It is possible that the older John Wetherley created the moat for Brick Place by quarrying for clay to make bricks for the house. Certainly they prospered from their enterprises in a way that suggests their income came from more than just farming their lands as yeomen. It is difficult to distinguish between the activities of father and son as they probably managed the business together.

The younger John Wetherley paid his fines for digging and became a constable in Hornsey Manor. His Will indicates that he not only owned the lease of Brick Place with its cottages, but also the freehold of a house, meadows and orchard in Finchley, the lease of a cottage held from William Cholmley of Highgate and a house in Highgate 'without the Gate' in the bishop's park in Hornsey parish. John Wetherley leased Highgate Chapel field and repaired both the school and chapel in 1601, although they had been built in brick as recently as 1576. John Wetherley may also have built the original Wollaston almshouses in brick on the adjoining site, but these were considered to be decayed and rebuilt in 1722 as a result of a further bequest from Edward Pauncefort which doubled the number of almshouses to twelve and added the girls' charity school in the centre of the range.[18] These are the buildings which survive in Southwood Lane today. A kiln and twenty five acres of brickworks existed in Southwood Lane where John Wetherley had been in trouble for digging pits. Most of the surviving brick houses in Highgate were built later in the seventeenth and eighteenth centuries. Many of these replaced earlier structures of brick of the Wetherleys' time which do not seem to have survived well. It may well be that of all those associated with Brick Place that the most influential in the story of the house and the locality in the late sixteenth and early seventeenth centuries are John Wetherley, father and son. Most remarkable is that because Brick Place was leased and not owned by them, we would be ignorant of their holding the lease if it were not for the Will of John Wetherley the younger proved in 1631. In the same year as John Wetherley's death, the ownership of Brick Place passed from the absentee landlord, Ambrose Aglionby to Richard Chambers junior who had been living in the house for some time.

Richard Chambers senior (died 1632-3)

Richard Chambers junior had connections with Hornsey as his father, Richard Chambers senior already held land here. Both father and son were girdlers and citizens of London as was the father of Elizabeth their wife and mother respectively. Girdlers had their own city livery company and made the ornamental belts which were highly fashionable among the rich and these were used to suspend weapons, purses and anything that later generations put in pockets or bags. When the coat with pockets came into fashion and weapons no were longer carried, the prosperity of girdlers declined. When Elizabeth Chambers (daughter of Samuel Armitage who died in 1636) herself died, Richard Chambers senior married again. In 1613, he had acquired a newly built messuage and an acre of land at Crouch End formerly called the "Grene Lettyce" which was eventually to form part of Crouch End School in Park Road (then called Maynard Street).[19] This was inherited by his second wife, Susanna, and then his son Richard. Shortly before he died in 1632, Richard Chambers senior played a part in conveyancing the land where Brick Place stood to his son. This provides the fullest description of the site available:

"At this court it is found that on 19 January, 1631, Ambrose Aglionby, esq., surrendered by the hands of Richard Chambers, senior, and John Wollaston, The Tower Place or Brick Place with buildings orchards and gardens, with a close called Home Close now separated into two parts and lying on the northern part of the said messuage containing 5 acres; with an orchard enclosed by the Moate and divers other parcels of land by the said Moate with the fish ponds containing 1/2 acre; a parcel of pasture called the Grove or Bushe Close containing 4 acres; a parcel of pasture called Primrose Meade containing 5 acres; a parcel of pasture now separated called Perrymeade containing 13 acres; which messuage etc. are in the occupation of Christopher Hoddesdon, gent.; with a cottage and meadow now in the occupation of Thomas Snow, Simon Day and Widow Wall, all which premises descended to Ambrose Aglionby as son and heir of Thomas Aglionby his father, deceased; with all that messuage and three acres of land of Lawrence Smith, gentleman, deceased, purchased by Ambrose Aglionby from Richard Gurnard, citizen and clothworker of London and now or lately in the occupation of William Benning, gent., to Richard Chambers, junior, citizen and girdler of London, for life with remainder to Katherine his wife."[20]

Richard Chambers junior (c.1588-1658)

The younger Richard Chambers inherited land from both his parents Richard (died 1632-3) and Susanna (died 1641).[21] In her Will,[22] Susanna left 'all that Cottage, garden, Plott or Yard lying in Hornsey to my eldest son Richard Chambers.' This was on the site of Linden House (now Linden Mansions) in Hornsey Lane. Like other wealthy Hornsey residents, Richard

Chambers was making his fortune in the City. His connections with the locality are seen in his marriage to Catherine Sprignell at Highgate Chapel on 4th January 1634. Catherine was the daughter of Robert Sprignell whose son Richard was to build Cromwell House in brick for his family a few years later. Cromwell House had twenty-five hearths in 1674 and Brick Place twenty-two, so they were comparable in size.[23] A ceiling at Cromwell House has the coat of arms granted to Sir Richard Sprignell in 1631. Richard Chambers was buried at Highgate Chapel on 17 January 1658-9, his wife in May 1661 and his sister Catherine Chambers in 1644. The following year, Richard Chambers settled Brick Place, nine cottages and thirty-six acres on himself and his prospective second wife, Judith.[24]

Richard Chamber's fortune as a merchant became embroiled in the political ferment of the seventeenth century between king and parliament. Richard opposed the imposition of the tax, known as tonnage and poundage, without the grant of Parliament in 1628. A case of silk grograms (a coarse fabric used to make girdles) brought to London by a carrier from Bristol and consigned to Chambers, was seized by the custom house officer, although he offered to give security for future payment *if the demand could be proved legal.*[25] Following his court appearance, the matter was referred to the Court of Star Chamber where the Attorney General stated:

"The said Richard Chambers of the City of London, Merchant, the 28 September last being amongst some other Merchants called to the Council-board at Hampton Court, about some things which were complained of in reference to the customs, did then and there, in an insolent manner, in the presence or hearing of the Lords and others of his Majesties Privy-Council, then sitting in council, utter these undutiful, seditious and false words, *That the merchants are in no part of the world so screwed up and wrung as in England; that in Turky they have more encouragement."* [26]

Whatever the original offence, Richard had managed to get himself into deeper trouble by "comparing his Majesties government with the government of the Turks, intending thereby to make the people believe that his Majesties happy government may be termed a Turkish Tyranny; and therefore the court fined the said Mr Chambers in the sum of 2000*l* [i.e. pounds] and to stand committed to the Fleet."[27]

There was a great difference of opinion in the court about the fine. Richard tendered an apology adding "Doth our law judge any man before it hear him, and know what he doth?" (John VII, 51). In Michaelmas Term 1629, Richard was brought out of the Fleet by Habeas Corpus on the grounds that Star Chamber "doth not give them any authority to punish for words only."

This increased his confidence so much that in his resentment he brought an action against the custom house officers in the exchequer for the recovery of his goods. But his plea was rejected, and his imprisonment continued for six years and the value of his goods seized for tax he estimated at more than seven thousand pounds. Undeterred, on his release he continued to campaign against ship-money and was imprisoned for nine months in Newgate. As a result he brought an action in the King's Bench against the Lord Mayor for false imprisonment in 1636. His fortunes seemed to change when the Long Parliament ordered Chambers £13,680 in reparation of his losses. He became a popular hero and was elected alderman in 1642 and sheriff in 1644. The compensation was never paid and he wrote a letter of petition concerning all he had done for the City and how he had suffered. Richard Chambers wrote in September 1654:

"The Petitioner . . . having consumed his Estate, hath been constrained to sell and morgage [sic] some part of his Lands to pay Creditors, and to maintain his Family, having a wife and nine children . . . but now after 26 years suffering whereof 12 years in fruitless and wearisome waitings . . . needs some speedy course to pay his Debts, and redeem his Landes . . . And in like manner for his Wives debt which is to pay Debts and Legacies."

His end is described by Rushworth: "The Petitioner being wearied out with twelve years attendance upon one Parliament, in hopes of reparation for his imprisomnent, troubles and losses, during the twelve years former interval of Parliament, in standing for the Liberty of the Subject, grew infirm, was reduced to a low estate and condition, he died in Summer 1658 being about the age of Seventy years." His death occurred at Hornsey.[28] In his Will Richard Chambers left his property to be divided among his wife and sons after debts were paid, then a spate of selling followed his death. In the Hornsey Manor Court Rolls[29] a number of different tenants are named as occupying the extensive property. This all passed in 1662 to Christopher Joyner and included "that brick messuage with appurtenances, . . . that great barn being upon the 'Comon Greene'", as well as meadows, cottages, together with "all and singular the barns stables buildings gardens orchards and courtyards". In the same year John Musters was renting Brick Place, though the ownership of the house and land remained with Christopher Joyner and his heirs.

Sir John Musters (died 1690)
Very little can be learned of Sir John Musters and his family except from the entries in the parish registers[30] and from the memorials formerly in Hornsey church.[31] It is unfortunate that the earlier families before Sir Richard Chambers cannot be traced in Hornsey parish registers for these do not exist before the mid seventeenth century. Through the recording of baptisms, marriages and burials, parish registers provide an invaluable indication of

11. Francis Musters (1664-80) knew Brick Place as his only home. When the last St Mary's Hornsey church was built (where St Mary's Infants School now stands) this monument to the boy was moved from the chancel of the old building to the north-east porch of the new church, which has since been demolished. A wall monument in marble with cherubs supporting a crown above the kneeling figure and a cartouche-of-arms above.

the local presence of families. In the records of gifts to the church, Lady Musters made a gift of plate to the church in 1641, which shows a link with the area well before her husband became associated with Brick Place. He was elected a governor of Highgate School in 1675. Francis Musters (his only child by his third wife, Jane who may have been responsible for the memorial) was born on 1st May 1664 and baptised on 18th May, and died on 16th April 1680 and was buried the next day, so it is likely Brick Place was his only home. His monument (see illustration) was removed from the chancel of St. Mary's church to the porch of the new church until that was too was destroyed in 1969, when the monument was reputed to have gone into store, and its whereabouts are unknown. However it was photographed and recorded.[32]

Sir John died in 1690 when his son and heir (of a previous marriage), also named John had already died. The Manor Court Rolls recorded: "It is found that on 5 June, 1690, was granted to Millicent Musters, widow, late the wife of John Musters, esq., and mother and guardian of Mundy, Thomas, Charles and Francis Musters, licence to lease the Tower Place and 11 Acres of land to Lady Jane Musters, widow and relict of John Musters, knight, for 30 years if she live so long."[33] However, Lady Jane died on 17 September 1691 aged 67 and was buried in Hornsey church. Her gravestone may still be seen on the site of the nave at the foot of three steps leading to the base of the surviving tower. She was the daughter of Sir Francis Basset of Tehiddy in Cornwall. Her mother, Lady Basset, had been buried on 17 July 1682 at Hornsey following her death two days earlier at the age of 82. Mary Musters, presumably a member of the family, was married to Sir Richard Spencer at St. Mary, Hornsey, on 23 July 1672. There is no reference to a tomb or burial of Sir John Musters himself. Presumably he was buried elsewhere, perhaps where one of his earlier wives was buried. There he may already have made arrangements for his own funeral monument. At all events, Brick Place passed to his grandsons and was destroyed in a storm in 1703.[34]

The end of the moat

The land in and around the moat was used as pasture under a number of owners until the arrival of the railway, which was constructed through the site in 1847-50 burying it beneath a massive embankment. The moat appeared on Greenwood's *Map of Middlesex* in 1819, but was more carefully surveyed for the *Hornsey Enclosure Act* (1816) and may be seen on the accompanying *Enclosure Plan*[35] where the area of the land enclosed within the moat is recorded as being a little more than one acre.[36] (See p. 38)

In 1825, the first public railway opened between Stockton and Darlington. There followed epidemics of railway fever as investors sought to buy shares in hundreds of small ventures, principally in the coal producing areas. In 1838, a line was extended from York to London 219 miles long. In 1843, most of eastern England was without a railway. Instructions were given to promote a "Direct Northern" railway through East Anglia southwards from York to London and northwards to Scotland. Shortly afterwards another company proposed a more westerly railway from York to London, the "Great Northern Railway", and both companies were surveying routes and making plans for Parliamentary Bills necessary to acquire the land.[37]

There were no less than 224 railway bills awaiting the Parliamentary session of 1845. The Hornsey Vestry held a meeting on 9 January 1845, when its surveyor reported that the London and York Railway proposed to carry a line through the parish field, and the Direct Northern Railways Company intended to maintain a railway line through the parish a little further west. The Vestry

"Resolved that such above mentioned lines, while they cannot in any degree benefit the parishioners, are calculated to produce serious Injury to the value of Property in this Parish and to destroy the retirement of its locality and neighbourhood. Resolved that the undertakings seem to have originated more for the purpose of private speculation and gain than for any corresponding public advantage . . . That a deputation from this Vestry be appointed to wait upon the Lord Bishop of London as Lord of the Manor with a view to obtain his co-operation & support in furtherance of the above resolutions."[38]

The London and York Bill came through Standing Orders successfully while the Direct Northern was delayed with objections. The London and York Bill received the Royal Assent on 26 June 1846, the same day as Sir Robert Peel's Corn Law Repeal Bill. The Direct Northern had lost

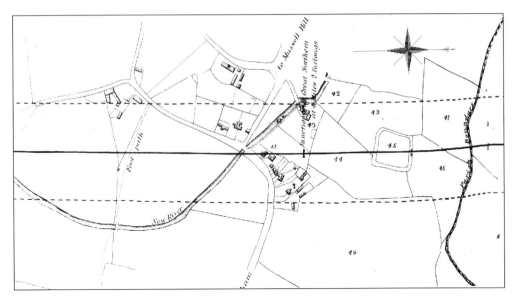

12. The course of the railway approved by Parliament shown on the *Deposited Parliamentary Plan* accompanying the London and York Bill (26 June 1846). The bold line marks the centre of the track and the dotted lines a fixed distance either side for use in considering claims for compensation; no indication of the width of the tracks, embankments or cuttings. St Mary's church is not marked, being at the extreme edge by the letters "to Muswell Hill".

the race and was never built. The Hornsey Vestry recorded nothing of this until February 1847 when it decided to appoint Mr George Prickett, surveyor of Highgate, to estimate the amount of claim in compensation to be sent to the Great Northern Railway Company.

At seven o'clock on the morning of 8 August 1850, the first public train on the line started from a temporary station at Maiden Lane (later extended to Kings Cross) on its way to Peterborough. *The Illustrated London News* reported: "The train having started, away it went in gallant style, darting into a tunnel of some length, emerged shortly after, and went skimming along a region of cornfields. This sudden transition from the busy haunts of life to quiet rural scenery, undisturbed even by the presence of a villa, is what chiefly strikes one at first starting on the new line. Nothing meets the eye but indifferent farming and a thinly peopled countryside. Passing through Hornsey, which is the first station on the line one goes through a second tunnel."[39]

The archaeological evidence for the origin and remains of Brick or Tower Place lie deeply buried beneath the railway. There are many thousands of moats in Britain, many, like Brick Place, covering a large area. Even those on the surface are not normally excavated as it is a large and costly enterprise rarely undertaken except when a site may be under threat of development. So we have had to rely on the limited documentary sources to tell what we can of its story. It is unfortunate that the house went as early as 1703 as there is no known picture or description so we have to be content with some account of its owners and occupants. I hope a little of the mystery of Brick Place has been solved, but there are still many unanswered questions.

Malcolm Stokes

References

1. John Lloyd, *History of Highgate* (1888), p.293

2. For examples of building in brick see Alec Clifton-Taylor, *The Pattern of English Building* (1972), chapter 9.

3. *VCH*, vol.vi, p. 155.

4. *VCH*, vol. vi, p. 123

5. Weinreb & Hibbert, *The London Encyclopaedia.*

6. *VCH*, vol. vi, p.148, note 3: CP 25(2)/74/ 630 no. 20; Cal. Pat. 1555-7, 413 (PRO)

7. Ormerod, *History of Cheshire*, p.638.

8. *Middlesex County Records*, 1, 86.

9. David Bethell, *Portrait of Cheshire* (1979), p, 53.

10. Guildhall MS 10312/04 mm.6-7.

11. *Middlesex Sessions Rolls*, p. 73.

12. Will of Thomas Aglionby, Prob. 1166 (P.C.C. 25 Butts).

13. Marcham, *Court Rolls*, pp. 7,15.

14. Marcham, p.59.

15. Marcham, *Court Rolls*, pp. 59 n., 80-1.

16. London County Council *Survey of London*, vol. XVII, St. Pancras Part 1, p.39

17. Peter Barber, Oliver Cox & Michael Curwen, *Lauderdale Revealed* (1993)

18. *VCH*, vol. vi, p. 203; Daniel Lysons, *Environs of London*, vol. III (1795), pp.75-6

19. Marcham, p.36.
20. Marcham, pp. 80, 81

21. *VCH*, vol. vi, p. 148

22. 28 July 1641 – P.C.C. 93 Evelyn (PRO)

23. Hearth Tax Returns; P.R.O. Lay Subsidies 143/370.

24. Marcham, pp. 36,48,101-2.

25. *DNB.*

26. John Rushworth, *Historical Collections* (1659).

27. Rushworth.

28. Marcham, p. 134; Smith's *Obituary*, Camd. Soc., p.47.

29. Marcham, p. 136-7.

30. GLRO

31. Frederick Cansick, *Epitaphs copied from Monuments*

32. Royal Commission on Historical Monuments *Middlesex* (1937), Plate 13 and p.78.

33. Marcham, p. 216

34. Daniel Lysons, *Environs of London*, vol. III, p. 2.

35. MR/DE/HOR/3; GLRO

36. la.Or.14p.

37. C. H. Grinling, *Hist. of the Gt. Northern Railway 1845-95* (1898), pp. 33, 46, 90.

38. *Hornsey Vestry Minutes* 9 Jan. 1845.

39. *ILN*, 10 Aug. 1850.

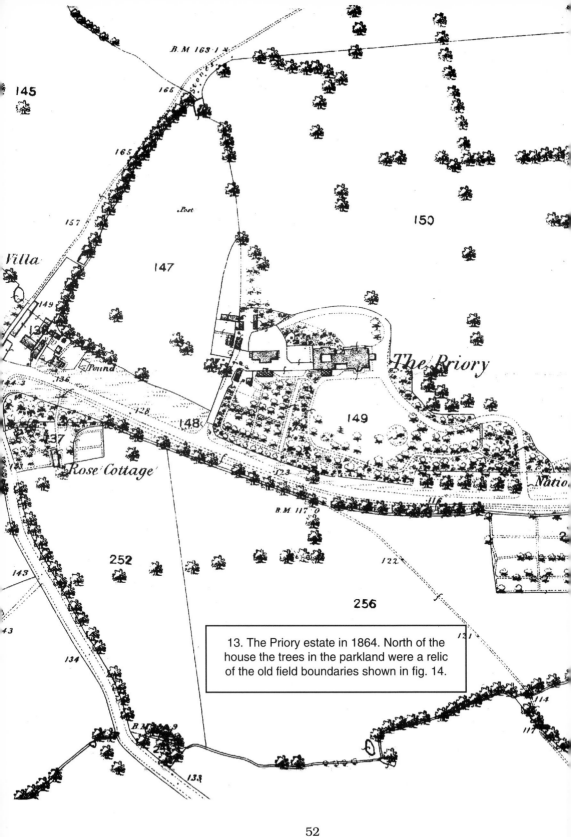

13. The Priory estate in 1864. North of the house the trees in the parkland were a relic of the old field boundaries shown in fig. 14.

Personalities and property: the development of the Priory estate

Sometime around 1849 William Keane, the landscape gardener, making one of his visits to the houses of the great and good of Middlesex, was at "Southwood" in Highgate and, looking towards the east made the following observation: "A short walk to the lower parts of the grounds, or an ascent to the upper rooms, or to the roof of the house, will open up to view a wide-spread landscape, graceful with hills, and dales and Bishop's Wood . . . and the Priory, the seat of Mr. Warner, in the valley, bordered by a distant horizon of wood-capt hills."[1] Such was the effect upon Keane of this panorama that he broke into a poetic stanza in praise of its beauty.

The house then known as the Priory stood on the north side of Priory Road between present day Warner Road and Danvers Road. An Edwardian house (number 98, Priory Road), also named the Priory, now stands on part of the site. As can be seen from a photograph taken in 1865 the house was part of a substantial group of buildings which included stables and other outbuildings., It stood on an estate of some 18 acres, the grounds of which were intersected by Priory Road, running east-west. The estate was bordered on the east by Nightingale Lane, and on the west by Park Road terminating near the spot now occupied by St. George's church, Cranley Gardens where once was an orchard owned by the Warner family.[2] The estate north of Priory Road extended to the grounds later occupied by Alexandra Park and, to the south, by an area now occupied by Farrer Road and Park Avenue South[3]. The estate was traversed from west to east by the little Moselle River.

The Early Estate

The house named by Keane as The Priory had at the time of his visit stood for some 25 years and although any earlier building save one is unknown, speculation has arisen that long ago a religious foundation stood on the estate. One writer commented at the time of the demolition of the Warners' house in February 1902, that "it was one of the prominent landmarks of North London" and that "it contained many dark passages, secret chambers, sliding panels, and other appurtances dear to the writer of romance."[4] This same writer claimed that The Priory was built on the site of a much older religious edifice, a seminary and retreat for members of the priesthood and prior to that a Cistercian monastery.[5] Another commentator has argued that the origins of the name The Priory derive from a monastery at Aldgate.[6] Quoting the 16th century chronicler, Stow, he states that friars were active in Hornsey by the mid-13th century with the permission of the Abbot of

Westminster.[7] This may well have been so, but whether a chapel was actually situated where the l9th century house came to be built is unlikely. Certainly any monastic foundation would have been well documented. The writer states that after the Dissolution of the Monasteries Sir Thomas Rowe of Muswell Hill purchased some land in Hornsey in 1658 and that in 1677 he was in possession of the remnants of the priory associated with the Aldgate Chapel of the Holy Trinity; it was in such a dilapidated condition that Sir Thomas ordered it to be pulled down and the materials sold.[8] However, whilst it is true that Sir Thomas did purchase land in Hornsey, on 20 April 1658, and was active in other land purchase at that time, there is absolutely no evidence that this land was that upon which The Priory was later built.[9] In the absence, therefore, of any evidence supporting the existence of a priory on the site this must be set aside as mere speculation and attention turned to the development of the estate.

The first evidence comes in 1682 when, on the 10th April "Paul Paynter, knight, surrendered a cottage of 18 acres of meadow late the land of Gregory Wilshire, gent., deceased, and aforetime of Susan Blackwell, widow, to Thomas Farley – Admitted – Fine £1.19.4d."[10] The "cottage" and estate had been in the possession of Gregory Wilshire (otherwise Grigorie Wilsheire, Wilsheere, or Wiltshire) although he may not have lived there since he was involved in many other land transactions prior to his death sometime around 1674. But in his Will dated 1 November 1672 and proved 1 October 1674, Wilshire left £3 to Mr. Lant, the Rector of St. Mary's, Hornsey, the parish in which the estate was situated, on condition that he, Wilshire, was buried near his wife in the chancel of the parish church. He left £3,350 to his four daughters and extensive lands in different counties to his sons Laurence and John.[11] Apart from this information and records of his land dealings, nothing else is known of Gregory Wilshire other than his marriage: "on 11th November 1616 Grigorie Wilsheire, of St. Antelynes, London, clothworker, married one Jane Worrall."[12]

It is tempting to endeavour to ascertain from whom Gregory Wilshire himself obtained the estate and there are indeed many references in the Manor Court Rolls to his transactions but unfortunately, they are not firmly identified with particular locations. There are, for example, his purchases of two separate areas of land in 1664 and 1665. Both were from one John Barnes, the first being for 8 acres and the second for 10 acres, making 18 acres which was the area of the Priory estate. However, this land was incorporated in other larger land transactions the acreage of which related to fields known as Lowdownes.[13] These fields lay between Middle Lane and what is now Hillfield Avenue.[14] This suggests that the Priory estate was not yet a distinct entity.

Sir Paul Paynter (or Painter), of "Pinnesnolhill alias Muswell Hill", was knighted at Whitehall on 8 August 1664 by Charles II; for what reason is unknown.[15] Like Gregory Wilshire he was much involved in land transactions in the Hornsey area and from 1676 until his death in 1686 was a governor of Highgate School.[16] Sir Paul died without issue and in his Will (dated 12 May 1682 and proved 6 July 1688) left the bulk of his estate to his wife, Lady Rachel, who died in 1695.[17] It seems certain that Sir Paul held some kind of public office, since, on 17 January 1677, he, together with five other worthies including a baronet and the aforementioned Sir Thomas Rowe, took an oath, "declaring that there is no transubstantiation in the sacrament of the Lord's Supper."[18] This was to conform with the requirements of the Test Act, 1673, designed to exclude Roman Catholics from holding public office. What kind of office Sir Paul held is not known although it may have been in connection with his governorship of Highgate School which he had assumed the previous year.

As with Gregory Wilshire Sir Paul may not have lived in the "cottage" on the estate. Thomas Farley, the next owner, immediately after his purchase, tried to secure his daughter's inheritance: on 21 April 1682 "Thomas Farley of St. Paul's, Covent Garden (who by copy on 20th April 1682, held a cottage and 18 acres of land) surrendered to himself for life remainder to Margaret his daughter, wife of John Braine for life."[19] Shortly after this transaction Farley seems to have died since it is recorded that, "Margaret, wife of John Braine and Thomas Farley deceased [was] admitted to a cottage and 18 acres of meadow."[20]

But by 1710, John Braine had died[21] and Margaret, his widow, taking what was by now a one quarter portion of the estate, married Abraham Coleman of London, merchant.[22] Over the next thirty years or so, Coleman managed to secure the remaining three-quarters of the estate, for by the time of his death around 1745, or sometime earlier, he stood possessed of the whole estate.[23] In his Will proved on 4 April 1745 Coleman mentions, "one Messuage, and . . . the Barns, Stables and Appurtances together with 18 acres of land formerly in the occupation of Widow Haynes."[24] Widow Haynes, between 1725 and 1732, occupied the "cottage" on the estate,[25] and it would appear that at least by the time of Coleman's death it was a working farm However, by that time Widow Haynes had departed, since in Coleman's Will it is stated that the cottage was in his sole occupation and that the copyhold of the estate was to pass to his wife Margaret; upon her decease it was to pass to their daughter Mary Fell, wife of William Fell, vintner and citizen of London.[26] Nothing else is known of Margaret or the Fells other than that Mary and William had one child, Elizabeth.[27] By 1795, they were both dead and the copyhold of the estate had passed into the hands of their daughter who had married but was a widow known as Mrs. Elizabeth Doubleday.[28] Mrs. Doubleday seems to have been in some dispute as to her right to inherit but it was resolved in her favour.

It seems almost certain that Mrs. Doubleday did not herself live on the estate since, in the following year, she surrendered her interest to Jacob Warner and, in the deed transferring the copyhold, dated 29 April 1796, she is described as being from the parish of St. Thomas the Apostle in the county of Devon. The deed of transfer describes the estate as being, "that Messuage or Tenement situate at the bottom of Muswell Hill within the Parish and Manor of Hornsey with the Gardens, Barns, Stables and Appurtances thereto belonging now in the occupation of Mrs. Garratt."[29] Mrs. Garratt, like Widow Haynes, was probably a tenant.

Jacob Warner's House

Judging by the description of the property in the deed of transfer it had acquired a status sufficient to meet the pretensions of a City merchant anxious to purchase a desirable country residence within reasonable daily travelling distance to his business. Such a one was Jacob Warner into whose family ownership of the house and estate had now come and was to remain.[30]

The earliest mention of Jacob Warner occurs in 1779 when, with his brother Joseph, he is described as a grocer with business premises at 23, Rood Lane, in the City of London.[31] Rood Lane itself was long established and is shown on a Tudor map of London as Roude Lane.[32] In various London directories Jacob and Joseph Warner are listed as wholesale grocers and by 1815 seem to have expanded to include someone by the name of Whitmarsh,[33] although this name subsequently disappears. The business continued at the same address and, even after Jacob Warner's death in 1831, continued in the name of Jacob Warner & Son until it disappeared from the records altogether.[34] What became of Joseph Warner is not known but in a codicil to Jacob Warner's Will mention is made of warehouses in Rood Lane which were left, together with Jacob's share of the business, to Joseph and to Jacob's son-in-law the Rev. Edward Linzee. He also left some share of his interest in Rood Lane to his daughter Caroline, the wife of the Rev. Linzee.[35]

Apart from business commitments, involving temporary absences, Jacob Warner lived at the house on the estate. How long this house had been in existence is not known but it seems to have been relatively new since an observer in 1816 could comment: "The village [Hornsey] contains many respectable dwellings, among which will be noticed the villa of Jacob Warner Esq. This is a spacious and well-built modern house, but of proportions altogether too lofty for a Country residence."[36] The view painted in 1817 with Hornsey Church in the background (cover picture) illustrates this house then known simply as Jacob Warner's house.[37] The engraving published by Hassell provides the only visual information relating to this house. Built in Georgian style and facing west, its three floors confirm Brewer's description of its rather lofty appearance.

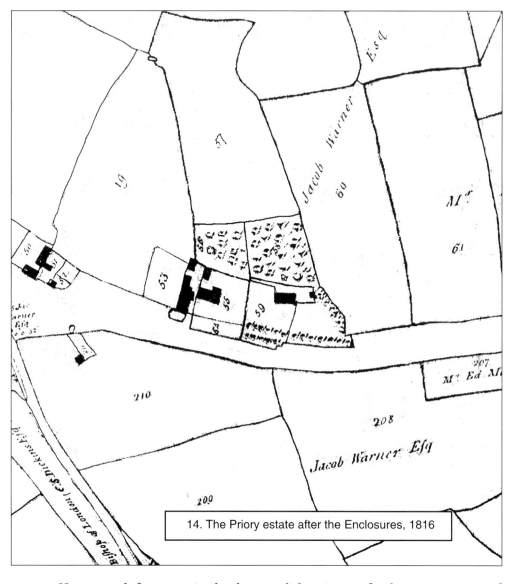

14. The Priory estate after the Enclosures, 1816

However, lofty or not, the house did not satisfy the aspirations of Jacob Warner and his family of four sons and one daughter. It would seem that something more substantial was required for such a large and prosperous family. In the early 1820s the erection of a larger building was embarked upon. The eventual house was occupied by Jacob Warner and his family but responsibility for the undertaking rested with one of Warner's sons, Henry, then in his thirties. In his Will Jacob Warner bequeathed the house to his wife Mary and so must have become the owner at some time after its completion. Most members of the family, including Henry, were in residence at the house by 1830.[38]

To build this new house, which became known as The Priory, the Warner family engaged the services of William F. Pocock, an architect whose business was located in the City of London. Born in the City in 1779, Pocock was the son of a London builder to whom he became apprenticed, since it was his father's wish.[39] Pocock was a reluctant apprentice and, one day, watching the laying of the foundations of a new building, the young Pocock observed "one individual ordering and directing the whole with a degree of dignity that quite fascinated his youthful imagination."[40] This person, Pocock soon discovered, was the architect and it was this path that he determined his subsequent career should follow. Thus inspired, Pocock's studious application to architectural drawing and design, for which he showed great aptitude, soon caused his father to cancel his articles of apprenticeship and place him under the tutelage of an architect, Charles Beazley.[41]

Apart from The Priory, Pocock's other works include the headquarters of the London Militia in Bunhill Row, EC1 in 1828 and the rebuilding of the Hall of the Worshipful Company of Leathersellers in the City. Those familiar with the former establishment, which still stands, will perhaps notice a certain similarity of style to The Priory, as shown in fig. 15 on p. 61, which was described by Pocock's son, himself an architect, as "a happy specimen of domestic Tudor."[42] Pocock was also responsible for the Almshouses of the Carpenters' Company at Twickenham, Christ Church at Virginia Water, and the Grammar Schools at Aldenham in Hertfordshire. In his early years he published several books relating to design and architecture. Among his lesser architectural works Pocock designed "The Pavilion" at Highgate (a conservatory for the Duchess of St. Albans at Holly Lodge) and a monumental column in memory of John, Duke of Bedford at Harford Climping parsonage; he was also responsible for villas built in both England and Ireland.[43] Between 1825 and 1827 Pocock exhibited at the Royal Academy.[44] According to his son, Pocock preferred "the useful to the ornamental, uniformity to variety, precedent to novelty. In arrangement he was simple and regular, bestowing much pains upon the plan. This he considered the ultimate of perfection."[45]

Unfortunately, with the demise of The Priory in 1902 and the non-existence of any interior or exterior plans, it is not possible to attach these attributes to the house in question. Little is known about the buildings on the estate. Beyond the print of Jacob Warner's first house and photographs of its successor, not much is available. Virtually nothing is known of the interiors. Much more can be written about people associated with the estate. The Ordnance Survey Map of 1864 gives an overview of The Priory and the surrounding estate but a description of the buildings has to be pieced together from scraps of information. The quest for enlightenment on the subject is not new. In 1887, for example, when the grounds of The Priory were opened to the public to celebrate the Jubilee of Queen Victoria the following was reported; "Daring ratepayers spread themselves . . . with a desperate determination. They trampled the flower beds, they invaded the greenhouse; they peered into the drawing room; they sought the secrets of the servants' loft; they poked their noses into the dustbin. All Hornsey was on the scent - here, there and everywhere."[46]

To return to the construction of The Priory; this coincided with the demolition of Wanstead House in Essex in 1822. The demolition followed upon the reckless profligacy of one of the Wellesleys who had married the heiress of a banker. This magnificent mansion in the Classical style had been built in 1715 but bankruptcy forced the demolition of the house and the contents were sold in 1822. The auction sale lasted for two days. Afterwards the house itself was sold for building materials.[47] It may be significant that in 1804 William Pocock had built a villa for one E. Warner at nearby Whipps Cross.[48] The Warners had family connections in this part of Essex[49] and it may well have been this which prompted Jacob Warner's family to take the opportunity to build a new house and to use some of the materials from Wanstead House.

The Priory and the Warner Family

The year after the Wanstead sale, 1823, builders began to demolish Warner's house and to build The Priory. By 1825 the new house seems to have been completed and ready for occupation.[50] It was of imposing appearance and was surrounded by some fine trees standing in very extensive grounds.[51] In the interior were many items taken from Wanstead House: oak panelling, window frames, bevelled plate glass in metal sashes, balustrades, architraves of doors, and mouldings.[52] One of the few features which was to survive the eventual demolition of the house in 1902 was the oak panelling and carving which was acquired by John Farrer who had it placed in the dining room of his house in Crescent Road, Crouch End.[53] Farrer was one of Hornsey's leading architects when urban development took place in the latter part of the nineteenth century and later. He was responsible for many houses on the Priory estate.

The wealth of Jacob Warner appears to have led him into land speculation in Hornsey and at one time he owned the adjacent Campsbourne estate. This passed to his daughter Caroline and her husband, the Rev. Edward Linzee, after the death of his wife Elizabeth Brooks Warner in 1833.[54]

In the 1800s Jacob Warner was an Overseer of the Poor in Hornsey and one of the Surveyors of the Highways.[55] In April 1804 he initiated, together with others as trustees, the purchase of a piece of waste land close to Hornsey Church to erect "a Protestant Charity School for the Education . . . of female children of the said Parish."[56] The school was extended in 1832 as a National School for girls and survived, later as an infants' school, till 1971.

59

In May 1806 Warner, together with another Overseer, purchased a small strip of land on the south side of Muswell Hill Road with the "purpose of erecting cottages for the use of the poor."[57] These cottages, virtual almshouses, remained till the 1890s.

In his Will drawn up in 1822 Jacob Warner mentions his four sons, Redston, Charles, George and Henry, and one daughter, Caroline, who was married to the Rev. Linzee.[58] Warner left his wife a sum of £500 to be paid immediately after his death together with a legacy of £10,000 at interest and much of his estate. To his four sons he left other lands. Mrs. Elizabeth Warner did not long survive her husband, dying two years[59] later in 1833. In her Will, apart from some minor bequests, Mrs. Warner left The Priory and the estate in equal shares to her children.[60] Of the surviving children and their spouses not a great deal is known. Caroline's husband at his death on 4 August 1842 at the age of 68, is recorded as the son of Robert Linzee, R.N., Admiral of the Blue, and Rector of West Tilbury, Essex.[61] Caroline Linzee died on 16 October 1840 at 56.[62] Caroline and her husband had suffered a sad loss with the death of a daughter, Augusta, who died aged 18 on 30 June 1831.[63]

George and Henry Warner lived at The Priory and they both died there; George on 29 October 1875 at the age of 86 and Henry on 4 September 1883 at 92.[64] Penelope Warner, wife of Jacob's brother Joseph was also at The Priory when she died on 2 August 1865 at the age of 86. Penelope was the mother of Harriet Brooks Warner who had married George, her first cousin.[65] (This gives some indication of the close knit structure of the Warner family at this time). Penelope was buried in the churchyard of St. Mary's, Hornsey on 7 August 1865 and appears to have been the first member of the Warner family to have been buried there; it is not known where Jacob Warner and his wife were buried. Later, other members of the Warner family were to join Penelope, including both George and Henry.[66]

Redston Warner was living at The Priory in 1841 but, thereafter, he disappears from the records apart from the use of his name by subsequent members of the Warner family.[67] No record has been found of what became of his brother Charles.

It is not clear who actually gained control of the business of Jacob Warner & Son. Although Jacob Warner left it in the hands of his brother and son-in-law, it seems that George followed in his father's footsteps for at the age of 62 George is described as a retired grocer.[68] However, the focus of George's business activities remains obscure although it might well have been in Rood Lane. In his Will, dated 11 January 1876, George's brother Henry refers to, "all my estate and interest in the lands, buildings, premises in or near Rood Lane in the City of London."[69] It is possible, therefore, that Jacob Warner's business continued after 1843 but under another name. Possibly George and Henry Warner entered into partnership with others who remain unknown.

15. The Priory in the Warners' day, *c.* 1865

The occupation of The Priory by the Warner family (which ended after the death of Henry Warner in 1883) was maintained in rather grand style. This is reflected in the number of domestic servants who were retained: no fewer than nine are recorded and at one time there were as many as eleven.[70] The Priory was the family home of George Warner after the death of his parents and he is always described as being the head of the household. But as we have noted, his brother Henry lived there too, and remained a bachelor. Living with George was his wife, Harriet Brooks Warner, and their children Joseph, the eldest (born 1836) and Arthur, Caroline and Edward, born between 1839 and 1853.[71] Not a great deal is known about this generation except for Joseph who became a barrister. His brother Edward too seems to have entered the legal profession. Joseph, Edward and Caroline were at The Priory in 1871 but there is no record of Arthur's presence. In 1881 Edward and Caroline were still at The Priory but Joseph seems to have left.[72] Joseph continued the family connection with the grocery trade and was Master of the Grocers' Company from 1873 to 1879. He was knighted in 1892. His son, Sir George Redston Warner (mentioned later) was born in 1879.[73] George Warner died at The Priory and in his Will (proved on 11

61

November 1875) he left the bulk of his estate as well as the house to his wife Harriet. He created a financial trust of which the interest was to be paid to his daughter Caroline. For his three sons he created another trust derived from various securities to provide interest in equal shares. It was also George Warner's express desire that his brother Henry could continue to reside at The Priory should he so wish.[74]

Mrs. Warner continued to live at The Priory with her brother-in-law Henry until she too died there on 7 May 1881.[75] The possession of The Priory then passed into the hands of the children. Henry Warner in his Will (proved 22 November 1883) makes no mention of the house and bequeathed his business interests in Rood Lane and the remainder of his personal estate to his nephews and nieces, i.e. George's children.[76]

Rather more is known of Henry Warner than the other members of the family since, among other things, he was at one time a churchwarden of St. Mary's, Hornsey and Treasurer of the Charities and Estates belonging to the parish. In 1869 he published an account of these charities which he presented to the church. It was perhaps his church associations that led him to donate the land at Muswell Hill upon which St. James's Church was built in 1842.[77] It would appear, therefore, that he had substantial means of his own.

Apart from his church work, Henry Warner sat as a J.P. at Highgate magistrates' court. He also had a long and successful association with the Middlesex Rifle Volunteers. This began on 2 November 1859 when Warner was transferred to the 13th Middlesex Rifle Volunteers (Hornsey) from the Oxford University Rifles where he had been posted as a Lieutenant in August of that year. He had, however, already attained the rank of Captain whilst with University Rifles and was gazetted as such with the Hornsey Corps on 21 April 1860.[78]

It would appear that Warner was something of a marksman since, in 1859 he had been one of the first volunteer officers to attend the Hythe School of Musketry where he had won first prize.[79] In June 1861 Warner gained further honours in shooting when he tied for second place in a competition to win a Whitworth rifle presented by J. Hoare, Esq., of Hampstead [80] These were no mean feats for someone then in his late 60s. (One wonders, in view of Warner's advanced age, whether he was representative of other officers or rather the exception.) He rose to become Lt. Colonel of the 2nd. Administrative Battalion of the Middlesex Volunteers and held this rank when he eventually resigned his commission at the age of 91.[81] Warner obtained further proficiency when, as a Major, he was attached, during the autumn of 1870, to the 91st Highlanders at Aldershot. Here he attended the School of Instruction where he obtained the first certificate of proficiency granted at that school and a certificate of special proficiency in military surveying.[82] Warner was able to combine his military activities with the benefits of residence at The Priory in lending its spacious grounds to the Volunteers for their frequent inspections and other events. Typical of these was the third annual meeting of the 2nd Battalion on Saturday 23 May 1863, "in the charming grounds of Mr. George Warner." Among those present were Miss Burdett Coutts as well as "gentlemen of the neighbourhood." Lt. Col. Wilkinson, the colonel of the regiment, paid tribute to Captain Warner for the way the meeting had been managed and to his father (sic), the proprietor of the grounds, for the welcome he had accorded the Volunteers.[83] In the following month there was, again, a large attendance of the local gentry to witness an official inspection of the 2nd Battalion by Colonel Morris, C.B. Captain Henry Warner was in command of 60 members of the Hornsey Corps.[84] The grounds of The Priory were not always used by the Battalion but in July 1869, following a change of venue from Alexandra Park, Mr. G. Warner allowed the annual inspection to take place in the picturesque and extensive grounds of The Priory." Once again there was a large assemblage, including Lady Waterlow, to inspect the very strong muster of ten companies.[85] The grounds of The Priory were used again for the annual inspection on 29 June 1872.[86]

With whatever military prowess he had gained, Henry Warner felt competent enough to address the Battalion in July 1874 on military tactics, offering criticisms and suggestions.[87] In October the grounds of The Priory were once again the centre for an inspection. This was to take place after a parade at Battalion H.Q. in Crouch End and a march to The Priory.[88] On 31st July of the following year another annual inspection took place at The Priory and on this occasion the officers of the Battalion were invited to be entertained by the 2nd Duke of Wellington at Apsley House. [89] It is unlikely that Major Warner would have refused such an invitation. By July 1876 he had been promoted to the rank of Lt. Colonel. [90]

The grounds of The Priory continued to be used for further drills and inspections and in 1881 Henry Warner carried out an official inspection of the Highgate detachment as commander of the Middlesex Volunteers. [91]

In December 1882 Warner stated his intention of resigning his commission owing to pressure of official work but was persuaded by Col. Kent, commanding the regimental district, to delay his decision and, instead, Warner was granted a year's leave of absence. [92] He finally resigned the following December and, on 21st May, [93] at the regimental dinner for officers held at the Holborn Restaurant, the new commanding officer presented Warner with an inscribed silver three-handed cup, a counterpart to a similar cup presented to him by the Grocers' Company. [94]

Warner had made a worthwhile contribution to the Volunteers but he had, upon assuming command as Lt. Colonel, introduced one measure which had some unfortunate consequences. This was an insistence that the same uniforms should be worn throughout all the battalions rather than the varied uniforms which had prevailed hitherto. The Enfield Company, representing some 50 per cent of the total strength, felt particularly aggrieved by this measure and the officer in command resigned in protest. [95] However, Warner got his way. He died soon after his farewell presentation.

The activities of the Volunteers at The Priory illustrates the fact that, in the absence of suitable open public spaces at that time, it was necessary to prevail upon the goodwill of the owners of local large houses for the use of their grounds. On more than one occasion the Volunteers made use of the grounds of nearby Crouch Hall. The demise of such large houses in the latter part of the 19th century placed increasing pressure on the local authority to provide suitable alternatives.

With the death of Henry Warner the next occupant of The Priory would not only strive to provide such open spaces but would also initiate other far-sighted projects. This champion of local amenities was Henry Reader Williams who became known as the "Father of Hornsey" and his residence at The Priory was the most celebrated stage of the mansion's existence.

Henry Reader Williams

Such were the achievements of Henry Williams in both philanthropic and local affairs that it would require a separate treatise to do him justice. Williams and his family took up occupation of The Priory some time after October 1884, when a letter of his to the local press shows he was living at

16. Henry Reader Williams, wine merchant and philanthropist, and last resident of The Priory

Oak Lodge, Jacksons Lane, Highgate,[96] where his next-door neighbour and business partner was the antiquarian J.H. Lloyd.[97] Williams, a member of Highgate Congregational Church, had lived at Oak Lodge for some twenty years. He had arrived on the Northern Heights from Hackney where his endeavours had been directed towards the re-building of Lower Clapton Congregational Church. He had come from humble beginnings, being born at Wapping on 25 January 1822; his wife Mary Anne had been born five years later in Mile End. [98] Williams began his working life at the age of 13 as a clerk in the City and showed remarkable energy and industry. At the age of 24, as well as working hard for his employers, he first began his philanthropic activities. [99] Indeed, it was because he was devoting so much time to voluntary work that he was given the option of relinquishing it or resigning his post. He chose the latter course and formed his own business as a wine merchant.[100]

Williams proved a successful man of business and the company, under the name of Henry Williams & Co., Wine & Spirit Merchants, became one of the best known wine houses in the country. Indeed, Gladstone, the Chancellor of the Exchequer, in his 1860 budget in which he proposed to modify the import duty on French wines, referred in the House of Commons to a very good ordinary claret which would thereby be 14 shillings per dozen. Although Parliamentary rules prevented Gladstone from naming the company, he privately informed M.P.s that it was Williams's firm. Such was the subsequent demand that it became known as Gladstone's claret.[101]

The centre of Williams's business activities was, in 1889, situated at 11, Queen Victoria Street, E.C. but, by 1895, it had removed to 6, Lime Street where it was to remain, still bearing his name long after his death, until at least 1923. Between that time and 1928 the business seems to have been absorbed by Standing, Sandeman & Hartley Ltd.[102]

It was the success of Williams's business that enabled him to undertake the expense of living at The Priory. However, Williams did not purchase the property but resided there on leasehold terms as a life tenant.[103] Ownership of the house and the estate remained in the hands of the Warner family. Williams and his family lived in style since he maintained a retinue of 11 staff which included a coachman, plus four other servants.[104] In 1891 he was living with his wife and one of his sons, Henry Edmund, then aged 36; he had one other son, Stanley, who followed him into the wine business.[105]

Williams' philanthropic work in the East End had begun in earnest when, in 1846, he accepted the office of Honorary Secretary and Superintendent of the King Edward Ragged Schools located in an old stable in King Edwards Street, Spitalfields. The 7th Earl of Shaftesbury (then Lord Ashley) accepted the office of president and this marked the long association between the two men.[106] Williams, together with the Rev. William Taylor, raised money to purchase a site in Albert Street, Mile End, for what was to become The King Edward Ragged & Industrial School and Eastern Refuge for 500 children, with dormitory accommodation for 40 girls. The building was opened by Lord Shaftesbury in 1851. Williams continued to hold the posts of Secretary and Superintendent until 1861 when he resigned from the latter post but continued as Secretary until 1868 when he undertook the duties of Treasurer.[107] Eventually, in 1872, the Ragged and Industrial schools returned to a new and larger building on their original site.[108] The building in Albert Street was then certified as an industrial school for 100 girls. By 1875 premises in Andrews Road, Cambridge Heath, were opened as a branch of the School in Albert Street with accommodation for 120 girls.

Williams arranged for the girls to make annual visits to the grounds of The Priory. Such visits had already been a regular occurrence at Williams's previous house at Highgate. Thus, in July 1895, the local newspaper could report: "On Tuesday afternoon for the 25th consecutive year, Mr. and Mrs. Williams entertained the girls of the King Edward Certified Industrial School . . . The visit to The Priory is the event of the year to the girls, to whom Mr. Williams' beautiful demesne is a fruitful source of delight. Holiday fare, too, and holiday games, are not forgotten, and the children are able to romp and play in the spacious meadows to their hearts' content. The weather on Tuesday was fortunately very fine and the children greatly enjoyed the drive from the school at Cambridge Heath, Hackney . . . As in other years a large company of residents of the neighbourhood had been invited to The Priory on this occasion, and while the children romped in the meadows at the rear of the house, Mr. and Mrs. Williams entertained their friends on the spacious and charming lawn in the front. A pleasant little al fresco conversazione ensued over the cups of tea, an excellent musical programme being given at the same time by the band stationed in the centre of the lawn . . . (a list of some 80 visitors then follows) . . . At half past six the whole of the children and a large number of visitors gathered in the large marquee where reports were presented, and rewards handed to the children who had earned them. The girls as they stood along one side of the tent in their neat dresses, white pinafores, and straw hats, appeared to be in the very pink of condition, and they all had rosy faces and smiling looks, the hymn 'Now thank we all our God,' having been sung in a very creditable manner."[109]

The Priory was to play host to other local celebrations. In 1887 it was the focus for Hornsey's celebrations of the Golden Jubilee. On Saturday, 25 June "the beautiful grounds of The Priory appeared suddenly to change into a fairy pleasure ground . . ."[110] The first to arrive on the scene were "nine gaily coloured coaches, containing the girls from the King Edward Schools. The latter, to the number of 150, accompanied by a band, rode through the village and into the grounds, where they awaited the entry of the others.[111] By noon a muster of some 2,500 children from the district organised by Col. Bird assembled in the High Street in preparation for the march to The Priory. They were accompanied by the Millfield Band and the men of Hornsey Fire Brigade and their band and at 1.00 p.m. the whole procession, over one mile in length, marched through the village and into the grounds of The Priory. At 2.00 p.m. athletics followed in the grounds whilst dinner was given to the aged poor in one of the marquees." H.R. Williams greeted them although, no doubt because he was teetotal, he asked the assembly to give three cheers instead of drinking the health of the Queen. Later in the afternoon the King Edward School children, preceded by their band, led a general exodus of all the children. Mr. Williams gave a concluding speech and, following music by

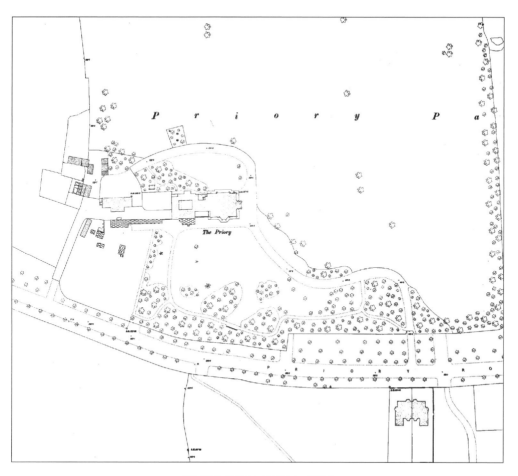

17. The Priory estate in 1894

the bands, was given three hearty cheers for himself and another three for his wife and family.[112]

Similar celebrations took place at The Priory ten years later for the celebrations of the Diamond Jubilee. The " Clerk of the Weather" had arranged a brilliant afternoon but illness prevented Williams from being present. Once again there was a large assemblage including 4,000 children from the district together with some 40 members of the Jubilee Committee. The children had mustered at their schools and then marched to Church Lane where, accompanied by the Church Lads' and Boys' Brigade the whole assemblage continued on to the grounds of The Priory accompanied by the bands of the 3rd Middlesex Rifle Volunteers. The afternoon was confined to children's sports under the supervision of 120 teachers. It was not until later that parents and friends were admitted to the grounds. The celebrations were not on the scale of those ten years earlier.[113] They were under the supervision of Williams's son Henry and perhaps were muted in view of Henry's father's illness. Henry Reader Williams died not long afterwards, on 29 September 1897, at the age of 75; he had suffered a long and trying illness.[114]

Apart from his business and philanthropic activities Williams was extremely active in local government affairs. The monument in recognition and appreciation of his public service is the Clock Tower in Crouch End Broadway which was unveiled in June 1895 by the Earl of Stafford.[115]

Limits of space preclude a full account of Williams's public service during his residence in Hornsey but there is no doubt that he played a major role in the development of the area. For twenty-one years Williams sat on the Hornsey Local Board of which he was the chairman for many years until he retired from this post in 1894.[116] He was also active in promoting public education including the formation of Board Schools in Hornsey following the Education Act, 1870. The first meeting of the Hornsey School Board, with Williams sitting as a Progressive Non-Conformist, was held at the Hornsey Local Board offices in Southwood Lane on 7 January 1875.[117] Williams remained on the Board until resigning in October 1878 but rejoined as its chairman, at the end of 1880, remaining as chairman until he finally stood down in 1887.[118]

It was Williams who in mid-1883 initiated the foundation of a residential school for incorrigible truants, a perennial problem.[119] This no doubt sprang from his experience with the King Edward Industrial School. Together with the school boards of Tottenham and Edmonton, Williams was authorised by the Hornsey Board to look for suitable premises. These he found at Walthamstow[120] and, largely due to his direction, the whole venture was up and running, with the official opening on 28 June 1884 by the Earl of Aberdeen.[121] Williams remained associated with the school, named the North London Certified Industrial (Truant) School, long after his retirement from the School Board. It proved its worth since, by 1903, 91.4% of children were in attendance at Hornsey's board schools, a 20% improvement over the previous 20 years or so.[122]

Although by 1894 Williams had relinquished his associations with both the Hornsey Local Board and the School Board he did not retire from public life. He allowed himself to be nominated as a candidate for Middlesex County Council and was duly elected. Politically Williams was a Liberal and was spoken of as a possible parliamentary candidate but he preferred to devote his energies to local work. Apart from this Williams was twice acting Master of the Fruiterers' Company.[123]

It was largely thanks to Williams's efforts that Highgate Woods were saved from speculative builders and remained open space. This involved a long and somewhat acrimonious campaign in which Williams was assisted by Ernest Hinscliffe Hindley, born at Lightcliffe House in Tottenham Lane in

1858, the son of a Park Chapel deacon. In 1889 Hindley married Williams's daughter, Amy, and he became a staunch ally of his father-in-law in the campaign to preserve what was left of Hornsey's open spaces.[124] To Williams, too, must be owed the eventual creation of Priory Park since plans had been submitted for the building of many small houses on what became the "Pleasure Grounds". Williams, who feared another Campsbourne or Abyssinia (tightly-packed working-class districts built up since the 1860s), negotiated with the owner of the land and it was purchased by Hornsey Local Board in 1891.[125] Williams also attempted to acquire the Alexandra Palace grounds for the local authority and thus secure them for public use. Although unsuccessful, he prevented, almost single-handedly, the southern part of the grounds from being developed by speculative builders.[126] Williams was also successful in making Hornsey the first district to insist on its roads being at least 40 feet wide.[127]

After Williams's death at The Priory the body was taken from there, on 30 September 1897, to a well-attended funeral service at Highgate Congregational Church and from thence to Highgate cemetery for burial.[128] Williams left an estate valued at the then gigantic sum of £89,134.7.8d.[129] In his Will Williams left the leasehold interest in The Priory and the estate in trust to his wife Mary, his sons Henry and Stanley and his business partner J.H. Lloyd, with the option for his wife of continuing to reside at the house. Williams also held two properties at Pembury Grove, Hackney, which passed into the trust.[130]

Whether or not Mrs. Williams wished to go on living at The Priory is not clear. At the time of Williams's death it was remarked that, "unfortunately the estate will pass into the hands of the builder. Already plans have been made, and a new town will shortly be opened up. Those who have passed many hours in the grounds will regret this." Perhaps none more than the girls of the King Edward Industrial School, of whom 120 had been present at the funeral.[131]

The development of the Edwardian estate

Why the surviving members of the Warner family embarked upon the destruction of The Priory and development of the estate for housing can only be surmised. No doubt the family foresaw the greater financial yields from leasehold rents from many properties rather than from one large house and its grounds. This, of course, was a common enough process at the time as one by one large houses and estates in the environs of London fell before the onward march of the speculative builder. There was a ready market, especially in Hornsey, which, largely thanks to the efforts of Williams and others on the Local Board, had earned the epithet of "Healthy Hornsey".

Whatever her personal feelings, Williams's widow left The Priory and the advertisement overleaf appeared in the local press in March 1898.[132]

The advertisement gives evidence of the high standard of living enjoyed by its last occupants. One item from The Priory which still survives is a bell, dated 1839 and weighing 77 lbs. which once hung from the building; it is currently in the possession of Haringey Council, at Bruce Castle Museum.

By 1899 Mrs. Williams was living with her son Henry at a house called "Shenley" in Shepherd's Hill, Highgate[133] where she remained until some time in 1906,[134] when it may be assumed that she had died; by that time she would have been approaching 79 years of age. H.E. Williams remained at "Shenley" for a further eighteen months or so until he moved to "Priory Lodge" (now number 3), Shepherd's Hill where he remained until at least 1931.[135]

Events on the estate moved fairly rapidly. As early as 1899 building operations had got under way and by 1902 The Priory had been demolished. It seems that the stables, including a clock-tower, were demolished some two years later. Unfortunately, no detailed plans of the buildings have been traced.[136]

A 1902 map shows all the forthcoming roads on the estate to have been laid out by that time.[137] Apart from Park Road North and Park Road South (north and south of Priory Road), the names of nearly all of them have very local connotations. Farrer Road and Farrer Close were named after the architect of the new houses. Priory Road which, in 1851, had been known as Muswell Hill Road and, at another time, as Broad Lane,[138] obviously derives its name from the old mansion and so likewise does Priory Avenue. (Incidentally, there had been proposals to widen Priory Road to meet the demands of growing traffic but vigorous local protests thwarted this move).[139] Warner Road derives its name from the estate owners whilst Redston Road is named after Jacob Warner's eldest son. Linzee Road derives its name from the Linzees. The derivation of the name of Danvers Road is rather more problematic although, in a codicil to her Will dated 5 January 1832, Jacob

Warner's wife, Elizabeth, made a bequest of £100 to a Mrs. Henrietta Danvers; no doubt she was a relative or close friend.[140] The origin of the names of Clovelly Road and Baden Road remains obscure although it may have expressed the desire to be associated with popular upper middle-class resorts, Baden-Baden being a fashionable spa in Germany at the time, and Clovelly a favourite summer retreat.

Building commenced on the eastern and southern sectors of the estate and moved in a westerly and northerly direction until, by 1909, much of the estate had been covered with mostly terraced houses, some 890 houses in all.[141] John Farrer, the architect, was much involved in the actual building operations. According to one account the many fine old elms which had stood on the estate were sawn up and used as gate posts for the houses.[142] The Edwardians wasted nothing, it seems.

The houses built on the estate varied in size although, in contemporary terms, most were bigger than average. There were, for example, four-bedroomed houses in Linzee Road at an annual rental of £42 whilst, for larger households, there were five-bedroomed houses in Priory Road at between £60 and £65.[143] Clearly, houses of this size and rental could only have attracted the more affluent. The properties were leasehold with the freehold remaining in the hands of the Warner family. They were officially, at that time, trustees acting on behalf of Arthur and Edmund Warner and Lady Wilhelmina Warner.[144] Today, in spite of the Leasehold Reform Act of 1968, the freehold of some of the houses and, in particular, the present row of shops on the south side of Priory Road and continuing into Park Road opposite the foot of Muswell Hill, is still in the hands of the Warner family. Many of the leaseholds will soon be due for renewal.[145]

One notable member of the family is Sir Edward Redston Warner, the son of Sir George Redston Warner to whom reference has already been made, who was a career diplomat.[146] Sir Edward followed the same profession, and was made a Knight of the Order of St. Michael and St. George in 1965; he had already received the O.B.E. in 1948 and the C.M.G. in 1965. Sir Edward, who was born in 1911, spent some 35 years working in the Diplomatic Service and, *inter alia*, was Ambassador to the Cameroon (1963-66) and, later, Ambassador to Tunisia (1968-1970). Sir Edward married in 1943 and had three sons and one daughter. He now lives in retirement in Gloucestershire.[147]

Thus a link with the Priory estate dating back 200 years still survives. However, whilst the rows of neat houses which cover the estate make a desirable suburb one wonders what the original purchaser, Jacob Warner, would make of the transformation which was wrought in such a short time.

Alan A. Aris.

References

1. William Keane, *The Beauties of Middlesex* *(1850)*, p. 87

2. C.J.M. Sidey, "Notes on Hornsey Church & District", vol.5, p.43; H.Lib.

3. Hornsey Enclosure Map, 1816; BCM.

4. Newspaper extract dated 23 February 1902; acc. 0874.188 (4846), BCM.

5. *HJ*, 2 October 1953

6. J.C. Marriott, "The History, Topography & Antiquities of the Borough of Hornsey" (unpublished m.s.), p. 135; BCM.

7. *Ibid.*, pp. 51-53

8. J.C. Marriott, "Notes on Highgate, Hornsey etc., which have been in the histories of the same," p.107; BCM.

9. Another commentator writing in 1910, having seen the then demolished house, offered a contrary view: "The Priory, invited inspection as a remnant of ancient days, but it was a fraud of modern erection, built of materials taken from a real priory at Banstead." It would appear that this commentator was confusing Banstead with Wanstead (see later text) and enquiries at Banstead have established that there has never been a priory in that area. *HJ, Christmas Supplement*, December 1910; Potter Collection, BM.

10. W. McB. & F. Marcham, *Court Rolls of the Bishop of London's Manor of Hornsey, 1603-1701;* p.190

11. *Ibid.*, p.170

12. W.McB. & F. Marcham (Editors), *Middlesex Parish Registers*, vol. 9, p.24

13. Marcham, *Court Rolls, op. cit.*, pp.145 & 147

14. *Ibid.*, p. 105

15. W. Shaw, *The Knights of England*, vol. 2, p. 240

16. *Highgate School Register 1833-1964* (6th ed.), p.50

17. Marcham, *Court Rolls*, p. 247

18. Acc. 203/16, G.L.R.O.

19. Marcham, *Court Rolls*, p. 193

20. *Ibid.*, p.210

21. Hornsey Manor Court Rolls; 10465/25, Gdl.

22. Court Rolls; 10465/61, Gdl.

23. *Ibid.*, 10465/61

24. *Ibid.*, 10465/61

25. 10465/40 & 10465/47, Gdl.

26. Prob. 11/745, P.R.O.

27. 10465/110, Gdl.

28. *Ibid.*

29. 10465/111, Gdl.

30. Information from H.G. Scott Esq., Surveyor to the Warner family

31. Kent's *Directory* for the year 1779

32. Copper plate map, c. 1553-1559, *Early maps of London;* Gdl.

33. *The Post Office Annual Directory* for 1815.

34. *P.O. Directory*, 1844

35. 1831, Prob. 11 1/91B, P.R.O.

36. J.N. Brewer, *The Beauties of England and Wales*, vol. 10, part 4, p. 211

37. J. Hassell, *Rides & Walks, with excursions by water, 30 miles round the British Metropolis*, vol. 1, p.30

38. MR/PLT/1970, p.4, G.L.R.O.

39. W.W. Pocock, undated memoir of W.F. Pocock; RIBA.

40. *Ibid.*

41. *Ibid.*

42. *Ibid.*

43. *Ibid.*

44. H.M. Colvin, *Biographical Dictionary of English Architects*, p. 465

45. Pocock memoir, *op. cit.*

46. *H & FPJ*, 2 July 1887; HHS

47. John H. Lloyd, *The History, Topography & Antiquities of Highgate*, p. 292

48. Colvin, p. 465

49. H.G. Scott, Esq.

50. Colvin, p. 465

51. Lloyd, *op. cit.*, p. 292

52. *Ibid.*

53. Sidey, *op. cit.*, vol. 3, pp. 36 & 38

54. 1833, Prob.11/1813, P.R.O.

55. J.C. Marriott, "Notes on Highgate, Hornsey etc.", p. 108 (quoting Hornsey Vestry Minutes)

56. 10465/119, Gdl.

57. 10465/121, Gdl.

58. 1831, Prob. 11/1791B, P.R.O.

59. *Ibid.*

60. 1833, Prob. 11/1813, P.R.O.

61. F.T. Cansick, *The Monumental Inscriptions of Middlesex (1875)*, p. 13

62. *Ibid.*

63. *Ibid.*

64. Enumerator's Returns, Census of Parish of Hornsey, 1841, 1851, 1861, 1871 and 1881; BCM.

65. *Who Was Who 1897-1905*

66. Monumental Inscriptions with index to St. Mary, Hornsey, p.10 (North Middlesex Family History Society Survey); HHS

67. 1841 census.

68. 1851 census.

69. Last Will and Testament of H. Warner, 1883; SH

70. 1851 & 1861 census

71. 1871 census

72. 1881 census

73. Boase, *Modern Biographies*, vol. 3, col. 1205. See also *Times* Obituaries, 7 and 19 July 1897

74. Last Will and Testament of G. Warner, 1875; SH.

75. Letters of Administration of Mrs. H.B. Warner, 1881; SH.

76. Last Will and Testament of H. Warner, 1883; SH.

77. *V.C.H.*, vol. 6, p. 175

78. E.T. Evans, *Records of the 3rd Middlesex Rifle Volunteers*, pp. 90 & 319; H.Lib.

79. *Ibid.*, p. 272

80. "   p. 183

81. "   p. 319

82. "   p. 198-199

83. *St. Michael's Highgate, Parish magazine*, May 1863; HLSI.

84. *Ibid.*, June 1863.

85. "   July 1869.

86. "   August 1872.

87. "   July 1874.

88. "   October 1874.

89. "   July 1875.

90. "   July 1876.

91. "   March & July 1877 & August 1878.

92. Evans, *Volunteers, op. cit.*, p. 14

93. (*Records of the 3rd Middlesex Rifle Volunteers*, p. 265) Unfortunately, the source recording the date of this dinner is incorrect since, as already noted, Henry Warner died on 4 September 1883 and could not possibly have attended a dinner stated to have been held on 21 May 1884. However, there seems no question that Warner did attend a farewell dinner, but it seems likely that the date was 1883 and not 1884. Incidentally, Warner was permitted to retain his rank as Lt. Col. and to continue to wear his uniform.

94. *Ibid.*, p. 272

95. *"For Queen and Country"*, Haringey Archives Committee exhibition catalogue; BCM.

96. Potter Collection, vol. XIV, p. 106; BM.

97. Census of Hornsey, 1881, P.R.O.

98. 1891 census.

99. *The Christian Age*, 10 August 1883; BCM.

100. *H & FPJ*, 2 October 1897 (Obituary)

101. *Ibid.*

102. Kelly's *Directories of Hornsey* – 1889, 1895, 1923, 1928 & 1930; Gdl.

103. Will of H.R. Williams.

104. 1891 census.

105. Will of H.R. Williams.

106. In 1884 Williams was presented with a portrait of himself which had been commissioned by Lord Shaftesbury. *Highgate Parish Magazine, op. cit.*, May 1884

107. *The Christian Age*, 10 August 1883

108. *Ibid.*

109. *H & FPJ*, 27 July 1895; HHS

110. Lloyd, *op. cit.*, pp. 422-425

111. *Ibid.*

112. "

113. *H & FPJ*, 3 July 1897; HHS.

114. *H & FPJ*, 2 October 1897 (Obituary).

115. *H & FPJ*, 29 June 1895; HHS. See Joan Schwitzer's pamphlet *Crouch End Clock Tower* (HHS 1995)

116. Newspaper extract dated 29 March 1894; acc. 90WIL, BCM.

117. HSB. Mins., vol. 1, 7 January 1875; BCM.

118. Alan Aris, "The Hornsey School Board, 1875-1903", unpublished M.A. dissertation, October 1979; King's College, University of London.

119. *Daily Telegraph*, 27 July 1883; BNL.

120. HSB.Mins., vol. 3, 8 May 1883; BCM.

121. HSB. Mins., vol. 4, 22 July 1884; BCM.

122. HSB. Mins., vol. 10 (Appendix); BCM.

123. *H & FPJ*, 2 October 1897 (Obituary)

124. Ben Travers, *The Book of Crouch End* (1990), p. 74

125. See James Savin, "Priory Park, its purchase and development," *HHS Bulletin 30* (1989), p. 40 ff.

126. *H & FPJ*, 2 October 1897 (Obituary)

127. C.J.M. Sidey, *op. cit.*, vol. 2, p.32

128. *H & FPJ*, 2 October 1897 (Obituary)

129. Will of H.R. Williams; SH.

130. *Ibid.*

131. *H & FPJ*, 2 October 1897 (Obituary)

132. *H & FPJ*, 5 March 1898; HHS

133. Kelly's *Directory of Hornsey* 1899-1900

134. *Ibid.* 1905-1906

135. *Ibid.* 1907-1908, 1908, 1909, & 1931.
    The name of the house was probably
    due to the *other* "Priory", which had
    stood nearby, a mansion demolished
    c. 1901 to make room for the Public
    Library and a row of Edwardian houses,
    of which Priory Lodge was one.

136. H.G. Scott, Esq.

137. *H & FPJ*, Christmas supplement,
    December 1902.

138. C.J.M. Sidey, *op. cit.*, vol. 4, p.133, &
    J.C. Marriott, "Notes on Highgate,
    Hornsey etc.", p.109

139. C.J.M. Sidey, *op. cit.*, vol. 4, p. 133

140. Prob. 11/1813; P.R.O.

141. Kelly's *Directory of Hornsey* 1909

142. C.J.M. Sidey, *op. cit.*, vol. 5, p.43

143. *H & FPJ*, 22 April 1899 & 7 September
    1901; HHS.

144. HUDC Mins., 18 February 1901; H. Lib.

145. H.G. Scott, Esq.

146. See *Who's Who*, 1948

147. *Who's Who*, 1996

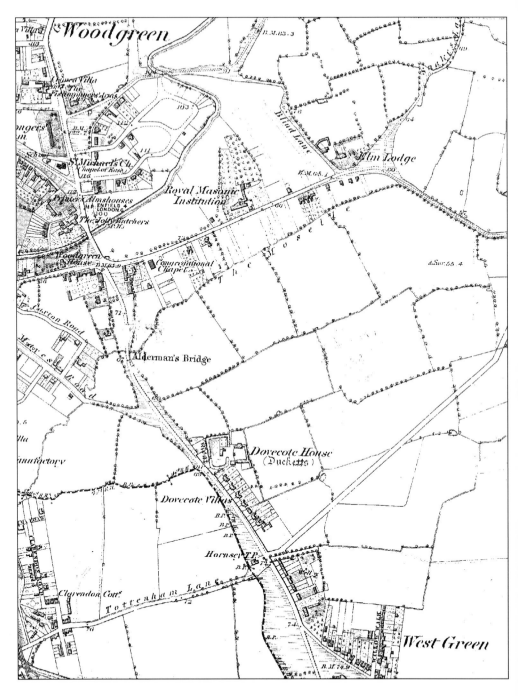

18. Ducketts and Green Lanes in 1873 with the moat clearly visible.
'Tottenham Lane' to the south is modern Turnpike Lane.

The origins of a manor: Duckett's, Green Lanes

Editor's note: Documentation to trace estates back to their beginnings, sometimes as portions of larger estates existing at or even before the Norman Conquest, is rarely available. When it is, only the most persistent of researchers with a command of palaography and medieval Latin and almost unlimited time can tease out the facts. Such a seeker after knowledge was Cecil Harris, a long-standing member of both the Edmonton Hundred Historical Society and the HHS for whom the history of the Manor of Ducketts became an enduring interest. He used a wide variety of sources – from State Papers to little-known ecclesiastical and private collections. Unfortunately, he died suddenly and unexpectedly, after agreeing to contribute to this book. His Ducketts typescript duly came to the HHS but no list of sources has come to light.

Cecil Harris had already contributed parts of his paper to our Bulletin where they were published under the titles of "Duckett's Manor and the King's 'Great Matter'" (No. 34, 1993), on the Tudor period, and "Ducketts in Stuart times" (No. 35, 1994). These articles and the overall length of the paper precluded complete publication, and it was decided to print a section only. This passage amounts to less than 15% of the author's complete history of the Manor.

Ducketts Common by Turnpike Lane Underground station at one time formed part of the great expanse of Ducketts Manor and Farm. Ducketts Manor was one of the seven lordships of Tottenham. The farmhouse of Ducketts stood at the site of what is now the eastern end of Dovecote Avenue which runs from the High Road, Wood Green into Bury Avenue. From the 1619 map of the Earl of Dorset's Survey the house looked a substantial building. It consisted of ground floor and first floor with four windows on the first floor. There are two entrance doors, and a barn or outhouse is also shown. There is no sign of a moat around the house although later one appeared. From the *History of the Manors of Tottenham* by Lord Coleraine *c.* 1650-1680 the mansion house is described as being like that of Mockings and moated round. It had great barns and was planted about with fruit trees. It also had good out-housing and a large pigeon house and was surrounded by water for its greater safety, "as Faulkners know very needful for such as keep hawks." Bordering on to Ducketts Farm was a

'Hawkwell Park' and it is very likely that hawks were kept at Ducketts to go hunting in the park. Inventories of household furnishings for this building are no longer in existence; inventories up to the middle part of the seventeenth century were lost in the great Fire of London in 1666.

19. Ducketts farmhouse *c.* 1846

In the mid-nineteenth century when William Robinson was preparing his *History of Tottenham*, an original engraving was made of Ducketts farmhouse for inclusion in his work. This shows the moat with a wooden bridge crossing it. The house at this period consisted of basement, ground floor and first floor. There were steps leading up to the front door and a side entrance and a conservatory. The front of the house is partially obscured by trees and bushes. There is a painting of the farm house in Bruce Castle Museum.

On the Tithe Commissioners' map of the Tottenham district dated 1844, the house, outhouses and the moat are clearly seeen, also the bridge. Robinson in his *History* states that the moat was connected to the New River and that a yearly rent was paid to the New River Company although no trace of these payments has been found in Company records. (A lot of information has been destroyed by fires at N.R.C. headquarters).

On the Ordnance Survey map of 1864, Ducketts is shown as

Dovecote House and the moat can still be seen. There are also thirteen houses adjoining it fronting the Green Lanes (now High Road, Wood Green) called Dovecote Villas – a sign of the oncoming rush of property builders and speculators. When the Ordnance Survey map for 1894 was issued all things appertaining to Dovecote House or Ducketts had been completely erased and Noel Park Estate was in its place.

The early years – Laurence Duket the elder
The beginning of Ducketts Manor and Farm was sometime before 1256. In a Grant dated 1256/7 160 acres of land in Woodlegh, Tottenham were granted by James de Stevinton and Isabella his wife to John Renger. This John Renger was Henry the Third's King's Clerk. A later grant, not dated, grants the land, 'in Woodeley, Tottenham', to Laurence Duket and Matilda his wife. This Woodeleye or Woodlegh would be today's Wood Green.

Laurence Duket was a relation of Nicholas Duket who was Chamberlain of London, Sheriff in 1191 and 1196 and was made Bailiff of the City of London on 28th September 1197. In the Charter Rolls of the 7th year of King John, 1206, Nicholas Duket is described as the son of Ranulfe Duchet or Duket – a man mentioned in the Great Roll of the Exchequer 1131.

Laurence Duket was a goldsmith by trade, and lived in turbulent times. In 1263 Simon de Montfort led forces against Henry the Third and rebellious citizens in London demanded the overthrow of the ruling merchants. In 1272 Laurence was caught up in the murder of a William le Fromund and was only pardoned of the deed by the intervention of the King's nephew, John de Valencia.

Further trouble was in store for Laurence which eventually led to his downfall and death. He was locked in a vendetta with Ralph Crepin, who became the first recognisable Common Clerk and in 1280 reached the aldermanic Council, the first specialised civic adminstrator to do so. Laurence was of good family and he had supporters drawn from a respectable milieu of goldsmiths and vintners. In 1273 his sister had sold houses to Crepin and the feud may have originated in a loan. For Crepin was a money-lender and though connected with the cadet branch of the Gloucester family, a new man in the patriciate.

There was a woman involved named Alice atte Bowe, who apparently kept a tavern in Mark Lane. She was a member or dependant of the Laufare family, a clan of cutlers and cordwainers who had been prominent among the rebels in 1263. They were active supporters of Crepin. So was his nephew Peter, another cordwainer, and John Tolesan, grandson of one of the City aldermen who had been deposed in 1258.

Both sides resorted to violence and their clashes disturbed the peace. But while both employed professional thugs, Crepin could rely on fellow clerks within the administration to cover his tracks. In 1284 Laurence Duket met with Ralph Crepin in Cheapside and grievously wounded him. Fearing reprisals, he fled for sanctuary to St. Mary-le-Bow church, but Crepin's friends surprised him there and hanged him so artfully in one of the windows that the coroner's inquest gave the verdict of self-murder, suicide, and ordered the body to be drawn by the feet and buried in a ditch outside the City. However a boy had also taken refuge in the church and had lain with Duket but had concealed himself. Later he gave information against the murderers and many were apprehended. Sixteen were hanged and a woman, said to be the contriver of the murder, was burnt alive. Persons of distinction concerned in this action were given pecuniary fines. Laurence Duket's body was taken up from the ditch and buried decently in the churchyard. Ralph Crepin was arrested and imprisoned in the Tower and his goods and chattels were taken and given to the King. But on swearing his innocence before the Bishop of London, he was acquitted and all his goods and chattels returned to him.

Laurence Duket's association with Tottenham was well-established as there are five property documents in existence bearing his name as a witness. [Details omitted.] Laurence Duket is also mentioned in the Rolls of the City of London in the year 1275.

After the death of Laurence Duket all his lands in Tottenham passed to his son, also named Laurence. He became Coroner of the county of Middlesex until his death in either 1300 or 1301. This Laurence also received lands in Tottenham and Hornsey from William-le-Brun, King's Yeoman. This new acquisition, amounting to one hide of land, twelve acres of meadow, four acres of woodland and 12d. rents, helped to swell the Duket holding.

In September 1314 Laurence Duket's son John granted all the land of his father's in Tottenham to a William Furness and Cecilia his wife. For how long is not known, but in 1331 John was again in possession and made a grant of all his lands and 'tenements' etc. in Tottenham and Hornsey to a Matthew le Palmer. Some evidence of John Duket's association with Tottenham is on a note of debt dated 13th July 1332 which reads:

"John Duket of Tottenham acknowledges that he owes to Walter Neel, citizen of London, £20; to be levied, in default of payment, of his lands and chattels in county Middlesex."

Duckett's Manor
The first time the actual Manor of Duketts is mentioned is in a Power of Attorney by which John de Yakesle, tent maker to King Edward the Third, appointed Henry de Chireton

"to receive livery of seisin [possession] of all that Manor called Dukets (from the family of that name) in the county of Middlesex which Lord Matthew de Palmer recently granted to him and endowed with Charter."

The date was 1334. Sale of the manor's stock occurred in the same year.

In 1346, Sir John de Stonford, Knight, obtained possession of the Manor of Duket from John de Yakesle. He leased the property to a member of the original Duket family, Thomas Duket. How Sir John came into possession of the property is uncertain, but is seems Isabella de Yakesle, wife of John Yakesle carried out a number of suits and actions to stop this new ownership but to no avail. Sir John was a judge at the Court of Common Pleas from 1342 to 1372, and acted as Chief Baron of the Exchequer in 1345. He is stated to have been born at Stonford, or Stowford, in the parish of West Down, Devonshire. He married Joan, co-heiress of the Traceys of Woolacombe. He and his wife held lands at South Petherton and Drayton, Somerset. Their cousin, also named Joan, married William de Brightlegh of Devon who was "a man well read in the laws" and to whom the ownership of Ducketts Manor passed on the death of de Stonford.

In 1360 William de Brightlegh leased Ducketts Manor and farm to Robert de Gayton and Reyna his wife and John Doget "for ever" for a payment of 10 marks annually. When Robert de Gayton died, a clause in his will stated that John Doget de Boterwyck was to release to Reyna the whole of Ducketts Manor; the will is dated 1361. Doget is another form of Duket. Boterwyck was another form of Butterwick and it is believed that John Doget was associated with the Manor and farm of Butterwick, an estate in the parish of St. Peter's, St. Albans, Hertfordshire. Also in Herts. was a John Doget of Aldenham, mentioned in 1378, and an inheritor of the Manor of Bourne Hall, Bushey named Doget (1384). A John Doget also inherited land from the de Windsore family in Oxhey during the fourteenth century.

There are varius grants and documents dating from 1369 until 1399 where the names John Doget or John Doget of Boterwyck appear either as witness or in the main part of the document. These are to be found among the Close Rolls of Edward the Third and Richard the Second, and also among the records of Westminster Abbey. In 1374 Reyna, widow of Robert de Gayton granted to John Doget and Alice his wife 'one messuage, 300 acres of land, 50 acres of meadow and 40 acres of wood, etc., in Tottenham and Hornsey' which she held of William de Brightlegh on lease.

In 1388 Joan, the widow of William de Brightlegh left the 300 acres of arable land but only 15 acres of meadow and 14 of wood, with 4d. rents, in Tottenham and Hornsey to John Doget and Alice. The Dogets now became the owners and freeholders of the manor and farm. The year 1389 saw a lease being granted to "Henry atte Fforde", a Citizen of London, by "John Boterwyck alias Doget, of the Manor of Dogettes" (Ducketts) for a period of

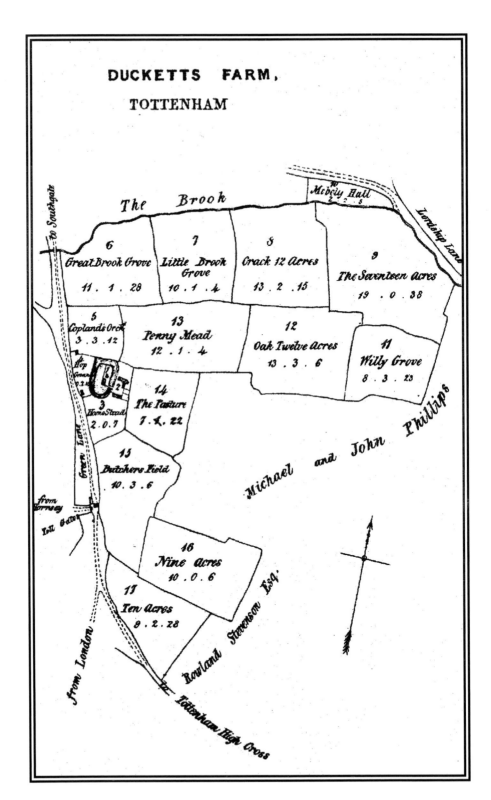

DUCKETTS FARM,

TOTTENHAM

ten years. In the early years of the fifteenth century, after the death of John Doget, the Manor and Farm passed to his son William Rote. (It is strange that the son should have had a different surname; perhaps he did not like a name which included the word Dog.) He married, and on his death left his lands to his wife Elisabeth. She granted all his lands in Hornsey and Tottenham to Robert Canndyssh, sergeant at law, Thomas Carbonell de Agmondesham, Robert Warner of London, Richard Sturgeon and William Hall of Kensington.

On 16th March 1454, Richard Sturgeon and William Hall, the other co-owners being deceased, granted all these lands to John Lorchyn and Nicholas Bayley. Early the next year John Lorchyn gave up his part of Ducketts and Nicholas Bayley became the sole owner.

Nicholas Bayley was the Executor of the Will of Richard Sturgeon and was involved in two Proceedings in Chancery over failing to make over the estate to St. Bartholemew's Hospital in west Smithfield. [The petitioners acting on behalf of the hospital claimed that Sturgeon had intended the land to finance the building of a new chapel and the maintenance of a priest. These had been duly provided but had been paid for by Nicholas out of his income from the farm.]

"Our said beseecher oft time since the death of the said Richard hath willed and required the said Nicholas to make sufficient estate of the said place called Ducketts, with his appurtenance, according to the said first intent, will, and foundation, the said Nicholas will not do it, but so to do it utterly refuses."

[Nicholas was supoenaed to appear, and lost the case. The result was that in 1458 the Manor of Ducketts was put into the hands of Hospital trustees, including Nicholas Bayley. This arrrangement was licensed by the Abbot of Westminster as Chief Lord of the Fee on 7th November 1463. The priest who had been appointed to sing prayers for the souls of the departed Richard Sturgeon and his wife and relatives was to continue as long as the value of the property was being amortised.] In 1464 the Manor and Farm were granted by the Trustees to John Wakering, Clerk in Holy Orders and Master of the Hospital of St. Bartholemew.

The Tudor age was now dawning. It was to see Ducketts taken away from the hospital and once more given back to private ownership, and to come into contact with some of the eminent people of the day.

Cecil Harris

(Left):   20. The Ducketts fields *c.* 1846, with names identifying those shown on the
           Ordnance map of the 1870s (fig. 18)

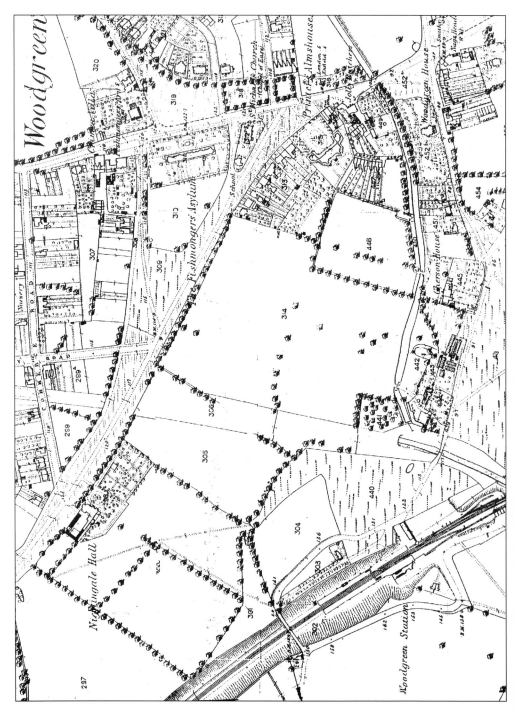

21. Nightingale Hall and Wood Green in 1864. Urban development had started to the north of St Michael's church with the coming of the railway.

'Clearance in the Wood':
the Nightingale Hall estate

The residential development of Wood Green began to gather pace in the 1860s following the advent in 1859 of the Wood Green GNR railway station (now Alexandra Palace Station). This development was initially concentrated between the Bounds Green Road and the High Road to the north of St Michael's Church. Subsequent development took place in the 1870s in the vicinity of the railway station to the west and later with the Barretts and Noel Park estates to the east, these latter being encouraged by the presence of the GER railway terminating at the former Palace Gates Station from 1878. Prior to this period much of the area was farmland claimed from the great Middlesex Forest which predominated in earlier times.

Before the urban development there were few distinctive buildings in the Wood Green area. One of these was Nightingale Hall which was situated on the south west side of the Bounds Green Road (covering the site now occupied by the Adventist Church in Northcott Avenue) with its outbuildings and gardens extending over what are now Northcott and Cornwall Avenues. In 1864 the Hall, its outbuildings and ornamental gardens occupied an area of 2.3 acres and formed part of an estate of over 70 acres. The earliest recorded evidence of Nightingale Hall by name is found in Rocque's map of 1754[1] and the house remained a feature of all subsequent definitive maps until it was demolished in 1894-5. It was undoubtedly also a distinctive local feature for well over 300 years and the original building was thought to be of Elizabethan origin.[2]

Early origins: Woodriddings and Austynsreddings

The Nightingale Hall estate was, however, of much earlier origins and can be traced back over several centuries. Nightingale Hall was situated on land originally called "le Woderedynge" which had been cleared from the eastern flank of Tottenham Wood in medieval times. Woodriddings (or Woodreddings: meaning "clearance in the wood") as the estate was subsequently known was manorial land and the record of its ownership through copyhold tenancies as well as its occupancy and size can be traced through the Tottenham Court Rolls from the time of Richard II (1377-1400).

The earliest reference to "le Woderedynge" was in 1392 when the land was held by John Northampton who was lord of the manor of Daubeneys at that time and sometime Lord Mayor of London.[3] By 1515 (the sixth year of the reign of Henry VIII) the ownership of "a close called Woodriddynges containing by estimation sixty acres of land more or less abutting Burnys Grene (Bounds Green) on the east and the Lord's wood called Tottenham Woode on the south . . . " had passed to a George Brymande described as a "gentleman".[4] There were several different owners during the early 16th century all of whom were prosperous citizens of London. In 1545 Jasper and Margaret Pheasant surrendered "all their lands tenements and herititaments called Woodredinge . . . to the use of William Locke citizen and mercer of London and his sons".[5] This appears to be the earliest reference to the existence of a building, possibly the precursor of Nightingale Hall. By the early Elizabethan period the copyhold tenancy had passed to Elizabeth Locke the grand-daughter of William Locke.[6] In 1619, as Mrs Elizabeth Candeler, a widow, she had succeeded her husband, Richard Candeler J.P., as a prominent land-owner in the Parish of Tottenham: the Candelers, who lived at Tottenham Green, are commemorated by a fine veined marble monument in All Hallows Church, Tottenham. The Dorset Survey of that year indicates that the land was leased to a Robert Morris but provides no information about a building although the farm itself is clearly indicated in the related parish plan.[7] During the 17th and 18th centuries the copyhold tenancy was held by several prominent citizens who were substantial land-owners not only in Tottenham but elsewhere. None of these "tenants" appeared to live on the estate and the land, mainly pasture, was leased probably for grazing. During the 17th and 18th centuries the description of the estate in the Court Rolls became clearer. For example, an entry in 1628 describes Woodredding

"as comprising about 60 acres abutting the Tottenham Wood on the Western part and Bakersfield [now Nightingale Gardens] and Dears Pightell [now St Michael's Terrace/Dorset Road] on the Southern part and Bounds Lane [now Bounds Green Road] on the East part and Danfors Wood [now Durnsford Road] to the North".

An entry for 1732 refers to "That tenement with barns, stables and out-buildings called Reddings at Wood Green farm with several parcels of pasture comprising 72 acres."

In 1769 John Giles, described as "a gentleman" and also a Tottenham resident was admitted as Copyhold Tenant of

"all that Messuage or Tenement commonly called or known by the name of Woodridding otherwise Wood Green Farm situate in Bounds Green Lane . . . together with the yard, garden, orchard, barns, stables, outhouses and buildings..and also all those eight several Meadow or pasture fields to the said farm now in the tenure of Matthew Twydall (at a yearly rent of eighty pounds) and containing 61 acres 3 roods and 16 perches . . . bounded to the West by Tottenham Wood and the freehold lands of the said John Giles purchased by him of the said John Sawbridge called Aust Reddings".[8]

22. Plan of "Awstereadinge" drawn by Israel Amyce in 1599. This grove of about 12 acres of woodland became part of the Nightingale Hall estate in 1769, by which time it was pasture.

The indenture[9] for the purchase of these freehold lands was dated 22nd August 1769 and relates to land claimed from the eastern flank of Tottenham Wood in earlier times. In fact, an early reference to "a pasture and grove called Austynsredynge" is made in a grant[10] made to one Gilbert de Fox de Tottenham and others in 1356 (in the 28th year of Edward III) and which is also attractively displayed in a plan by Israel Amyce made in 1599.[11] This plan allows "Awstereadynge" to be located at the north west extremity of the estate. The plan also states that the underwood was of four years growth indicating that coppicing was being carried out at that time. These additional freehold lands comprised 14 acres thereby extending the estate to over 70 acres. A further entry in the Court Rolls in 1769 describing Woodreddings refers to

"Brickhouse, Barn, Stables, Cowhouse and Carthouse with the Garden, Orchard, Yard and Hoppet[12] thereto adjoining"

indicating a well-established homestead.

The earliest specific reference to Nightingale Hall by name in the Court Rolls appears to be in 1808 with regard to the Will of John Giles which was dated 19th May 1804 and refers to Nightingale Hall Farm[13]. The Wyburd Survey of Tottenham was carried out in 1798 during the ownership of John

Giles and records the size of the estate at 71 acres and that the Hall and land was occupied by a Thomas Dale, the son of a stablekeeper of Chiswell Street in London.[14] The Poor Rate Assessment Books suggest that the same Thomas Dale, no doubt a farmer, tenanted the land from at least 1798 to 1817 and probably owned or rented other land in the area.[15]

As we move into the 19th century it is possible to relate the estate to the present day features. The Wyburd Survey was based on a plan[16] which shows the estate extended on the north west as far as Tottenham Wood Farm and its northernmost extremity (i.e. "Austynsredynge") would now be the Recreation Ground in Albert Road. To the north and east the boundary followed a stream (parallel with what is now Albert Road), which ran down from Tottenham Wood to the New River, to a point on the Bounds Green Road now occupied by the Ambulance Station (previously a Fire Station). On the south-west it followed a line approximately along what is now Clifton Road, Victoria Road, Palace Gates Road and Bridge Road. Its south and south-eastern boundary were what is now Avenue Gardens (originally part of Wood Green Common) and Cornwall Avenue respectively and the eastern flank was the present Bounds Green Road.

Nightingale Hall in the nineteenth century
In the 19th century the changes in ownership and occupation of this ancient property can also be traced.[17] On the death of John Giles in 1807 the estate was divided equally between his sister Sarah Giles, his nephew Francis Dalton and his niece Mary Dalton and at that time a Thomas Green was recorded as occupant of the Hall.

Between 1820 and 1840 the ownership passed by marriage from the heirs of John Giles into the Woodward family. Mary Ann Woodward, the daughter of Francis Dalton, became the copyhold tenant but she too was an absent landlord. In 1820 reference is made to the pastures being in the occupation of Thomas Rhodes who also appeared to have occupied the Hall and the farm for some time during 1825-1840. This Thomas Rhodes was a dairy farmer and owner of the adjacent Tottenham Wood Farm, and was also an uncle of Cecil Rhodes of Rhodesia fame. A large part of his farmlands were later to become Alexandra Park.[18]

In 1841 Thomas Pearson, described as independent, had become the tenant at the Hall together with his son, also named Thomas, a solicitor, and his daughter-in-law Bella Goss Pearson; two female servants and one male also lived in.[19] The ownership of the estate by Mary Ann Woodward and the occupancy of the Hall by Thomas Pearson is confirmed in the Tottenham Rent Charge Book for 1843, with the further information that the estate had been extended by a further 10 acres to include two fields on the southern flank[20]. These acquisitions brought into the estate two very old entities, namely "Dears Pightell" and "Bakersfield" which were not only mentioned in the Dorset Survey of 1619 but were also the subject of a grant[21] by Henry VIII to Henry Audeley and John Cordall in 1544. "Dears Pightell" is now occupied by St Michael's Terrace and Dorset and Terrick Roads, and "Bakersfield" (or at least part of it) is now Nightingale Gardens, a public open space lying between Park Avenue and Braemar Avenue. The size of the estate was now 88 acres overall and at this time Thomas Rhodes was tenanting 76 acres of pasture adjacent to his own farm and Thomas Pearson the remainder in the vicinity of the Hall.

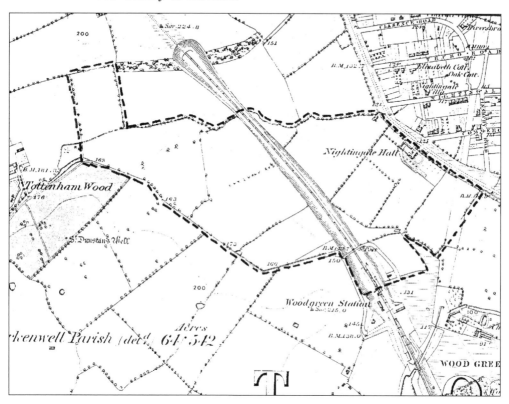

23. Nightingale Hall estate in the mid nineteenth century. The estate boundary of 1843 is superimposed on the O.S. map of 1873. This shows the maximum extent of the estate. In 1848 the Great Northern Railway divided the estate in two. Thomas Rhodes of Tottenham Wood Farm bought the 29 acres to the west of the railway in 1850.

The coming of the railways

The Great Northern Railway Act of 1846, which facilitated the building of a trunk railway from Kings Cross to the north, operational from 1850, was to have a major impact on the fortunes of the Nightingale Hall estate. The railway required a strip of land running in a north-westerly direction through the middle of the estate to provide the track for the main line. The amount of land involved then was 5 acres, 3 roods and 5 perches which was sold to the GNR for £2660 in 1848.[22] The railway effectively divided the entity known as Woodriddings for almost 500 years into two almost equal parts This was followed in 1850 by the purchase[23] by Thomas Rhodes of 29 acres, 3 roods and 20 perches to the west of the GNR railway for a sum of £1,900 and the purchase of the remainder to the east, including Nightingale Hall, by the younger Thomas Pearson for £1,800. Both Thomas Pearson and Thomas Rhodes were admitted as copyhold tenants for their respective holdings in 1850 and Thomas Pearson became the first owner (copyhold tenant) to actually reside at Nightingale Hall.[24]

Despite its long life only limited evidence describing the appearance of Nightingale Hall has been found and, undoubtedly, the building underwent various structural modifications over the years. Comparison of the 1798 Tottenham Plan with the 1844 Tithe Map suggests that a major re-building could have taken place between these dates and again during the Victorian era. In papers[25] recording the admission of the younger Thomas Pearson as copyhold tenant in 1850 the following description of Nightingale Hall itself showed it to comprise:

Ground Floor:	Dining, Drawing and Breakfast Rooms
	Conservatory and Billiard Room
	Kitchen, Scullery and Offices
	Basement and Cellars
First Floor:	5 Bedrooms and one Dressing Room
Second Floor:	2 Bedrooms
	Large Organ Room

There is also reference to an additional residence possibly referring to the farmhouse comprising 4 bedrooms and dressing room, 3 sitting rooms, 2 kitchens and dairy. The early plans do in fact indicate two separate buildings on the site.

In 1864 a further description of the Hall is similar except that three garrets replace the second floor and the yard is described as comprising "stables with coach and cart horses, cow houses and piggeries".[26] At this time the house, gardens and hoppet covered 2 acres, 1 rood and 11 perches.

Further loss of land adjacent to Nightingale Hall followed in 1853 resulting from the culverting of the New River along its eastern flank through what is now Nightingale Gardens. This transaction involved about 2 acres of land sold[27] to the New River Company for £2,600.

Mrs Pearson-Kidd and St. Michael's Church

In 1861 the younger Thomas Pearson had become head of the household and in addition to Mrs Pearson and a young nephew of Thomas's there were three domestic staff and a shepherd and his wife in residence.[28] Thomas Pearson died in 1862 and Mrs Pearson became the owner[29] in 1864. In 1871 Mrs Pearson and an elderly aunt were living at the Hall along with two cousins and three domestic staff.[30] By 1881 Mrs Pearson had remarried and had become Mrs Pearson-Kidd, her new husband being John Kidd, a printing ink manufacturer and presumably a founder of the firm Mander-Kidd Ltd. of Wolverhampton, formerly major ink-makers in the UK. Other residents at the time of the 1881 Census included Mrs Pearson's ageing aunt and three other relatives and four domestic staff and a nurse. The domestic staff were drawn from Somerset, Norfolk and Devon as well as from London.[31]

Mrs Pearson who owned several properties in Wood Green was a substantial benefactor, particularly to St Michael's, Wood Green, the parish church. She was an aunt of the wife of the Rev. John Thomas (the incumbent between 1866-1907) and had a reserved seat in the choir stalls. In 1872 Mrs Pearson laid the foundation stone for St Michael's Senior Schools (now rebuilt as St Michael's Junior School) in the Bounds Green Road having already given the site valued at the time at £1,000.[32]

Mrs Pearson-Kidd died in December 1890 and Nightingale Hall, by then a freehold property, and her other freehold properties in Wood Green, including The Grange described as "an old fashioned dwelling house, garden and paddock in 3 acres" at the eastern corner of Park Avenue and Station Road, and a plot of land adjacent to St. Michael's Vicarage (now occupied by the Church Hall) as well as various leasehold properties in central London, Westminster and Chelsea, were put up for sale by auction[33] in December 1891. In her Will Mrs Pearson-Kidd directed that the proceeds from the sale of Nightingale Hall and the other properties she owned in Wood Green, such as Avenue Lodge, Holly Lodge and Wood Green Cottage, be invested for the benefit of Mrs Bella Laura Burt (sister or cousin?) and her children.[34]

By the time of the death of Mrs Pearson-Kidd further erosion of the estate had already occurred with the building of the Enfield branch of the Great Northern Railway in 1871 skirting the north and west of the Hall and the widening of the main line GNR track. The Great Eastern Railway Act 1874 made provision for a line from Barking with a terminus at Palace Gates Station (formerly in Dorset Road) and associated sidings lying between the GNR line and the Bounds Green Road. This resulted in the sale in 1877 to the GER of a 14-acre strip of land on the southern border of the estate.[35] The sale plan of 1891 shows Nightingale Hall and its immediate surroundings as comprising only about 10 acres.[36] In the same year Mrs Pearson-Kidd's servant Joseph Barnard and his widowed daughter and her children were the only residents at the Hall and he was probably acting as caretaker prior to the sale.[37]

The few known photographs (c. 1890) show a castellated facade with a large conservatory, probably Victorian modifications, on the south-west facing side with a suggestion of an earlier building style in the background.[38] The 25 inch O.S. Map of 1864 shows that the main frontage to the Hall faced

24. Nightingale Hall *c.* 1890 seen from the south west.
A 'gothic' facade had been added to an older building in the early nineteenth century.

south-east and was approached by a short carriage drive from the Bounds Green Road and also shows the extent of the formal gardens adjacent to the Hall.[39] A contemporary account of 1891 makes reference to the Hall being "very gay for the Jubilee, with flags and coloured lamps" (presumably Queen Victoria's Golden Jubilee in 1887) and to the "large stables for the hunting stock" and also describes other features:

"the staircase had some fine large paintings on its walls and being so wide that you can go up six abreast. The music room was fine with a large organ which I believe was sold to the Wesleyan Chapel in Trinity Road."[40]

The Wesleyan Chapel became the Greek Orthodox Cathedral of St Mary. Attempts to trace the organ were thwarted by a tragic fire which destroyed the contents in the 1980s.

The end of Nightingale Hall and after
The Nightingale Hall site was acquired by an Aaron Withers of Brighton and subsequently purchased by Albert Walter Gamage, proprietor of the famous

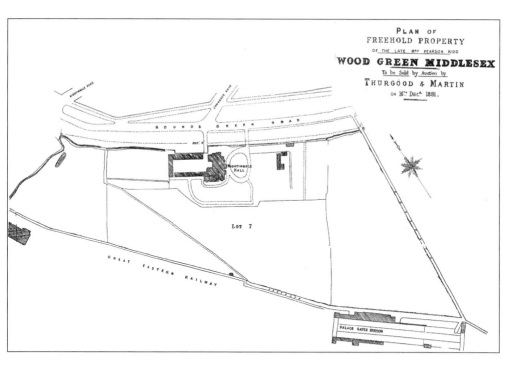

25. The Sale plan of 1891 shows the residue of the estate, about 10 acres, which became the North London Cycling and Athletic Grounds in l895.

Holborn store, in 1895.[41] The Hall was then demolished to make way for the building of the North London Cycling and Athletic Grounds[42], of which A.W. Gamage, a keen cycling enthusiast, was also the principal shareholder.[43] The cycling track was opened in June 1895 but had a relatively short existence (1895-1900) and as a result of the pressure for urban development was replaced by the present terraced housing on the south side of Bounds Green Road, built between 1900-1907.[44]

Although Nightingale Hall is long gone the name "Nightingale" is well preserved for posterity in such local names as Nightingale Road, the Nightingale Arms, Nightingale Gardens and Nightingale School. The earlier name of "Woodriddings" is also preserved in Woodriddings Court in Crescent Road. It is also interesting to pose the question of whether there is any connection between the references to "Nightingale" in Wood Green and those in Hornsey, i.e. Nightingale Lane and the Nightingale Tavern, or indeed any connection between the Nightingale Hall in Wood Green and the one which existed in Edmonton.[45]

Albert Pinching

References

1. *Topographical Map of the County of Middlesex* by John Rocque, reprinted by LMAS, 1971.

2. *VCH*, vol. v (1976) pp. 316-319

3. TMCR, vol. ii (1377-1399)

4. TMCR, vol. vi (1510-1531)

5. TMCR, vol. vii (1531-1546)

6. TMCR, vol. xi (1558-1582)

7. Field Book accompanying the Earl of Dorset's Survey; transcript at BCM

8. TMCR (1625-1792); Acc.695/1, BCM

9. MDR (1769), 5/237

10. BCM Grant, P/3

11. Survey of woods and groves in Edmonton, Tottenham and Enfield in Middlesex for the Dean and Chapter of St. Pauls by Israel Amyce, Surveyor, 1599; Gdl, MS 18798

12. Hoppet: an enclosure, yard or paddock (OED)

13. TCMR (1787-1823); Acc. 695/7, BCM

14. Field Book accompanying the Wyburd Survey, 1798; BCM

15. Tottenham Parish Poor Rate Assessment Books (1777-1843); BCM

16. Copy of Plan of Tottenham 1798 (for Wyburd Survey) by Henry Piper Spurling, by Jonathan and William Newton, 1817; BCM

17. TMCR (1787-1823 and 1824-1852); Acc. 695/ 7 and 8, BCM

18. *HHS Bulletin. No. 29.* (1988), pp. 22-26

19. Enumerators' Returns on microfilm, BCM and PRO

20. Tottenham Rent Charge Book, 1843, BCM

21. *Tottenham and Edmonton Historical Notebook* by William James Roe

(Percy Press, 1952)

22. TMCR (1824-1852); Acc.695/8, BCM

23. *Ibid.*

24. *Ibid.*

25. MDR (1850), Acc.1016/358

26. MDR (1864), Acc.1016/360A

27. MDR (1854) 2/945

28. Enumerators' Returns; PRO and BCM

29. TMCR (1864); Acc.695/3, p. 244, BCM

30. Enumerators' Returns: PRO and BCM

31. *Ibid.*

32. *St. Michael's: A Record of One Hundred Years of Life and Work 1844-1944* by H.C. Pearcey (1954). St Michael's Wood Green, Parish Records

33. Auction notice in *The Wood Green Herald,* 11 Dec. 1891

34. Principal Registry, SH

35. MDR (1877), 16/501

36. Sale Plan, Property of Mrs Pearson-Kidd, 1891, by Thurgood and Martin; BCM

37. Enumerators' returns; PRO and BCM

38. Ref 927NIG, BCM

39. *O.S. of Middlesex, Parish of Tottenham,* 25 inches to 1 mile, 1st edition

40. Typescript; Ref 927 NIG, BCM

41. MDR (1895) 9/6 and 9/7

42. *HHS Bulletin. No. 34* (1993) pp. 18-19

43. Dick Swann, *The Life and Times of Charlie Barden* (Wunlap Publications, 1965)

44. *Kelly's Directories for Wood Green*

45. VCH, vol. v, p. 139

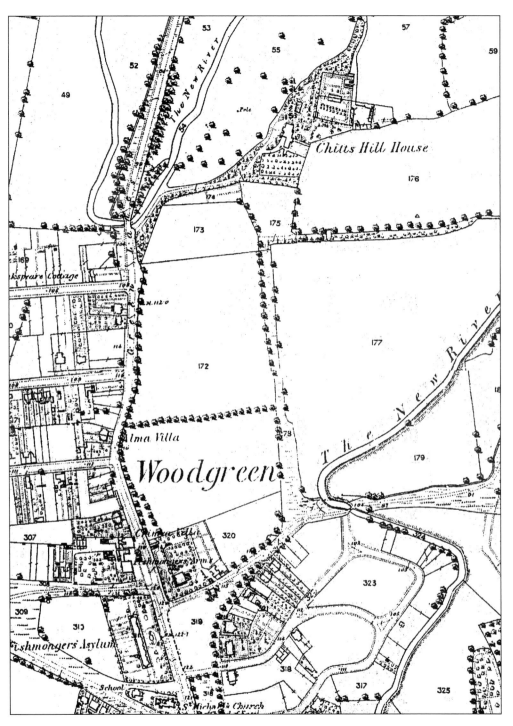

26. Wood Green in the 1860s was still largely rural, particularly to the east of the High Road (shown as Green Lanes on this O.S. map).

95

From farming to philanthropy: Chitt's Hill and its Regency house

E ven before the urban development of Wood Green began in the 1860s a number of substantial houses existed alongside or overlooking the New River as it wound its meandering path through the area. One of these was Chitts Hill House, in what was then the Parish of Tottenham, situated between what is now Arcadian Gardens and Woodside Road on the east side of the High Road, Wood Green, to the north of Woodside Park. In 1864 the house stood in 48 acres of land extending between the High Road (then Green Lanes) and Wolves Lane, with the New River being a feature on both its western and eastern flanks. Indeed, the 25 inch 1864 O.S. map[1] conveys the idyllic position of the house with its slightly elevated position with respect to the river and its surrounding fields. Chitts Hill itself lay to the east of the High Road with its summit (120 feet above sea level) at the junction of what is now Woodside Road and Cross Road.

Chitts Hill: early references

In early Tudor times reference was made to "Shetyshill" (or "Shuthyll" and "Shitthyll") described as "the Lord's Common"[2]. This common or waste land was approached by a broad green lane ("Shutteslane") north from White Hart Lane and from the High Road (to Southgate) from the west. By the later Tudor period it was known as "Shotes Hill" or "Shottishill".[3] In Stuart times the name "Chits" Hill featured as a topographical reference in the Dorset Survey[4] of 1619 but it does not appear by name in the related Tottenham Parish Plan.[5] Rocque (1754) makes reference to "Chits" Hill Lane (now Glendale Avenue) but still gives no indication of a house or building on the site.[6] Spurling's Plan of Tottenham (1798) also makes reference to "Chits" Hill but gives no evidence of any buildings.[7] The smaller scale Cary (1801) makes no reference.[8]

The Original Surveyor's Drawing[9] for Hampstead (1807-8) – upon which the first Ordnance Survey maps were based – shows evidence of buildings at Chitts Hill, and Greenwood (1819) delineates the estate clearly and confirms the presence of a building.[10] The first O.S. map (1822) also shows a cluster of buildings on the site.[11] These maps indicate that the original building(s) at Chitts Hill appeared at the very beginning of the 19th century. A later Parish Plan of 1844 gives evidence of a substantial building and outbuilding(s).[12]

Early origins of the estate: Sprotmans, Shuttesfield and Belsars

At the end of the 18th century the land in the vicinity of Chitts Hill, in common with that around Wood Green generally, was farmland which had replaced the earlier woodlands of the great Middlesex Forest. A survey in 1798 showed that about thirty acres of land which was to become the core of the Chitts Hill estate was owned by a James King and was being farmed for wheat and hay by a Thomas King, probably a relative.[13] This parcel of land formed more or less a rectangle with its northern boundary abutting the parish boundary between Edmonton and Tottenham and the east and west boundaries being what are now Wolves Lane and the High Road respectively. Its southern boundary would correspond with the present Woodside Road. An attempt has been made to trace the earlier origins of this freehold land.

A Tudor reference described Chitts Hill as "lying between Sprotmans and Shuttsfield" although the exact location and extent of these is not clear.[14] This land was bounded on the north by the Manor of Bowes, the major part of which lay in Edmonton but parts of which extended into the parish of Tottenham to the east and west of Chitts Hill, and which was then held by the Dean and Chapter of St. Paul's. The Court Rolls during the Elizabethan period also refer to certain lands to the south of Bowes Manor as "Sprotlands"[15] or "Sprotmans".[16] In 1649 a survey of the manor refers to "the land of Benjamin Garfield to the south".[17]

In the early part of the 18th century this land was in the possession of George Wanley, a City goldsmith, who lived at Tottenham High Cross and owned large amounts of freehold and copyhold land not only in Tottenham and Edmonton but also in London, Middlesex, York and Lincoln.[18] He had purchased the land from Edward and George Downes (c.1715) and subsequently it had been in turn in the tenure of a William Pannell, Samuel Payne, Anne Speak, and Joseph Brown. Indentures of lease and release from George Wanley to his son-in-law, John Sawbridge, of 1728 and relating to various freehold properties in Tottenham worth £36,000 include reference to:

"And all that messuage or tenement called Belsars with its appurtenances lying in Edmonton . . . now in the tenure of Anne Speake, widow . . . And all that piece of meadow ground called Dodds Hill . . . And all that parcel of land called Mark (or Marsh) Grove with the appurtenances in Tottenham . . . And all those three fields called Sprottmans or Sprotsmans or Shottesffield in the said parish of Tottenham."[19]

A later indenture of 1771 describes the property as:

"All that messuage or tenement with the appurtanances called by the name Belsors otherwise Belsars and all houses outhouses edifices (etc) . . . lying and being in the Parish of Edmonton . . . And also all that piece of meadow . . . called Dodds Hill near or adjoining to the said messuage lying and being in the Parish of Edmonton . . . Also all that parcel of land called Mark Grove . . . and also all those three fields and groves called Sproton otherwise Sprotmans and Shotters ffield . . . lying in the said Parish of Tottenham . . . which are or so now seem to be divided into the several closes or partitions following Wood Ground . . . the Grubbed ffield . . . the Middle ffield . . . the Barnffield . . . the Plowed ffield . . . Chitts Hill ffield . . . and the slip below the New River"

all of which fields together totalled 30 acres 1 rood 27 perches.[20] Thus, it appears that the land adjacent to Chitts Hill was part of a farm which straddled the boundary between the parishes of Tottenham and Edmonton to the north but the location of the house called Belsars,or the full extent of the farm, has not been established. However, a clue to this is indicated in a map of Edmonton (c.1600) which features "Belsers Lane" located in what is now Tottenhall Road in Palmers Green.[21] Later indentures refer to "the farm called Belsars" comprising the fields situated in the parish of Tottenham as previously described but no further references are made to property in Edmonton, suggesting that this may have become a separate entity. It is also tempting to speculate whether the land around Chitts Hill did at some even earlier (medieval) time also form part of the historic Manor of Bowes.

Late 18th century developments

During the 1770s and 1780s Alexander Lambley, a Churchwarden of All Hallows, Tottenham owned the land at Chitts Hill and was allowed to enclose a small piece of the adjacent common or waste land "on payment to the Churchwardens of one shilling annually for the benefit of the poor of the parish for ever"[22]. This was the first of a series of legal enclosures; illegal encroachments had been recorded more than two centuries earlier.[23] Generally, enclosure of waste land for small scale building became commonplace before the full-scale urbanisation in the late 19th century.

In 1786 the "farm called Belsars" was sold to an Arthur Miller of Southampton who had also leased part of Bowes Manor.[24] The same Arthur Miller also registered an indenture of lease and release on the property involving Josiah Wedgwood FRS, the renowned Staffordshire potter and man of the Enlightenment period, as mortgagee in the sum of £1,500.[25] Josiah Wedgwood retained ownership for almost ten years until his death in 1795. In the following year the property was sold by his son, John Wedgwood, as executor, to Henry Townley Ward, described as a gentleman, of Soho Square for £1,500 plus interest.[26] Five years later the property was purchased for £3,000 by William Wrangham of Palmers Green[27], who had interests in the island of St Helena, and who had already purchased in 1796 the long-established property known as Wood Green House (once situated in what is now Station Road, Wood Green) and also a further 53 acres of pasture and 32 acres of woodland in Tottenham.[28] The Wyburd Survey shows William Wrangham as owning 80 or so acres situated to the west of Chitts Hill lying between the High Road and the Bounds Green Road which were being farmed by the previously mentioned Thomas King at an annual rent of £150. This triangle of land was to become the first site for the residential development of Wood Green within the following fifty or sixty years.

William Wrangham died in 1802 and his Will instructed that his estates be divided into moieties of one-sixteenths to be shared between his various heirs and dependants. This applied to the "farm called Belsars" and to his other properties in Tottenham and Edmonton and his estates in St Helena.[29]

The origins of Chitts Hill House

In May 1805 a James Clark, described as an oilman (i.e. oil merchant), of Hollywell Street in the City of London, purchased the farm known as Belsars for a total of £2,650 from the various dependants of William Wrangham. At this time the property was described as:

"All that farm called Belsars adjoining to Five Elms in the road leading to Bowes Farm . . . consisting of those several fields . . . commonly called by the names Woodfield, Barnfield and the Middle Field consisting of 14 acres, 1 rood and 27 perches . . . and all those other fields known by the several names of Chitts Hill Field, Ploughshed Field and the Grubed Field therein one and the meadow below the river containing by estimation 16 acres, 1 rood and 4 perches . . . Together with all and singular buildings, barns, stables, yards, backsides, orchards, gardens, ways and appurtenances".[30]

Clearly, the farm was well established consistent with the definitive maps of that time but there was still no mention of a dwelling house. It is most likely that James Clark could have been the originator of Chitts Hill House itself. He represented a class of wealthy London merchants seeking a desirable country home near to the City. On 26th September 1806 he sought leave of the Tottenham Vestry to "enclose further common land which led to his house at Chitts Hill " and also a strip of land fronting the High Road. Although he was granted permission to enclose two pieces (totalling 1a 2r 15p), on payment of £2 annually, it was for less land than he requested. He was also required to ensure that the right of way to the public was not impeded seeing that the waste land constituted an old road.[31] A related Vestry Plan shows the location of the house and the land requested which was no doubt required for the carriage drive to the house.[32]

The only known but undated photograph of the house shows a splendid two storey Regency-style facade with steps leading down to the lawn.[33] Comparison with the 1864 25-inch map suggests this view is from the north-west and is most likely the original building. Details of the builder and the interior lay-out of the house have yet to be located.

99

John Overend and the entrance lodge

By February 1822 John Overend had acquired[34] the estate from the descendants and executors of James Clark and a related indenture of release of 1815 refers to:

"all that capital mansion dwelling house, coach houses, stables, out houses, barns and other buildings erected and built upon said parcel of land".[35]

In the previous year (1821) John Overend sought leave of the Tottenham Vestry to enclose a further piece of the waste land (1a 3r 24p) to provide the carriage drive from the High Road to the house. This was granted (at a rate of £5 annually) but with the proviso that a passage of 25-foot width was left open to provide for access from the High Road to the lane to White Hart Lane to protect the public right of way.[36] It would therefore appear that John Overend had succeeded in enclosing the land previously denied to James Clark. It was at this sitting of the Vestry Committee that mention was made of the possibility of a lodge being erected at the end of the carriage drive. Since the waste land was manorial John Overend also had to seek permission for the enclosure from the Tottenham Manor Court which was granted to him and his heirs "unto the full end and term of one thousand years from the 4th May 1822 . . . paying yearly to the said Lord (of the Manor) . . . one peppercorn if demanded". For this generous grant John Overend paid a 'fine' of £203 and 15 shillings. The same Court Rolls bearing the date 4th May 1822 records the fact that the entrance lodge had been erected on part of the designated waste land.[37] Thus, a total of 3 acres 39 perches of the former waste land, had now been incorporated into the estate.

John Overend and the Quaker connection

In an early edition of Pigot's *Directory*[38] John Overend was listed under "Gentry & Clergy". In fact, this John Overend who had become the owner of Chitts Hill House was an extremely successful Quaker businessman, being the founder of what was to become one of London's largest merchant banks of that era. He was born in Settle, Yorkshire on 2nd June 1769 the son of John and Isabel Overend, his father being a woolcomber. He later demonstrated how the Quaker qualities of shrewdness, determination and perseverance, coupled with 'connections', can be successfully applied in business. His brother, Hall Overend, achieved eminence as a surgeon in Sheffield.[39]

John Overend worked his way to London and became a clerk in the Quaker firm of Smith and Holt & Co., woollen factors and bankers. This brought him into contact with John Gurney, of the Norwich Bank, another Quaker. It was to John Gurney that he put his plan for simplifying and revolutionising the discount system which was to be of particular advantage

27. John Overend of Overend, Gurney & Co. from a contemporary print by Richard Dighton, 1820

to country banks at that time. With the backing of John Gurney and in partnership with Thomas Richardson, another Tottenham Quaker, he set up the discount and bill-broking business of Richardson, Overend & Co. in 1805. Samuel Gurney (son of John Gurney) became a partner in 1807[40]. This firm subsequently became Overend, Gurney & Co., after the retirement of Thomas Richardson (in 1830).[41] It had remarkable success as a "bankers' bank" and an alternative depository to the Bank of England. During its hey-day John Overend was described as "one of the shrewdest and wealthiest of the London money lenders". The company thrived long after its founders' demise and by 1860 held deposits of £8 million and was making a profit of £500,000 a year. But it crashed dramatically in 1866, partly as a consequence of the introduction of the Joint Stock Act of 1826, and, it has been suggested as a result of less caution and business sense of the heirs to the business. This story provides a good example of the influence of the Quakers in British business life of which there were many others during the same period.[42]

As a consequence of their success John Overend and his partners became very wealthy men. Overend moved to Southgate from the City in 1807 and married his partner's sister, Martha Richardson, in 1809 but the marriage only lasted six months, with his wife's death at the early age of thirty. On moving to Chitts Hill he took as housekeeper his friend Mary Kitching, who had been a close friend of his former wife. Mary Kitching also had a Quaker background and became the second Mrs Overend on 22nd June 1831 at Winchmore Hill[43]. This marriage also was only destined to last six months with the death of John Overend, at the age of 62, on 17th January 1832. He was buried in the Quaker Burial Ground at Winchmore Hill.

John Overend made generous provision in his Will for his wife, sister-in-law, nephews and nieces and not least his domestic staff and the Quaker schools at Arkworth and Croydon. In accordance with a codicil to the Will dated 11th June 1831 indicating his intention of marriage to Mary Kitching he bequeathed the following to his intended wife:

"all my freehold, copyhold and other real estates in the several counties of Monmouth, Middlesex, Yorkshire and elsewhere in England and Wales to have and to hold the said estates to my said friend and her assigns for and during the term of her natural life . . . and to have receive and take the rents issues and profits of the said estates for her sole use and benefit."

In addition to inheriting these estates under trust, Mary Overend also received a sum of £10,000 to be held in trust for direction under her own Will. John Overend also directed that after the decease of his wife that all his estates should be sold by his executors with all the profits therefrom going to his personal estate from which provision was made for its disbursment to his nieces and nephews in the form of trusts.[44]

Mary Overend

Mary Overend was born on 14th March 1783, in Darlington, Co. Durham, the daughter of William Kitching an ironfounder. Her brother, John Kitching, a draper in Whitechapel was to reside at Stamford Hill and become a well-known Quaker philanthropist.[45] It is said that in her early days circumstances were limited and as a result she gained insight into the problems of the poor to which she later turned her attention. She herself had poor health and as a consequence did not enjoy a high profile in society and was to remain a widow for thirty years. Nevertheless, "the suffering and afflicted often had substantial proof of the good use she made of the abundant means at her disposal."[46]

In 1841 Mrs Overend employed two male and two female servants who lived at the house. At that time four other ladies of independent means, possibly relatives or visitors, were also in residence. The lodge was occupied by her coachman and his family.[47]

In 1844 Mrs Overend owned and occupied 31 acres to the north of Chitts Hill, *i.e.* the original estate, of which the house, gardens etc. then totalled over 4 acres. She also occupied a further 20 acres to the south and east then owned by a Mary Robinson which were subseqently added to the estate.[48]

In 1850 the house attracted the attention of William Keane who wrote:

"Chitshill - The seat of Mrs Overend
Is contiguous to Bowes Manor. The house is seated on rising ground and is approached by a winding carriage drive from a pretty Gothic lodge on the right hand side of the high road to Southgate. At a short distance from the house is a span-roof

28. Chitts Hill House from the north west. Probably the original building with a Regency facade. Undated photograph.

conservatory surrounded by pleasure grounds, and in front flows the New River which is spanned by a pretty Gothic Bridge."[49]

The amenity of the New River was to be short-lived with the short-circuiting of the Tottenham loop of the river in 1852 by the tunnel between Myddleton Road and Station Road. As a result the course of the river as it passed Chitts Hill House would gradually dry up.

In 1851 and 1861 Mrs Overend employed a cook, two housemaids, gardener, coachman and gatekeeper. By 1861 Mrs Overend's cook (Anne Larman), gardener (Richard Cuthbert) and her gatekeeper (Mary Fryer) had been in the Overends' service for over 30 years having already been acknowledged in John Overend's Will of 1830. The servants were generally of local or home counties origin.[47]

Mary Overend died on 20th August 1862, aged 79, and was buried at Winchmore Hill, like her husband. Her death notice in a local newspaper read as follows:

"On Wednesday 20th at her residence Chitts' Hill, Mrs Mary Overend, many years an inhabitant of Tottenham who, by her large benevolence, and repeated kindness, had won the esteem of all who knew her."[50]

Mrs Overend left a personal estate approaching £25,000 and made good provision for both her and her late husband's families, her long serving employees and various charitable institutions including the Tottenham

103

Monthly Meeting of Quakers and the Invalid Society of Stoke Newington.[51] In 1859 Mrs Overend had established a trust fund, when she conveyed stock (in the Stockton & Darlington Railway) worth £1250 to trustees (members of the Society of Friends) to distribute income to residents of Tottenham especially widows.[52] This charity remains in operation today and since 1992 it has been administered by the Family Welfare Association. In 1995 the beneficiaries were occupants of the almshouses in Philip Lane, Tottenham administered by the Josiah Forster Trust. It is understood that these two related trusts are likely to be merged in the near future.[53]

Samuel Page and late 19th century developments

Following the death of Mary Overend the estate was sold, in accordance with John Overend's Will, by her husband's surviving nephews, to Thomas and Robert Sidney, the former of Bowes Manor, Southgate, and it was subsequently conveyed to Samuel Page, a City tea dealer, in August 1863. By this time the estate comprised 44 acres of freehold and almost four acres of copyhold land.[54]

Both the 1864 25-inch O.S. map and the margin plans in the indentures of 1863 give a clear indication of the buildings and surroundings at that time. In addition to the substantial house with adjacent stable yard and orchard there was a separate conservatory, a walled kitchen garden with greenhouse and an adjacent farmhouse and yard. The main access to the house was by a carriage drive from the High Road opposite what is now Sidney Road with another (tradesmen's?) drive to the rear of the site also from the High Road but further north. By the early 1860s the development of Wood Green as a residential suburb was well underway, particularly to the north of St.Michael's Church and between the High Road and the Bounds Green Road, but Chitts Hill House and estate still retained its rural park-like character to the east of the High Road.

Samuel Page, was born in Stanton in Nottinghamshire, one of five brothers. His business premises at 4, King William Street in the City was the location of Ridgeway & Co., the tea importers, in which he was probably a partner.[55] He was to have some influence on both the house and the local community. A Vestry Plan of 1876 gives a clear indication of substantial alterations to the house carried out under Samuel Page's tenure. Extra wings were added to the east and west of the main building and a large conservatory to the north end of the house to replace the previous one which had been a separate entity.[56] This conservatory, built by Messrs J. Weeks & Co. of Chelsea, prominent horticultural builders, received much praise in the gardening press of that time:

"Both the elegant and varied exterior(see illustration) and the capacious and convenient interior show a marked advance, as regards tasteful construction, beyond

29. The conservatory at Chitts Hill House, from a contemporary print of 1876

the ordinary dome-shaped or the rectangular curvilinear structures which were the types seen in former days . . . This is, moreover, a striking example of the way a skilful designer should and does encounter any obstructions, adapt himself to any conditions of site and glean from them new ideas of form and beauty. At a short distance from the house, directly behind the octagon end, as seen from the exterior view, stands a very fine specimen of the Araucaria, and its retention the proprietor very properly made a *sine qua non*. Now the most obvious and ordinary way would have been to stop the conservatory short of this tree, but this very condition in skilful hands suggested the narrowing of the building at this point, so as to escape the tree, and led to the erection of the elegant octagonal dome represented in our view. The size of the portion adjoining the residence is, in this case, 30 feet by 25 feet, with a height in front of 12 feet inside the building, the ventilating lantern being 24 feet high. The domical portion is an octagon of about 15 feet diameter, with an extreme height of about 30 feet . . ."[57]

This innovation suggests that Samuel Page must have had more than a passing interest in horticulture.

The original gatehouse known as The Lodge took the form of a round house which still exists today and is now incorporated in Woodside Park. For many years it was the residence of the employees of the estate. Interestingly, the Census returns of 1871, 1881 and 1891 reveal that there were two such lodges, the second lodge not being evident in the earlier returns. The location of the second lodge was at the other entrance further north along the High Road opposite what is now Lascotts Road.[58] It seems reasonable to assume that the second lodge was erected during Samuel Page's tenure.

The 1871 Census shows that Samuel Page and his son were in residence at the house with a cook and two housemaids. The Lodge was well occupied by the coachman, his wife, six children and a lodger and the second lodge by the gardener and his wife. Later in August 1871 Samuel Page lost his oldest son, William, at the age of 21, his wife having died only a few years earlier. The following testimony was recorded:

"The inhabitants of Wood Green have been cast into a state of gloom on the 10th ult. through the death of William H. Page, the only child of Samuel Page Esq. of Chitts Hill who during the time he has possessed the property has gained the goodwill and respect of all. The deceased has but recently attained his majority: he had endeared himself to all who knew him by his kindness of heart, and his memory will long be cherished in the neighbourhood."[59]

Samuel Page also continued the tradition of seeking to enclose the remaining waste land on the boundaries of the estate involving a strip of land (2 roods 13 perches) on the southern boundary[60] and a give and take alteration along the Southgate Road.[61]

The rateable value of the house in 1870 was £225 and in 1881 was £315, the latter reflecting the alterations that had taken place.[62] In 1873 a major part of the estate was still rented out for farming, the annual income from 38 acres of the estate that year being £499.[63]

Samuel Page subsequently remarried. A younger woman from his native county of Nottinghamshire, by 1881, when he was aged 70 and had retired from business, she had five young children then between the ages of one and six, all born in Wood Green. The domestic staff had increased to six to include a nurse and under-nurse. The coachman and his wife and five children were still in residence at the lodge including one addition since the previous census. Two of the coachman's older sons were now employed on the estate as groom and gardener respectively. Another gardener and his wife occupied the second lodge. The occupancy of the house and the estate at this time had probably reached its apogee.

Samuel Page and St. Michael's Church
In common with their benevolent predecessors at Chitts Hill House the Page

family "contributed so munificently to the enlargement and enrichment "of the parish church of St. Michael, Wood Green.[64] Both Samuel and his first wife subscribed to the first rebuilding of the church initiated in 1863.[65] This was to be followed in 1873 by Samuel Page covering the cost of the tower and spire (both designed by Sir George Gilbert Scott) together with the clock and a peal of six bells dedicated to the memory of his first wife and eldest son. These benefactions were heralded in a leading article in the local press as follows:

"The Tower and Spire of Wood Green Church are, we are pleased to learn about to be erected forthwith, Samuel Page Esq. of Chitts Hill having munificently undertaken to defray the whole cost . The work to be executed will be of a much more elaborate character than was originally proposed.The old estimate amounted to about £1200 but at Mr Page's request fresh designs have been prepared, and one adopted which will cost between £2000 and £3000 to carry out. There are also to be a peal of bells and a clock to the tower of the Church, the expense of which Mr Page will defray, so that ere long Wood Green will be able to boast of a Parish Church worthy of the neighbourhood. It is not often that we have had the opportunity of recording such an act of munificence as that we have referred to and we are sure we shall be echoing the feelings of the parishioners of Wood Green and Tottenham generally when we say that Mr Page deserves the gratitude of the public for his great liberality."[66]

The same bells can still be heard ringing out over Wood Green on Sundays and on Monday evenings during bell-ringing practice.

Decline and fall

The Chitts Hill estate was not to remain immune from the onward march of urban development. In June 1881 the first part of the estate was sold for building purposes which involved an east-west strip of land of just over eight acres on the northern boundary of the estate which was in due course to become Lyndhurst Road.[67] Later in 1881 Samuel Page and his family moved to Bayswater and the remainder of the property, now known as the Chitts Hill Park Estate, comprising 35 acres, was sold to the Freehold Cottage Dwelling Company Limited. The indenture[68] recording this sale dated 20th December 1881 also included the adjacent property of Earlham Grove (formerly known as Westbury House) comprising seven acres (which had been acquired by Samuel Page in 1875[69]), the house being occupied by Thomas Bywaters Smithies, author and editor of *The British Workman*. Earlham Grove House subsequently became Wood Green Town Hall (in 1890) and remains in municipal use today as Woodside House.

Plans were already in hand for the development of the estate for building by this time: one plan showing the proposed road lay-out designated the principal Lodge as the estate office.[70]

Samuel Page died on 12th April 1886, aged 76, leaving a personal estate of £140,160 the bulk of which, apart from various legacies, went to his surviving wife. He also left instructions that he should be buried at the Great Northern Cemetery, Colney Hatch in the same vault as his first wife and son.[71]

The house may have still been in use in 1887, possibly rented, under the ownership of the Freehold House Property Company who sought, and were granted, a diversion of the right of way to the house from the High Road.[72]

By the late 1880s the development of Wood Green was proceeding apace particularly to the west of the High Road and by 1888-89 occupation of housing in the new roads which had been laid out on the east of the High Road had started but Chitts Hill House and some of its outbuildings remained with access via the new road system, but the carriage drive and the "old road" had by now disappeared.[73] The once splendid views to the west over the New River were also no more having been superseded by terraced housing on the west of the High Road. In 1891 the only occupants of Chitts Hill House were a caretaker of the building estate company and his wife. Both lodges at this time were occupied by respectively a road foreman and a bricklayer and their families, both presumably involved in the development of the estate.

Further development of the new housing, spreading eastwards from the High Road took place over the next decade. Chitts Hill House was probably demolished between 1895 and 1900 and Sylvan Avenue (later Sylvan Road) covering the site of the house was occupied by 1905.[74]

Only the Lodge survives today

Both lodges remained in residential use until 1894 at least but the northernmost lodge (opposite Lascotts Road) was probably demolished around 1910 to make way for the existing parade of shops on the High Road. The original lodge with the small triangular piece of land surrounding it, which still exists today, formed part of a conveyance of almost seven acres including Earlham Grove House from the Freehold House Property Company Limited to the Wood Green Local Board in 1894.[75] It is most likely that this conveyance led to the suggestion that the lodge had always been associated with Earlham Grove. An additional three and a half acres of land fronting Woodside Road was the subject of a separate conveyance between the same parties.[76] This latter became part of the municipal recreation ground (c.1900) known then as Town Hall Park (now Woodside Park) and the original lodge took on a new lease of life as refreshment rooms which it remained until the late 1960s. In the early 1970s it was known as "The Childrens' Mushroom Playhouse" then under municipal auspices. This lodge, which remains in Council ownership, is not only one of the oldest surviving buildings in Wood

30. Entrance lodge in the Edwardian period, situated in the High Road, Wood Green. Built in 1822, it still exists today.

Green but also of unusual "mushroom" construction, and was Grade II listed by the Department of the Environment in 1974. Although the building has suffered certain indignity in the recent past it is about to have a second lease of life as a cafe, under lease from the Council, having been recently renovated under an English Heritage grant.[77] It has, nevertheless, been identified by English Heritage as a building at risk.[78]

As for the name Chitts Hill itself? This has only been retained in the name of the local church of St Cuthbert's, Chitts Hill and the allotments also in Wolves Lane which are known locally as Chitts Hill Allotments and Gardens Society.

In relation to many other vintage Wood Green properties *e.g.* the nearby Woodside House, the life of Chitts Hill House was relatively short but it represented a style of living during the 19th century, which invariably vanished as a result of urban development. Nevertheless, the owners of such houses have often left permanent reminders of their contribution to the local community and to society in general.

Albert Pinching

References

1. *O.S. of Middlesex, Parish of Tottenham*, 25 inches: 1 mile, 1st edition

2. TCMR (1510-1531), pp. 3, 155, 158; transcript at BCM

3. TCMR (1547-1558), p.119; transcript at BCM

4. Field Book accompanying the Earl of Dorset's Survey; transcript at BCM

5. Dorset Survey Map of Tottenham, 6 inches: 1 mile; BCM

6. *Topographical Map of the County of Middlesex* by John Rocque, reprinted by the LMAS (1971)

7. Copy of Plan of Tottenham 1798 (for Wyburd Survey) by Henry Piper Spurling, by Johnathan and William Newton, 1817; BCM

8. *A New Map of Middlesex* by John Cary, 1801

9. Facsimile of the *Ordnance Surveyors' Drawings of the London Area 1799-1808*, OSD 152/Serial No. 104 Hampstead 1807-8, Scale 2 inches:1 mile; London Topographical Society Pub. No. 144 (1991)

10. *Survey of Middlesex 1818-19*, 2 inches: 1 mile; by C. Greenwood; Gdl.

11. *O.S. 1822, Sheet 71 London* (David and Charles Edition, 1969) (This was Sheet 7 named London in the "Old Series" of 1 inch O.S. maps)

12. Parish Plan of St. Michael's, Wood Green, 3.5 chains: 1 inch: Acc 981/4e, GLRO and BCM

13. Field Book accompanying the Wyburd Survey 1798; BCM

14. TCMR (1510-153; p. 158): transcript at BCM

15. Reference to TCMR dated 2 July 1601 in the Dorset Survey (Ref 5)

16. Bowes,Barnford and Foorde Court Baron dated 3 May 1578: Gdl. MS 25296

17. Parliamentary Survey of the St.Paul's Dean and Chapter Estates – Folio 21; Gdl. MS 25631

18. TCMR, 24 December 1736; Acc 695/1, BCM

19. MDR (1728), 1/344 and 1/345; GLRO

20. MDR (1771), 3/140; GLRO

21. *VCH*, vol. v, p.132

22. Tottenham Vestry Minutes dated 31 December 1777; 1/PT/2A/5, BCM

23. TCMR (1510-1546), p.158; transcript at BCM

24. MDR (1786) 3/271; GLRO

25. MDR (1786) 3/272; GLRO

26. MDR (1796) 1/431; GLRO

27. MDR (1807) 4/268; GLRO

28. MDR (1803) 7/377; GLRO

29. MDR (1807) 4/271; GLRO

30. MDR (1806) 4/310; GLRO

31. Tottenham Vestry Minutes, dated 26 September 1806; 1/PT/2A/6, BCM

32. Tottenham Vestry Plan (1822) No.43; BCM

33. Photograph at BCM: ref 927 CHI

34. MDR (1822) 2/491

35. MDR (1815) 5/231

36. Tottenham Vestry Minutes, dated 15 November 1821; 1/PT/2A/7, BCM

37. TCMR (1787-1822); Microfilm G/2, BCM

38. Pigot's *London, Commercial and Provincial Directory*, 1826-27; BCM and GLRO

39. Biographical Catalogue, London Friends Institute 1888; FHL

40. *Friends Quarterly Examiner*, 1891, p. 521; FHL

41. Dictionary of Quaker Biography; FHL

42. *Quakers in Commerce* by Paul H.Emden, pp. 105-107; *The Quaker Enterprise* by David Burns Windsor (Fredk. Muller, 1980); FHL

43. Tottenham Monthly Meeting, Register of Members (1797-1839); FHL

44. Last Will and Testament of John Overend proved 14 February 1832, (PROB 11/ 1796): PRO Chancery Lane

45. *My Ancestors* by William Penney, pp, 162-163, 204-205 (Privately circulated, 1920); FHL

46. Biographical Catalogue, 1888, *op.cit.*; FHL

47. Enumerators' Returns; BCM and PRO

48. Tottenham Parish Rent Charges Returns 1844; BCM

49. *The Beauties of Middlesex* by William Keane (1850)

50. *Tottenham and Edmonton Advertiser*, 1 Sept. 1862; BCM

51. Last Will and Testament of Mary Overend proved 9 September 1862; Principal Registry, Somerset House

52. *VCH*, vol. v, p. 379, and Tottenham Vestry Minutes

53. Family Welfare Association: private communication.

54. MDR (1863) 4/745-747; GLRO

55. *Kelly's London Directory*, 1863

56. Tottenham Vestry Plan (1876) No. 135; BCM

57. *The Gardeners' Chronicle*, 5 February 1876

58. MDR (1881) 29/814; GLRO

59. *Tottenham and Edmonton Advertiser*, 1 September 1871; BCM

60. TMCR dated 11 August 1865; Acc 695/3, BCM

61. Tottenham Vestry Plan (1880) Nos. 49, 51; BCM

62. Parish of Tottenham Rate Returns, 1844; BCM

63. Returns of Owners of Land, Middlesex, 1873; GLRO Library

64. *St. Michael's Church, Wood Green, 150th Anniversary Brochure*, 1994

65. "The Earlier History of the Parish Church of St. Michael, Wood Green" by Frank Theodore; BCM

66. *Tottenham and Edmonton Weekly Herald*, 31 May 1873; BCM

67. MDR (1881) 29/814; GLRO

68. MDR (1882)1/749; GLRO

69. MDR (1875)14/793; GLRO

70. Tottenham Vestry Plan (1886) No. 126; BCM

71. Last Will and Testament of Samuel Page proved 26 May 1886; Principal Registry, SH

72. Tottenham Vestry Minutes, 17 March 1887; 1/PT/2A/13, BCM

73. *O.S. Parish of Tottenham*, 25 inches: 1 mile, 1894-96 edition; BCM

74. *Kelly's P.O. Directories for Hornsey* (1889-1899) and *Wood Green* (1900-1910) and *London* (1967)

75. MDR(1894) 15/256; GLRO

76. MDR(1894) 15/63; GLRO

77. Haringey Council Planning Dept., private communication

78. *The [Haringey] Advertiser*, 1 May 1996

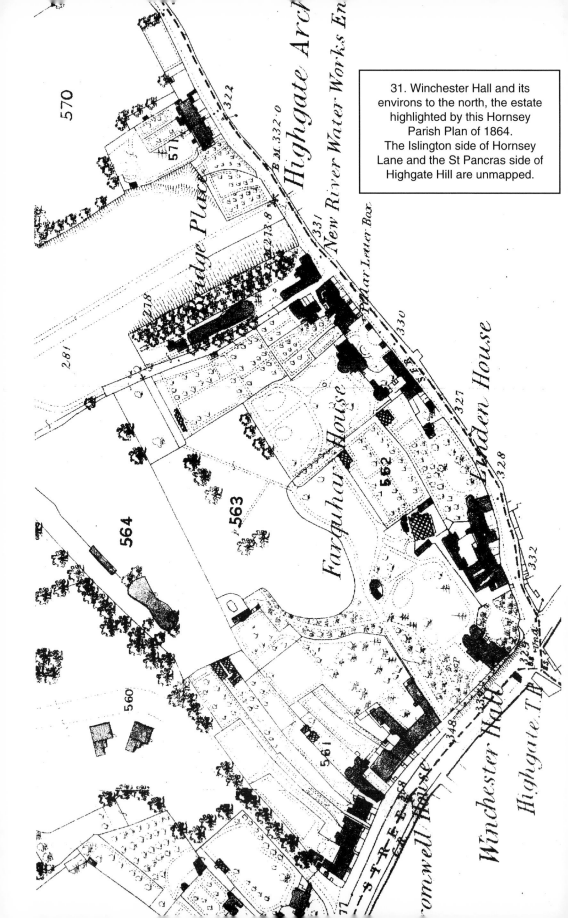

31. Winchester Hall and its environs to the north, the estate highlighted by this Hornsey Parish Plan of 1864.
The Islington side of Hornsey Lane and the St Pancras side of Highgate Hill are unmapped.

A Country Residence for City Men: Winchester Hall over Three Centuries

Winchester Hall was a large redbrick house that stood just below Cromwell House, the seventeenth century mansion on Highgate Hill, on what is now the top of Cromwell Avenue. That street did not exist then and Winchester Hall filled the corner between Highgate Hill and Hornsey Lane, and its grounds stretched over several acres to the rear.

The original mansion and its owners

The Winchester Hall estate can be traced back to the beginning of the reign of James I, although the house that stood on the site then was different from the one the Victorians knew. In that year, 1603, the copyhold property was inherited by Ann (or Anne) Smith from her late husband Robert Smith (or Smythe), who had died a short while before in his mid-thirties. Robert was the fifth son of Thomas 'Customer' Smythe (1522-1591) who was the collector of customs duties in the Port of London and one of the leading commercial figures of Elizabethan England. Thomas's father-in-law was Sir Andrew Judde (c.1495-1558) who was Master of the Skinners' Company six times, a founder of the Muscovy Company, and Lord Mayor of London in 1550. Thomas Smythe, a wealthy man, commissioned portraits of his wife and children and they were painted in 1579/80. Some of the portraits have survived, including Robert's. Robert was born in 1567 so his shows a boy of twelve. His thin intelligent face with dark eyes and hair gazes out of the picture, the head surmounting an elaborate ruff and richly embroidered doublet. Robert married the daughter and heiress of William Lynford and came to live in Highgate.[1] It is reasonable to surmise that the first Winchester Hall was built for the young couple. When Anne became a widow the house was regarded as only recently built.[2] It may have been timber-framed but was more likely built of brick, like Cromwell House and other seventeenth century Highgate residences.

When Anne died in 1627 her son John succeeded to the estate[3] and lived in the house.[4] But in the 1630s he was induced to let it to Sir John Wollaston,[5] the City goldsmith who lived very near by, in Cholmeley Lodge, and who was to become Lord Mayor and a powerful figure in London and its environs during the Civil Wars. He and John Ireton gained virtual control over Highgate for the Parliamentarians, Wollaston acquiring the Manors of Hornsey and Finchley from the Bishop of London and Ireton the Cantelowes side of the township, but we know little of the local sequence of events during the Commonwealth. John Smith died in 1656,[6] four years before the restoration of the monarchy, and his widow, another Anne, in 1665.[7] Some of John's relations through his mother's second marriage, the Vaughans, became the new owners,[8] but they were not the occupants. A widow called Susanna Winch lived there,[9] and it was her name that stuck to the place. Throughout the eighteenth century the house was referred to as 'the Winches house'. The name 'Winchester', whether prefixing 'House' or 'Hall', probably became current from the 1820s only.[10] One attribute of the house is certain; it was large, for in 1674 it was recorded as possessing nineteen hearths.[11]

In 1683, Edward Beeker, a City of London cooper, bought the house, sixteen acres of land round it and several cottages from the Vaughans, and about four acres from other vendors.[12] To be on the safe side, Beeker also bought a two-foot wide strip of land taken from the Manor's 'waste' all along the edge of his garden next to the King's highway,[13] because people squatting on vacant land were a constant threat to anyone trying to create or maintain an attractive property.

The late seventeenth century house
By 1691 the old mansion was gone and Beeker had had a new house built.[14] In his Will, dated 30th June of that year, he left the house and 23 acres of pastureland to his wife Elizabeth; after her death the estate was to pass to their daughter Elizabeth and her husband John Cooke and then to their grand-children. Beeker died three years later.[15] In 1701 his daughter Elizabeth, by then a widow, and her son were recognised as the lawful owners of the Winches house by the Manor court.[16]

Unfortunately for Elizabeth, she found herself encumbered by debts, most likely incurred by her father and not discharged by her husband. To acquire some ready money, she mortgaged what remained of the Highgate property to two lawyers. This was the re-built Winches house with its gardens, orchards, stables, barns and other out-buildings and six acres of pasture, and the nearby four-acre farm or nursery garden known as Merralls after the name of a previous owner and occupied by Peter Smith, described as a 'gardener'. The tenant of the big house was Thomas Lewis, a City merchant. Elizabeth re-married, becoming the wife of Robert Bumpsted of Bishops Hall in the then rural parish of Stepney. Her property would have come to Robert on their marriage, but he would have gained no immediate advantage from a mortgaged estate. So in 1710 the tenant of the Winches hall, Thomas Lewis, was offered the whole estate for the duration of Elizabeth's life, on condition the mortgages were re-paid. He agreed to this arrangement, but immediately re-mortgaged the property to someone who had become interested in it, Thomas Rogers, the owner of an inn in St James's, Westminster. (The relevant documents are printed in the Appendix.)[17] Lewis must have got it back for he later entered into a private agreement to sell the estate for £1500. He died without heirs, and the purchaser under the agreement, Richard Boulton, was able to bequeath the estate to a nephew, his namesake. It is not known whether Robert Bumpsted was able to contest any of these arrangements.

32. Winchester Hall from the south. An Edwardian drawing based closely on a photograph, but omitting Victorian decorative ironwork round the roof and emphasising the Georgian aspect of the house.

In 1738 the younger Richard Boulton sold the property to Thomas Rogers, who would seem to have been waiting in the wings for the chance to acquire it. He was given leave to take down the existing house and re-build.[18] Whether he actually carried out this plan is dubious, as no subsequent reference to it has been found. Rogers died in 1745, and after the death of his widow Mary a cousin and his wife, George and Margaret Rogers, became the new owners.[19] They lived in Southampton so were absentee landlords, and in 1764 they sold out to John Lucy of Stockwell.[20] He seems to have come to live in the house, but in 1775 he sold it to Alexander Anderson who likewise wanted it for his own occupation.[21] In 1793 he in turn passed it on to Henry Peter Kuhff, a City business man.[22] Kuhff died intestate but his son Henry was officially declared the owner in 1798.[23] Henry and his wife Lucy went to live in Islington and in 1801 sold the Winches house to Charles Ranken of Lawrence Lane in the City.[24] He lived only a few months longer and his widow sold the property to another City man, Nathaniel Harden, or Arden as he was often known, of Crosby Square.[25]

Harden must have lived at least part of the time in Highgate for he became Commandant of the local Volunteer force during the Invasion scare of 1803,[26] only a year after he had acquired the Winches house. His estate was now defined as the house itself and its immediate grounds, amounting to over two acres, and the "Paddock" and the "Long Meadow", each of more than an acre. After a few years he decided to sell. From 1811 the new owner was Peter Poland (1760-1827), a City furrier who had come to England from Bavaria as a young man[27] and had lived in Islington. He paid £5,250 for his new home.[28] But Peter and his wife Sarah considered a modern house more suited to their requirements, and they moved to the recently erected Farquhar House in Hornsey Lane (on the site of the present reservoir). They made a small profit in selling the Winches house for £5,900.[29]

The residence of Thomas Hurst

The purchaser in 1818 was Thomas Hurst, a publisher from Paternoster Row, the street of booksellers near St Paul's Cathedral. He maintained a town house in Bloomsbury,[30] and had an affluent life-style. He was no newcomer to Highgate for since at least 1812 he had occupied a semi-detached house, now known as Ivy House, higher up Highgate Hill.[31] He and his neighbour, George Lackington, another publisher, living in Northgate House, the other half of the c.1700 building, were friends, and they had bought the property together.[32] Hurst had thrown himself into local life and in 1817 became a Governor of Highgate School, a position he held till he resigned in 1832.[33] Later he was to reflect that he had used up much of "his fortune and his leisure" in trying to be "a hospitable Neighbour and an active member of the Hamlet."[34]

Hurst certainly spent a great deal of money in Highgate. In addition to his original home on Highgate Hill and then Winchester Hall, he bought Cromwell House next to it in 1823. He also invested in the corner site opposite Winchester Hall, *i.e.* land between Hornsey Lane and Highgate Hill formerly belonging to The Old Crown (at that time further down the hill).[35] He found a tenant for Cromwell House so that the major expense was undoubtedly Winchester Hall. He had a special fondness for the old house. According to his own estimate, given to Mrs Gillman in whose house his friend the poet Coleridge lived, he had spent £12,000 altogether on the property – the purchase price plus the cost of "improvements".[36] These improvements were considered remarkable at the time and were duly noted by *The Ambulator* in 1820. The contiguity of Cromwell House and Winchester Hall presented him with an opportunity to plan the two gardens together. Behind the two houses Hurst created a sweep of lawns and paths to provide delightful vistas and walks. The main elements of the Winchester Hall garden that can be seen on the large-scale Ordnance Survey maps of forty years later were devised by Hurst – the lawn with its specimen trees, the sheltered kitchen garden in the angle between the gardens of Linden House and Farquhar House, the path to the shrubbery, and the flower beds and pool at the edge of the higher ground. A contemporary plan[37] shows these features and also that the garden had been extended to incorporate land that later went back to Cromwell House. This was always referred to as the melon ground, so presumably Hurst had hotbeds for the production of these exotic fruits to grace his dinner table.

In 1826 Thomas and his older brother John went bankrupt. But it was not so much the result of private extravagance as of business mismanagement. Their firm of Hurst, Robinson and Company had speculated recklessly, especially in the hops market, and when debts accumulated Hurst had given in to the temptation of making out promissory notes in the name of Longman, the publishers with whom they were in association. Thomas was made personally responsible for outstanding bills, and Winchester Hall had to be put up for sale.[38]

Some of Hurst's friends rallied round to help. Coleridge wrote several times to a prospective buyer, Charles Tulk, in the late summer of 1826, urging him to buy.[39] The contents were up for auction and a date had been fixed for the sale but Coleridge mentioned an overall figure of £6,500 for the entire property which it was thought would be "accepted at once". He pointed out that the value of the house and grounds (£6,000), the fixtures (£400), "the Furniture (i.e. Wine, Books, Pictures, &c., as per Catalogue)" (£1,300) and the two cottages ("let at present for 35£ a year, but would fetch 40£: the present tenant having been Mr. T. Hurst's Coachman") – all these added up to a figure much in excess of the suggested £6,500.[40] After the contents sale had taken place, he did not give up and mentioned the significantly high prices paid for the furniture:

"Of the Books the only one that sold cheap was the Unique Copy of the Encyclopaedia for 100 guineas, thought to be worth 200 at least. The prices given for the Pictures made me stare . . . All together, you would certainly have had an excellent bargain."

The house, fixtures and two cottages were still available, Coleridge pointed out, possibly for only £6,000.[41] He also tried to interest Tulk in buying Cromwell House as well "if a respectable tenant could be secured before hand . . . for a lease of years & at a rent that would pay good interest for the purchase money." This would avoid "the possibility of an unpleasant neighbour as an occupant of Cromwell House."[42]

Dr Gillman too, Coleridge's medical advisor and long-standing host, seems to have taken some responsibility from their broken friend's shoulders. He was involved in the abortive attempt to interest Tulk in the property; according to Coleridge, Gillman would gladly "have taken a run down to Brighton" where Tulk lived or met him in Town to discuss the project, and Tulk was asked to make any offer through the doctor. Hurst's own financial acumen had obviously lost credibility; whereas Gillman was to Coleridge "a sensible man of business" Hurst had become "our worthy but not very clear headed Neighbor [sic]".[43]

The liabilities of the Hursts and their partner Joseph Ogle Robinson took several years to sort out. Tulk did not buy Winchester Hall and pending a longer term solution it was let to Thomas Tegg, the print-seller. Cromwell House continued with the same tenant. Hurst went back to live in Ivy House for a while,[44] but by 1833 his address was Waterloo Place, Pall Mall.[45] George Lackington with Andrew Spottiswoode, Thomas Dickinson and three others formed a panel of "Assignees" who had the task of disposing of the various assets in the most advantageous manner. Hurst had property in York as well as in London and this was duly confiscated. Friends and acquaintances being in the driving-seat made the consequences of his folly slightly less painful. An elderly local resident, Richard Nixon, bought Cromwell House in 1833, paying only £3,000 for the house and £944.17s.6d. for the garden and the melon ground. At the same time Sir William Poland, one of the three sons of Peter Poland, the previous owner, bought Winchester Hall for £3,500.[46] Two years later he acquired a further 6 acres between Cromwell House and the Archway Road.[47]

The Polands and the Redmaynes
William Poland (1797-1884), who had gone into the family fur business and been successful, had become Sheriff of London and Middlesex in 1831 and had been knighted the same year. Buying Winchester Hall was a homecoming, for his family had moved there when he was 14. He had four sons whom he enrolled at Highgate School, three of them in 1833 and one in 1834.[48] This was during the Headship of Rev Samuel Mence whose conduct of Sir Roger Cholmeley's Grammar School had been heavily criticised, and was an act of faith in an establishment which had only recently been converted from a virtual primary school to a grammar school once more.

So Sir William Poland had an independent mind, but otherwise little is known of him. His sons were Richard who followed his father in the firm,[49] Alfred who became an eye surgeon at Moorfields Hospital, James who was a surgeon in the Navy, and Frederick who went into the Church.[50] The Polands stayed at Winchester Hall for five years and then in 1830 moved to William's parents' old home, Farquhar House in Hornsey Lane. They sold the Hall to Giles Redmayne, a silk mercer with a shop in New Bond Street.[51] The price he paid in 1838, £2,980,[52] was low compared with the figure of £5,900 paid by Hurst in 1818, after the Napoleonic War.

Giles Redmayne was a man in his forties and he and his wife Mary, who was a little younger having been born in 1800, had been living in

Highgate for some years with their young family, in Greenwood Cottage at the foot of West Hill (although it was then regarded as being in Kentish Town). From there Redmayne had commuted to the West End every day on horseback and the children had thrived in a rural setting. They kept a cow, pigs and chickens, grew their own vegetables and maintained a vinery, and they had an old black barn serving as stables, coach house and hay loft.[53] But with increasing affluence the Redmaynes were looking for a bigger house. Winchester Hall with its acres of grounds promised ample scope for children's play. After the family moved, Greenwood Cottage disappeared, to be replaced by a house built for the new owners; later, in 1852, part of the garden became the site for St Anne's church.

Redmayne was a Northcountryman who had come to London in his youth and worked hard at his business of selling silks, linens and lace. Later, when his son John joined him, he was to acquire additional premises in Conduit Street, where ladies' shawls were the speciality.[54] It was not Redmayne's preferred career; he would have liked to have become a preacher, but having been apprenticed to the silk trade and married young he found himself virtually trapped. His son Robert could not remember his father ever taking a day's holiday. But Giles Redmayne was keenly interested in politics and was called a radical by some. Once established at Winchester Hall, he delved into local affairs, sampling the Hornsey Vestry meetings,[55] and becoming the first Treasurer of the Highgate Literary and Scientific Institution which was founded in 1839, the year after his arrival.[56] He gave money towards the re-building of the Highgate church school and was elected as a Foundation Manager.[57] (It was in that capacity that he averted a further split between the clerical and lay factions.[58])

Apart from these outside commitments, life for the Redmaynes revolved round the family, with summer holidays spent with Redmayne's sisters who lived in the Lake District. There was no intimacy with other Highgate residents (being in 'Trade' did not help) and dinner parties were rare. To Robert, dinner parties seemed to be given out of a sense of duty to acquaintances they did not particularly like. In contrast warm hospitality was often given to young men from the northern counties who were embarking on careers in London or were about to emigrate to Australia. A fixed point in the week however was the reading round the fire on Sunday afternoons by the whole family, one verse at a time, of the Bible. Apart from that, religion was instilled not by words but by example. It was a happy family, with a relaxed household in which the children were allowed considerable freedom. To Robert, looking back, life in Winchester Hall was Paradise.[59]

The house itself must have seemed very large after Greenwood Cottage. With its frontage facing Hornsey Lane, it was four-storeyed, with the basement containing the kitchen and ancillary offices. Because of the steep

33. The garden side of Winchester Hall where dining room and drawing room had bay windows

slope up Highgate Hill, the ground floor was approached by front steps, made in stone, but was level with the garden at the back. The entrance hall occupied the centre of the house, the wide staircase having a half-landing forming a kind of gallery. On the left of the door (viewed from outside) was a cosy breakfast room which was also the library, looking towards the front and so facing south-east. On the right were the dining room and drawing room opening by low bay windows on to the garden. On the first floor were six bedrooms and dressing rooms. The top floor was given over to nurseries for the children, maids' bedrooms, a playroom and a storeroom fitted up for apples.

The best part of the property, for the children, was outside. Hurst's lavish planting had matured, and there were mimosas, a tulip tree, arbutus, medlars, peaches and many unknown varieties of trees. Specially impressive were the cedars and a mulberry tree of very ancient origin that fruited heavily. An elaborate 'grotto' covered in imitation rock that served as a summer house, with French windows and stained glass, was roofed in lead, affording the intrepid climber a magnificent view over London, with St Paul's and the Thames clearly visible. The grotto may have been made at Hurst's direction, but the sundial formed from one of the balusters of old London Bridge was probably installed by the Polands. Redmayne made no alterations at all. There was enough land for cows, pigs, chickens and rabbits to be kept, and the various outhouses and their lofts, including the stable, coach house, hay barn, woodhouse, toolhouse and laundry, gave endless opportunities for play. Robert and his younger brother Marriner regarded the rabbits as their pets, while their older brother Giles was allowed to keep pigeons. However much they got to know the lanes and footpaths round about, they always preferred their own domain. One of their few local contacts was with the Poland boys at Farquhar House, a rather unruly lot, who treated their parents with disrespect. Their garden was to Robert in miserable contrast to his own, as it contained a large number of classical statues. He remembered being with the boys when they threw stones down on to the coaches in Archway Road from the top of Nash's balustrade that was only a few hundred yards along Hornsey Lane.

Mrs Redmayne was a Londoner and sometimes escaped to Town by taking a 'fly' (hansom cab) from a jobmaster's below the Old Crown. (The family coach remained in the coach house unless needed for the rare visits to the railway station to go North, and the gig, a 'Tilbury', was driven to the West End daily by Mary's husband.) To keep order in her absence she had a nanny, cook, parlourmaid and housemaid.[60] At the time this would have been considered the minimum number of staff for such a large house. Not surprisingly, Robert's memory of his mother was that she was always busy. The staff were devoted to the family. Robert recalled James Whitlock,

"Gardener, Coachman and friend of the family, who would have soon thought of changing his place as of committing suicide, and who remained with us till we ceased to have a garden, in the year 1851 or '52 and was then in his declining years set up in an eating house in the East of London." [61]

Schooling for the Redmayne children was fairly local, very much so in the case of the girls, Ellen and Margaret, who attended Mrs Addison's finishing school for young ladies next door in Hornsey Lane. Giles went to Mr Holloway's Gordon House Academy in Kentish Town, which moved to Notting Hill where Robert later boarded, while Marriner went to the Highgate Commercial Academy nearby on The Bank in Highgate. Robert left Mr Holloway's and was sent to Tunbridge School before going on to Trinity College, Cambridge.[62]

We do not know why the Redmaynes left Winchester Hall in 1853 after living there for fifteen years. Perhaps Mary found Highgate too quiet, and according to Robert she had never been interested in the garden. Their new address was near Portman Square. The Redmaynes' business continued to flourish and became a limited company. It continued until the first world war.[63]

The Redmaynes sold Winchester Hall in 1853 to Francis Parkyn, a builder from Haverstock Hill: the house, the four acres of pleasure grounds and the six acres of pasture.[64] Nothing is known about his intentions. By 1857 he had died and his widow Agnes let the property to one George Sharp,[65] who also did not stay long. By the spring of 1861 the big house was empty except for a caretaker[66] and in June it was bought by J. William Jeakes for £8,010.

William Jeakes: voluntary service and outdoor entertainment

Jeakes was the Director of C. Jeakes & Co., "Engineers, Stove and Range Manufacturers, Domestic Metal Workers, and General Ironmongers", of Great Russell Street.[67] Jeakes was one of the beneficiaries of the new iron age, when not only were public buildings constructed round an iron framework but multifarious domestic appliances formerly made in wood or earthenware were now made in iron. In the 1850s his shop had gained the

attention of the Press, through his service to the British troops taking part in the Crimean War. He had supplied a drying cabinet for wet clothes as sought by Charles Dickens after he became indirectly in touch with Florence Nightingale; she had written home to a mutual friend (Angela Burdett-Coutts) about the sodden misery of the soldiers. Jeakes not only coped with the unprecedented requirement of shipment in parts for customer assembly but incorporated a wash-boiler and spindrier into the design. Six feet high and seven feet wide, iron inside a wooden cabinet, capable of drying 1000 articles at once, Jeakes's washing machine was depicted in the *Illustrated London News* as a new wonder. Dickens declared it was the only 'administrative' thing connected with the War that had been a success.[68]

34. John William Jeakes, London ironmonger and Highgate benefactor, who made Winchester Hall his home in 1861

After Jeakes moved into the Hall, he extended the estate so that the grounds were back to the early eighteenth century size. Some of this was the result of a purchase in 1865 of five acres of meadowland west of Archway Road used by Mrs Frances Turner of Hornsey Lane Farm for her cows.[69]

Jeakes and his wife, their son and three daughters, lived in far greater style than the Redmaynes, who had had simple tastes and old-fashioned furniture. Jeakes was a man of about the same age as Giles Redmayne when he had moved in, but he employed six resident servants.[70] He took a leading part in community life. He was Treasurer of the Highgate Dispensary[71] which gave free medicines to the poor, supported by private subscriptions. He was a magistrate who presided at the Highgate police court. He was President of the Highgate Working Men's Club.[72] He was one of a group of prominent residents who between 1864 and '67 defeated a move to build on Pond Square and at the same time were providing affordable housing elsewhere.[73] He got the Public Health Act applied to the Parish of Hornsey by helping to create a Local Board; in 1869, two years after it was formed, he became its Chairman.

With all these activities and Jeakes's status as an officer in the Volunteers, allied to a certain softening of social attitudes, the new owners of

35. The entrance hall

Winchester Hall became accepted members of the Highgate gentry. One of the memorable events arranged by Colonel Jeakes, as he always preferred to be known, was a field day for his old comrades in the Bloomsbury Volunteer Rifles (37th Battalion of the Middlesex Regiment) after he had become the Highgate Commandant, in October 1866. On the sixth, a fine afternoon, 200 men assembled at 3 o'clock in the yard of the Foundling Hospital, and marched off under Colonel Stedall of the Highgate Volunteers. Headed by a brass band, they marched up Highgate Hill and reached the Hall at about four. They formed three sides of a square below the terrace, the fourth side being reserved for the large number of guests. After a speech of welcome from their host, a display of army manoeuvres ensued. Then the arms were all put in a pile. The officers went indoors with the other guests for refreshments and toasts were drunk; the men were treated to a cold spread in a marquee. Eventually the force was back on parade and speeches were made to bursts of cheering. At 7 o'clock it was all over and the Bloomsbury Volunteers marched away.[74]

A year or so later, Jeakes was employing a landscape gardener to improve the estate.[75] His main contribution would seem to have been a new lower lawn, taken from a field, and some hothouses. These were lavish indeed. One, forty feet long, was for growing pineapples, and a smaller one was for grapes.[76] Cast iron had revolutionised the construction and running of hothouses and both coal and labour were cheap. Jeakes had the

36. The garden in 1873, with the first Alexandra Palace faintly on the skyline

advantage of being able to order large quantities of iron at trade rates. He also had an aviary and an octagonal beehive built.

It was entirely to be expected that Jeakes would become President of the Highgate Horticultural Society which had been founded in 1859. The presidency was usually a transitory office of which the chief duty was to provide the venue for the summer show. In June 1869 he duly lent his grounds. Two large tents housed the exhibits. As was customary with the society in Victorian times, the entries of fruits and vegetables had to be in classes according to whether the competitor was a 'gentleman', 'cottager', or schoolchild. For many of the more exotic exhibits – *e.g.* grapes, pineapples and orchids – no such classification was required for they came solely from gentlemen, like Jeakes himself, who employed gardeners. Two police bands had been hired for the occasion and seats for an audience were provided on the lower lawn while the upper lawn became a dance floor. About 3,000 people attended and the dancing continued until it was nearly dark. According to Jeakes, not a single plant in his garden had been damaged. The prizes were presented later, on a July evening in a school hall, by one of Jeakes's daughters.[77] In 1873 Winchester Hall was again used for the Summer Show, and at the prize-giving the trophies were this time presented by a well-known public figure who lived locally, Lady Burdett-Coutts.[78]

Sale and re-development

Jeakes died suddenly on 15th February 1874, aged 57, and was buried in Highgate Cemetery. His son, John William Jeakes, inherited the Hall and two-fifths of the estate, with the proviso that the house was to be his principal place of residence. The remainder was divided between the girls with an annuity for their mother.[79] Unlike his father, who had been concerned to keep the property intact, John William was chiefly interested in its re-sale value. He set about acquiring six acres on the east of Archway Road, land divided since 1867 by the London, Highgate & Edgware Railway, but still occupied by a local farmer, Charles Turner. This speculative investment was undertaken in collaboration with J.F. Huggins of the Lion Brewery, Broad Street, and J.W.'s uncle, Rev. James Jeakes,[80] later to become Rector of Hornsey.

In 1881 the Winchester Hall estate was sold to the Imperial Property Investment Company, one of the agents of the increasing urbanisation of the area at this time. The subsequent auction sales revealed the attention that had been lavished on the property. Liberal use had been made of ironware, including the 1 1/2 miles of railings round the estate, the decorative wrought iron crowning the roof of the Hall, the columns in the entrance hall, and the heating systems in the hothouses. All the trees in the garden and the hundred oaks round the ancient field boundaries were offered for timber. There was one stipulation from the vendor: the grape house was not to be dismantled till after the grapes were picked.

The furnishings included many of the trappings of a stately home: heraldic shields, pairs of antlers, a deer's head, a breastplate, and claymores and other weapons. The paintings included a portrait of Queen Elizabeth by 'Zucchero', a portrait of Charles II, paintings attributed to Nicholas Hilliard and to Peter Lely, and three portraits of ladies by Godfrey Kneller. The furnishings were sold on 18th May 1881 at Foster's Gallery in Pall Mall.[81]

The building materials were auctioned on the premises on 20th July 1881. There were no powers to save the house and the Local Board accepted the proposed re-development, and creating new residential roads over the old estate. The Company also planned to widen Hornsey Lane and the row of elms outside the garden wall was doomed. Later they constructed a new pavement in continuation of the Bank on Highgate Hill and planted new trees.[82] One wing of the Hall was taken down during July and August 1881. The other wing was allowed to remain until September of the following year.[83]

As a direct consequence of the demolition, Cromwell Avenue and its side roads came into being and the area running north-east from Winchester Hall was built up. Only the names Winchester Road, Winchester Place, and Winchester Tavern in Archway Road serve as reminders of the old mansion.

Joan Schwitzer

References

1. The portrait of Robert Smythe by Ketel was exhibited in the "Dynasties" exhibition on "Painting in Tudor and Jacobean England 1530-1630" at the Tate Gallery in 1995/96. The writer is indebted to Peter Barber for drawing attention to the sitter's connection with Highgate. The information about Smythe's forebears comes from the exhibition catalogue edited by Karen Hearn (1995), pp. 108-109.

2. Marcham, p. 2

3. Marcham, p. 70

4. Marcham, p. 72

5. Marcham, pp. 76 and 90

6. Marcham, p. 131

7. Marcham, p. 155

8. Marcham, p. 182

9. Marcham, p. 249

10. Letter from S. T.Coleridge to Thomas Hurst at "Winchester House", 6 Aug. 1825, *Letters of Coleridge*, vol.5, p.488

11. Hearth Tax Returns of 1674; Marcham, p. xiv.

12. Marcham, pp. 193-194

13. Marcham, p. 200

14. Marcham, p. 216

15. Marcham, pp. 226-227

16. Marcham, p. 249

17. Hornsey Manor Court Rolls. 13 March 1709/10, 10465/25; Gdl. Printed in full, as a translation from the Latin original, in the Appendix. The author of this chapter is indebted to Ian Murray, former Archivist to

the London Borough of Haringey, for help in the interpretation of this document.

18. 10465/53; Gdl.

19. 10465/60; Gdl.

20. 10465/79; Gdl.

21. 10465/90; Gdl.

22. 10465/108; Gdl.

23. 10465/113; Gdl.

24. 10465/116; Gdl.

25. 10465/117; Gdl.

26. John Richardson, *Highgate Its History since the fifteenth century* (1983), p. 227

27. Info. from Gwynydd Gosling, Archivist of the HLSI

28. 10465/126; Gdl.

29. 10465/133; Gdl.

30. Holden's *Triennial Directory of London* 1817-19

31. Hornsey Rate Book, DR0 E20/E2/1; GLRO

32. 10465/131; Gdl.

33. *Highgate School Register 1833-1964*, 6th ed., p. 51

34. Hurst to C.A. Tulk, 8 Sept. 1826, *Letters of Coleridge*, vol. 6, p. 610-612

35. *Lost Houses of Haringey*, ed. Joan Schwitzer (1986), p.56

36. *Letters of Coleridge*, vol. 6, p. 609

37. Middlesex Deeds Register 1833, Book 3, Nos. 656 and 657; GLR0

38. *Letters of Coleridge*, vol.6, p.605

39. *Ibid.*, pp. 606-620

40. *Ibid.*, p. 613

41. *Ibid.*, p. 614

42. *Ibid.*, p. 620

43. *Ibid.*, pp. 614-615

44. Hornsey Rate Book, entries for April and September 1832, DRO 20/E2/4; GLR0

45. 10465/148; Gdl.

46. *Ibid.*

47. 10465/176; Gdl.

48. *Highgate School Roll 1833-1912*, 1st ed. (1913)

49. Potter Collection of North London Topography, VI, 99; BM

50. Boase, *Modern Biography* (1897), vol. 2, cols. 1568-1569

51. *Post Office London Directories, 1824-1838* eds.

52. 10465/168; Gdl.

53. Robert Robey Redmayne, "A Retrospect", unpublished MS memoirs, p.6; BL Add. MS 60740. Peter Barber kindly drew attention to this acquisition by the British Library. The preceding paragraph and the following six are based chiefly upon it.

54. Kelly's *London Directories*, 1850 and 1854

55. Hornsey Vestry Minutes, 1838; BCM

56. Info. from Archivist of HLSI

57. Building Committee vol., St Michael's School, North Rd., N6, archives

58. Managers' Minutes, St Michael's School archives

59. Robert Redmayne's "Retrospect"

60. Census of Hornsey, 1841 and 1851; PRO

61. Robert Redmayne's "Retrospect", leaves 7-8

62. Venn, *Alumni Cantabrigiensi*, part II, vol. 5, p. 264

63. Kelly's *London Directories* 1853-1930

64. 10465/168; Gdl.

65. 10465/176; Gdl.

66. Census of Hornsey 1861

67. For Jeakes's forebears, see *Lost Houses of Haringey*, p.60

68. *Ibid.*

69. 10465/189; Gdl.

70. Census of Hornsey 1871

71. *Highgate Directory 1870*, pub. by *Ham. & High. Express*; BL

72. *Highgate Parish Magazine*, March 1874, p. 40; HLSI

73. Joan Schwitzer, "The struggle for Pond Square", *Camden History Review 3* (1975)

74. *Highgate Parish Magazine*, Nov. 1866, pp.10-11; HLSI

75. *Highgate Parish Magazine*, July 1869, p.119; HLSI

76. *O.S. 1:2500*, 1st ed. 1870. See also Catalogue for Auction Sale 30 July 1881, Potter Coll., VII, 39; BM

77. *Highgate Parish Magazine*, Aug. 1869, pp. 138-141; HLSI

78. *Highgate Parish Magazine*, Aug. 1873, pp. 106; HLSI

79. *City Press*, 9 May 1874

80. 10465/189; Gdl.

81. Sales Catalogues, Potter Collection, VII, 39; BM

82. Hornsey Local Board Minutes, May to Nov. 1881; BCM

83. MS note in Potter Coll., VII, 35

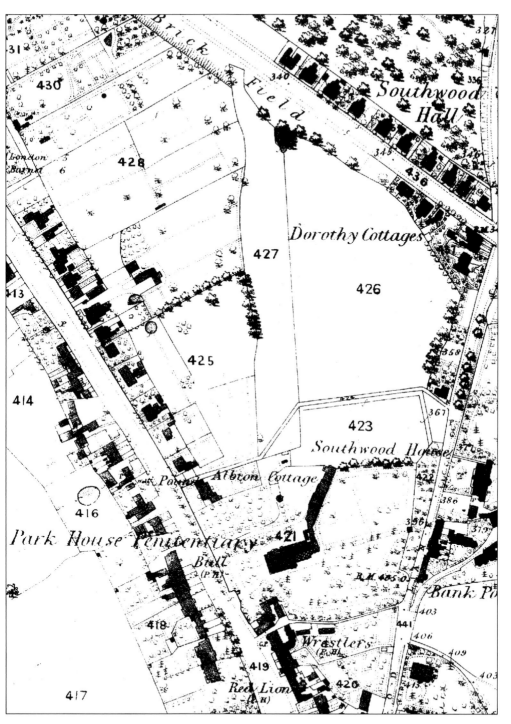

37. Park House and environs 1864. The house and garden were almost completely surrounded by trees. The estate's fields (numbered 423,426 and 427) were grazing land.

The evolution of a strategic site: Park House and its predecessors

Park House, Highgate is an example of a Regency mansion that survived until after the second world war through institutional use. It was transformed from private residence to charitable institution when only a third of its time span had elapsed and lasted almost a century more before being demolished in 1946. Today the site of Park House and its garden is occupied by seven six-storey redbrick blocks of flats built by the Borough of Hornsey as one of the first post-war Council housing schemes.[1] They stand on a plateau with a belt of trees round three sides, between North Hill on the west and Southwood Lane on the east. Several names round about are derived from that of the old mansion. The southern boundary of the estate is delineated by Park Walk, an alley running from The Wrestlers in North Road to Southwood Lane. The curved northern boundary forms one side of The Park, a road which is linked to North Hill by Park House Passage.

The Bulwarks

Perhaps the most striking feature of the estate is the steep and apparently embanked perimeter that rises above Southwood Lane and The Park, flattening out near North Hill so that the main entrance there is almost level with the highway. The steepness of the northern and eastern boundaries is emphasised by the terrain beyond falling away towards Archway Road. The name for the Council estate – Hillcrest – was well chosen. Its commanding position suggests that the land may have played an important role in the earlier history of Highgate. An investigation into the site must therefore precede an account of Park House and its occupants.

The slope now covered by The Park, Bloomfield Road and Bishops Road was until the 1860s open pasture land, the top part being known as Scrubs Meadow – evidently rough grazing. From the highest point of the plateau above there was an uninterrupted view north over the woods and towards the distant hills.[2] The vantage point was much bigger than today for the estate extended beyond the site of Park Walk embracing The Wrestlers and land further south. Another asset of the situation was that from the fourteenth century until about 1830 when the Archway Road bypass was completed the estate was flanked on the west by London's main road to the north. The strategic importance of the site is apparent to any observer who follows Hoskins[3], but has been unaccountably ignored by earlier historians.

The site was in fact envisaged as a stronghold by the War Office when a Napoleonic invasion was feared. Government plans were drawn up to make it part of a planned line of defence round London in which natural heights including the Hampstead-Highgate ridge were to be utilised. In 1803 the site was specifically recommended for "a strong redoubt in front of and connected with the entrenched village of Highgate, to command the Great North Road and ridge from Mazle [Muswell] Hill" for a force of four guns and six hundred men.[4] Was the plan or part of it ever put into effect? And was it based on past experience?

The Hornsey Manor Court rolls of the seventeenth century show that the second question at least can be answered in the affirmative. In 1664, only four years after the Civil Wars had ended, there is a reference to "the Bulwarks" of Highgate[5] and the cumulative evidence from this and eleven later references place these fortifications squarely on the Park House site.[6] There are no such references before the Cromwellian period, so that the inference must be that the site was fortified at some point during the Civil Wars. This should surprise no one, for at that time Highgate was virtually taken over by Parliamentarians and they would have wished to keep control over the chief routes in and out of London. The site for the bulwarks was part of Hornsey manor which had been acquired by a City merchant, Sir John Wollaston, from the Bishop of London.

Daniel Lysons, writing in 1795, refers to the bulwarks as "a small piece of ground with fortifications" – presumably a wall or stockade atop earthworks – but does not say where they were.[7] *The Victoria County History*, nearly two centuries later, identified the bulwarks with a garden wall at the back of The Grove,[8] but the Highgate windmill, a going concern before 1640[9], which the same volume refers to[10], would have helped to locate the site correctly. The windmill had been built in the usual place, near the brow of a hill to catch the wind, "at the north end of Chapel field". This was the tongue of land between North Road and Southwood Lane originally belonging to the Bishop which had been granted for the site for Highgate School and its chapel in 1565; only the end near the High Street had been used for this purpose. The 1664 Court record identifies a particular strip of waste land that had been recently leased out by its position "between the Mill House and the Bullworks upon the king's highway leading to Finchley."[11] We can therefore suppose the bulwarks to have been at the edge of the plateau, the windmill further back and the strip of land between them extending to North Hill. One indication of the proximity of the bulwarks may be the name Castle given to the eighteenth century inn that used to stand in North Road at the end of what is still called Castle Yard.

Before the sixteenth century the uses made of the bulwarks site, if any, are unknown. Records of the manor court earlier than *c.* 1560 have not survived. In medieval times the land was part of the Bishop's hunting park and was probably only leased out as a separate holding after a track was opened up through the park in or before the early fourteenth century, to become the main road to the north. The creation of North Road divided the park into two; Hornsey Great Park to the west, and on the other side the Little Park, bounded on the east by Southwood Lane. The Bulwarks site was therefore sandwiched between the two roads, but broadened out as the new road veered away to the north-west.

Going much further back, some significance may be attached to the find of Roman pottery kilns in Queen's Wood and of a hoard of Roman coins in Southwood Lawn Road[12] and another in Cranley Gardens.[13] All the locations are near Southwood Lane which runs past the bulwarks site, and which was a highway before North Road was opened to travellers; it led to the famed Mus Well and the medieval route to the north via Muswell Hill. It is possible that there was a Roman military presence on the Highgate heights and that the coins found were intended for the payment of troops. That there was settlement in the area in the third and fourth centuries A.D., mainly on the Highgate-Muswell Hill ridge overlooking the Vale of Hornsey has been acknowledged,[14] and protection for the incomers would have been needed. But any supposition about an actual fort is purely conjectural.

Highgate Brewery

Moving forward again to the time after the Restoration in 1660, we are on firmer ground. The bulwarks were redundant and the mill had gone. The fortified site was redeveloped with a brewery and living accommodation. The brewer was Humphrey Kettle, who seems to have been connected with a family brewing business in Islington.[15] A possible kinsman, Henry Kettle, had acquired a cottage and land near Hornsey parish church in 1648[16] and Humphrey took over this holding in 1667.[17] About the same time he was buying Highgate property.[18] By the mid 1670s he was ensconced in the Highgate Brewery, where he had his own residence with a garden entered by gates on the west side.[19] Soon after, however, he leaves the scene, perhaps through retirement or death, and Humphrey Ambler, described as a Gentleman, occupied the 'mansion house'. He put up posts and railings on the North Road where he managed to reclaim a strip of land from Thomas Dickens, Steward of the Manor and property dealer, which had separated his garden from the highway.[20]

In 1685 we have the first reference to a new dynasty of brewers, the Townsends. Edward Townsend, whose wife was called Elizabeth,[21] had been active locally since the 1670s, buying cottages and a former alehouse near Muswell Hill and serving as a juror at the Court Baron.[22] In 1701 a complaint was lodged against him that he had unlawfully cut down six trees in the Bishop's Little Park on the Southwood Lane side.[23] During his time or perhaps that of a successor, Joseph Townsend, the Brewery was re-modelled and thereafter referred to as "the New Brewhouse" or "Townsend's Brewhouse". Large brick underground tunnels were constructed for the storage of beer. Two of these were accidentally re-discovered in 1984,[24] one of them almost intact running along the front of the estate, parallel with the road, and preserved through being well away from the foundations of the twentieth century flats. It seems likely that the Townsends used the ditch that formed the outer boundary of the Little Park for making the tunnel. Several warehouses and a large barn with 'vaults' underneath were constructed.[25] Premises for plumbers, smiths and foundry men were on site, and the brewery maintained its own wagons, carts and drays with the requisite number of horses for the collection of raw materials – malt, hops, and so on – and the delivery of casks of beer to public houses. The Townsends were successful and respected entrepreneurs and two members of the family became Govenors of Highgate School – John Townsend in 1719 and William Townsend in 1741.[26] John Warburton's 1725 and 1746 Maps of Middlesex include a Townsend coat of arms amongst their embellishments.

By 1732 Joseph Townsend had died and the brewery was taken over on a lease by a partnership of two merchants, Joseph Cotton and Francis Gillow. Joseph's widow Mary had leased to them other property of the Townsends' as well, including The Angel in Pond Square and land in Swains Lane.[27] The brewery at this time is shown as a large L-shaped building with two smaller buildings nearer the road and a large oblong, next to what became Park Walk, which may have been the 'mansion house'.[28] In 1749 another Joseph Townsend, of Hannington in Warwickshire, leased the whole property to Gillow alone with all stock-in-trade and equipment.[29] But three years later Francis Gillow, who was a City cornfactor, sold out to John Southcote,[30] following up the transaction with a comprehensive disposal of his other Highgate property.[31] The man actually running the brewery was Gabriel Cox; he was succeeded by his son Robert Thilbye Cox.[32]

For the next half-century the Brewery was owned by the Southcotes. By 1800 the most recent of them, George Southcote, had died and there was no obvious family successor. The business was being run by John Addison who was also the proprietor of what was then called Brewhouse Wood, now called Highgate Wood.[33] He became an officer in the local Volunteer defence force of 300 men formed in 1803,[34] and his commission probably had something to do with the cellars under the brewery. They were very similar to tunnels used as barracks in at least one seventeenth century purpose-built fortress,[35] and it seems not unlikely that during the Napoleonic invasion scare the tunnels would have been regarded as ready-made accommodation for the augmented number of troops envisaged by the government plans referred to earlier.

On 30 January 1806 Sarah, George Southcote's widow, and Elizabeth, widow of Thomas Southcote, surrendered all their interests in the Brewery and in various other parts of the estate to Addison.[36] He however was soon to leave Highgate and a man called John Cooper emerges from obscurity. Lloyd relates a story of his walking to London to seek his fortune, finding employment at Addison's Brewery, and having prospered and bought the brewery, changing his name from Cooper to Cooper Cooper.[37] Part at least of the story is true; he did buy the brewery. Addison seems to have concentrated his brewing operations at Homerton and in 1809 John Cooper bought the Highgate premises, composed of three parcels of land for £1000 (£480 + £420 + £100), presumably the brewery and yard, the house, and a piece of land.[38] When he redeemed the Land Tax in 1813 the estate was stated to amount to twelve and a half acres with vacant possession and one and a half acres occupied by one Dutton.[39] (This 1.5 acres may well have been the strip of land referred to in 1664 as between the bulwarks and the mill, presumably the beginning of the short-cut from North Road to Southwood Lane now known as Park Walk, since "Dutton's Alley " was the name by which the short-cut became known at first.[40]) Addison still hung on to the Brewhouse Wood, and in 1809 bought the pub called The Lord Nelson's Head, otherwise known as The Lower Wrestlers,[41] which was situated on the wide verge of North Hill with the Brewery at the back of (see plan below). Meanwhile Cooper proceeded to have the old brewery residence pulled down and to build a new mansion.[42]

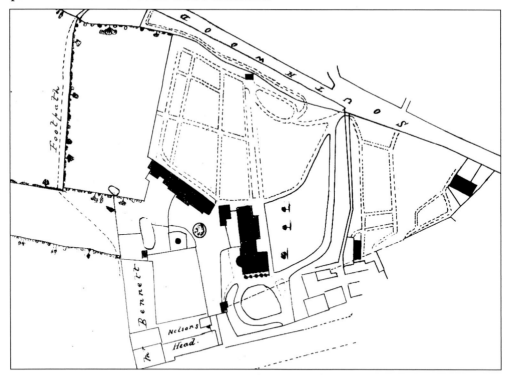

38. Former and existing property.
A plan prepared in 1861 for Park House's changeover from copyhold to freehold tenure the following year. Amongst the demolished buildings previously standing between the mansion and North Road, was The Lord Nelson's Head, an off-shoot of the Highgate Brewery.

Regency Residence

Before turning to the history of Park House we will try to elucidate some aspects of the first owner's family. John Cooper, whether his wealth was inherited or acquired, was by 1817 a member of the landed gentry. Besides his Highgate property, he had a country seat at Toddington Manor in Bedfordshire. It was however not he but his son-in-law who had the double-barrelled name. He, the son-in-law, was originally William Dodge Cooper Heap, being the son of a Rev. John Heap and having been given his mother's family name of Cooper to precede the patronymic. (This followed precedent, for his mother had been Anne Dodge Cooper, *her* mother having been a Miss Dodge.) W.D.C. Heap was a cousin of Elizabeth, daughter of John Cooper, and he married her. Their first child, another William, was born in 1810. John Cooper made Elizabeth heir to his property by his Will of 21 October 1817[43] and in 1818 her husband changed his surname from Heap to Cooper by Letters Patent; hence Cooper Cooper. William and Elizabeth had several more children: a second son, James Lindsay, and five daughters, Jane, Elizabeth, Amelia, Caroline and Lucy. Two of the girls married into the fringes of the aristocracy: Elizabeth, whose husband was a Dutch count and Lucy who became the wife of Sir Henry Robinson.[44]

W.D.C. Cooper took a leading part in Highgate life, chairing the Assembly at the Gatehouse Inn where balls were held,[45] and being Treasurer, *i.e.* Chairman, of the Governors of Highgate School and remaining so for twenty years after his appointment in 1837.[46] He was on the Management Committee of the local National School[47] and had at least one Book Society meeting at Park House.[48] He was a Middlesex magistrate and was also active in Bedfordshire, being a magistrate there and Deputy-Lieutenant of the county, having succeeded his late father-in-law, John Cooper, as Sheriff in 1824. He was aware of the deprivation suffered by rural labourers as a result of the Enclosures and was one of the early advocates of the allotment of land to them,[49] providing a number of plots from his Toddington estate.[50] When he died in 1860 this amounted to 3,388 acres.[51]

The Coopers' suburban residence was positioned quite differently from the old brewery house. It was placed centrally instead of to one side of the site, with the main entrance facing North Hill. On that west front it had a portico with six pillars extending the full width of the house. Leave was given by the Lord of the Manor to take down the old pub (the Nelson's Head) and various disused buildings and outhouses that lay between the mansion and North Hill.[52] The main part of Park House was almost square except for a large bay on the north side, and was surmounted by a domed turret. The house had three storeys. The east wing had a conservatory built along the south side. Running diagonally to the north-east was a long building of roughly the same ground area as the house, presumably the coach house and stables.[53] By the 1860s this was linked to the house by a single-storey

39. Park House in institutional use *c.* 1849.
Young people with learning difficulties were the first inmates.

building, probably the laundry, built for later occupants[54] Little is known about the interior of Park House, except that it contained family portraits and paintings done by some of the Coopers.[55]

Institution

W.D.C.Cooper and his wife were still living at Park House in the mid 1840s[56] but soon after retired to their country estate. The property was then sold to "The Asylum for Idiots" which had been founded by Rev. Dr. Andrew Reed (1787-1862). He was an extraordinarily energetic activist on behalf of the disadvantaged and founded two orphanages and a Hospital for Incurables besides being Pastor of Wycliffe Chapel (in Commercial Road) which was largely his creation. In 1847, in a favourable climate of Reform in many fields of public health and welfare, Dr Reed had gathered together a group of philanthropic individuals who felt that hitherto 'We had done nothing for the Idiot'. Park House sounded ideal for a new leaf to be turned.[57] Candidates for admission were to be 'neither pauper nor payment cases' and the 'moderate' fees were to be subsidised by subscribers.[58]

When the first inmates and their nurses were received, on 26 April 1848[59], they would have seen a large house standing back from the main road and screened from it by huge elm trees. Several rooms downstairs had been

40. Dr Andrew Reed, founder of the 'Asylum for Idiots'.
A pioneering fund-raiser for neglected causes, he also founded two orphanages and a
hospital, besides working as a Congregational minister.

adapted to form a schoolroom for Drawing and Singing lessons. The upper floors had been converted into dormitories. At the back of the house was a large playground with swings and other equipment. The Superintendent was Dr. Forman, who allowed visitors once a week. By 1849, there were sixty patients, mostly boys. In March of that year, Prince Albert came to inspect, and pronounced himself entirely satisfied with the conduct of the charity.[60]

By 1851, the number of inmates had grown to seventy-one – 58 boys between the ages of five and twenty-seven, and thirteen girls between six and twenty-six.[61] The penalty of success was that the asylum was outgrowing Park House. So it was transferred to larger premises at Earlswood in Surrey.

The institution that took the place of the Asylum was a 'Female Penitentiary'. The idea of rescuing prostitutes from a life of vice and misery had by then taken hold of public opinion. It had its roots in the eighteenth century which had produced special places of correction for those on the streets, and hospitals which treated patients with venereal diseases. In 1807 the London Female Penitentiary was established in a house in New Road, Pentonville[62], and by 1815 subscribers to it numbered about 2,500 nation-wide.[63] With Wilberforce as President, the object was reclamation and a fresh start. This was to be achieved through the traditional formula of Training 'to qualify them for Service' and comprised 'Household work in all its branches and particularly the Business of the Laundry'.[64] Such ventures did not however greatly appeal to the general public until Henry Mayhew's investigative articles into the causes of prostitution appeared in the *Morning Chronicle* in 1849-50. These seem to have contributed to a change of heart and by the mid 1850s the number of rescue homes in England had mushroomed to sixty.[65] One of these was Park House, Highgate.

Highgate's 'House of Mercy' owed its existence to the Church Penitentiary Association founded in 1852. By 1880 the C.P.A. was to be in charge of 25 penitentiaries and 13 temporary refuges. Such an association had been campaigned for by the Rev. John Armstrong (1813-1856), the vicar of a Gloucestershire parish, who wanted what he called 'Houses of Mercy' to be run by the Church. An immediate objective for the newly formed association was a London Diocesan penitentiary, and a large sum towards it was donated by another clergyman, Rev. R. Magee, in 1853. The money was insufficient for the purpose and an appeal committee under Charles Blomfield (1786-1857), Bishop of London, was formed in March 1854. Temporary accommodation was found at Hampton Court and then at Sunbury before the committee finally acquired the Park House lease.[66] The House opened in 1855, a few weeks before Christmas. The number of supporters grew to 600 in the first two years. Of the larger donations, the Church Penitentiary Association gave two grants of £250 each, Lord Dufferin (a local resident and trustee) twice gave £100, and Blomfield and W.E. Gladstone each gave £50.[67]

The House was under the general supervision of a Council of 46 and an Executive Committee of 22 whose authority was vested in a Warden. Rev. Magee was the first Warden but he did not stay long. The second was Rev. John Oliver, born in 1804, helped by his wife Ann. Oliver had been Chaplain of King's College Hospital in London[68] so he was familiar with institutional life and he stayed until his death in 1883. The day-to-day administration and the instruction of the girls was in the hands of unpaid Sisters, for the Houses of Mercy conceived by Armstrong, who was an Anglo-Catholic, were rather like nunneries. The Sisters were assisted by some 'permanent penitents' who wished to remain in the House after their course of instruction was over: they were known as Magdalens. Ladies would also come in as Assistant Sisters and help to organise the Needlework. Charles Dickens and his patron Miss Burdett-Coutts, who had set up her own refuge for prostitutes at "Urania Cottage" in West London, did not approve of this type of management, which contrasted with her reliance on paid professionals. To Miss Coutts such 'a permanent Asylum put a premium on vice'. Dickens considered the regime "Pernicious and unnatural."[69] Certainly the sentimentality of the 'Magdalen' idea ignored the realities of unmarried motherhood and the women's need to care and provide for their children. Supporters of the Penitentiaries argued that the young must be protected from vicious influences and that re-habilitated mothers should support their offspring from a distance. There was no need, they maintained, to have orphanages attached to penitentiaries; they should be run quite independently, and the 'fruits of sin' would have to be boarded elsewhere.[70]

Life for the girls was regulated every hour of the day and contact with the outside world was not only forbidden but well nigh impossible. Recreation in the grounds was however encouraged and in the summer classes were taken outside. A visitor in 1865 described the prison-like exterior; entry was by a postern gate, which was unlocked after a bell had been pulled which sounded far off in the House.

"At last there is a step audible on the gravelled walk, then the jingling of keys and the door is opened by a grave but gentle portress in black".

When the girls were first admitted to the House, their own clothes were taken away and stored and they were issued with a rather drab dress in brown, and put into a probationers' class where they learned Needlework. After a few weeks, if found 'educable', they were issued with a blue dress with a white cap and apron. They were expected to stay for two years so the course of education was divided into four successive classes of about six months each. First came Needlework, then Laundry, then Domestic Work, then Cooking. Each class had a presiding superintendent and its own dormitory. Some aspects of the regime were harsh: girls were not allowed to talk on the staircase or in the corridor and they had to endure two daily periods of silence as well – between 11 and noon and between 4 and 5 in the afternoon. Attendance at Chapel three times a day and at Holy Communion on Sundays, Thursdays and Saint's days was obligatory.[71]

It is difficult to find out whether the treatment worked. The statistics are bald. For instance, in 1863, the Warden reported that of the 22 girls who had left the Home during the previous year, eight had gone into domestic service, one had married, two had returned home, two had left because of 'ill health' and eight of their own volition, and one was expelled.[72] A 50% success rate would seem a reasonable estimate. The girls were mostly teenagers,[73] sometimes as young as ten.[74]

The House with its carefully guarded residents, each with stories to tell that were outside the experience of most respectable women, exercised a peculiar fascination. One frequent visitor was Christina Rossetti (1830-1894), the poet. She spent several weeks of each year in the 1860s staying at Park House, dressed in the nun-like black habit of a Sister, with hanging sleeves, a muslin cap with lace edging, and a veil. Her sister Maria, who later became a real nun, stayed there at least once.[75] Their brother, Dante Gabriel Rossetti, was also greatly attracted by the theme of seduction and betrayal and portrayed it in some of his paintings. Christina's somewhat bleak private life, with two broken engagements, seems to have led to her living vicariously through the girls, and so sympathetic to their plight was she that she was offered the post of Lady Superintendent, which she however declined.[76] The sexual overtones of her concern for 'fallen' women are evident in some of her poems.

41. Christina Rossetti the poet who stayed at Park House several times as a Sister

Park House appeared to be an ideal background for rescue work, with its dormitories with separate cubicles, a large communal dining room (although the Sisters ate at separate tables from the 'penitents'), the garden with ample space for growing vegetables, and the laundry.[77] It is not surprising that the Warden wanted the Trustees to buy the property from

William Cooper. First, though, the estate had to be enfranchised, *i.e.* converted from copyhold to freehold tenure by agreement with the Bishop as Lord of the Manor. This was done in the autumn of 1862.[78] The following March the Park House estate became the property of the Penitentiary for £11,500.[79] Most of the purchase money had to be raised by mortgage, one of the trustees, the Marquis of Dufferin and Ava, standing as security.[80]

The new owners were quick to capitalise on their investment. Land south of Park Walk, not needed for the Penitentiary, was leased to the Parish for the purpose-built Local Board offices that were opened in 1869; Hornsey had adopted the Local Government Act two years before[81] and the Board's responsibilities had greatly increased. About the same time, land was leased to builders where Bishop's Road, The Park and Bloomfield Road were to be built.[82] The proceeds of the sales, together with the subsequent ground rents from house-owners helped to meet the interest on the mortgage and the gradual repayment.[83] In April 1870 the trustees felt confident enough to acquire more property as an investment; this was along Archway Road between Southwood Lane and Bishop's Road, bought from the Archway Road Company.[84] By 1875, funds were considered sufficient for a new chapel. The architect was Arthur Blomfield, son of the former Bishop of London, and brother-in-law of Charles Dalton, the Vicar of Highgate, who had married the Bishop's daughter. Blomfield had been responsible for Christ Church, Crouch End (1862) and All Saints', Highgate (1864). The new chapel was opened in 1877.[85]

By 1890 the situation had deteriorated. Running costs threatened to outstrip income. To meet the shortfall, land in North Hill on the northern edge of the estate was sold for a site for a new house and some more was sold in Southwood Lane.[86] A financial appeal was made, for funds to modernise the old laundry.[87] The Park House laundry, taking in local people's washing, made a substantial contribution to the funds, earning about half the running costs of the Penitentiary. The laundresses got extra food.[88] In contrast, the fine sewing and embroidery that went into trousseaux, babies' layettes, etc., produced a much smaller sum from sales. A new mortgage was entered into in 1893.[89] In 1897, a half-acre site at the bottom of Bishops Road was sold, and acquired by the Middlesex County Council for the new Highgate Police Station and Magistrate's Court.[90] The biggest worry was that the wave of Reform that had launched the Penitentiary might subside. Subscriptions were vital and were now insufficient to meet expected costs. In 1900 the Penitentiary was handed over to an order of nuns, the Sisters of Clewer near Windsor.

Park House in the twentieth century is still remembered by a few older residents as a place of seclusion and mystery. Occasionally scandals would surface in the Press about expectant mothers having to work in the laundry while in labour, but the charity was well supported. Ladies were still helping, especially with the summer Bazaar, where the doctor's wife would run a sweet stall. The Penitentiary seems to have changed little since Victorian times[91], except for the new commercial-type laundry. This was a well-equipped set of communicating rooms, comprising the main room, with two stoves in it for general warmth and for heating irons, and a six horse power gas engine providing power for the various machines; the wash-house containing three coppers for boiling white cotton articles; drying rooms with overhead racks; the dormitory and sitting room for the captive work force; and the lumber room and fuel cellars. There was also a carpenters' workshop with a 6 h.p. steam engine, for breakdowns and repairs.[92]

In the early days penitentiaries had concentrated their efforts on prostitutes rather than destitute mothers. The London Female Penitentiary, in 1808, had even forbidden entry to pregnant women[93] although this policy was obviously impossible to enforce and was abandoned.[94] But there was always criticism of the 'rescue' policy. E.B. Pusey (1800-1882) thought the real need was for orphanages for little girls, and castigated his contemporaries for not helping those in danger of falling into prostitution while running penitentiaries where girls were made to leave "to make room for fresh victims". Park House seems to have become aware of some of the pitfalls for penitentiaries; the two-year residence rule was not inflexible and some girls stayed for a third year and in the 1920s were rewarded by being given "a rather better outfit before being sent out once more into the world".[95] By this time other agencies had started to be set up for the welfare of very young girls, so entry to Park House was restricted to those over 18, and the girls came not only from Refuges but were sent from hospitals and prison.

Despite its steadfastness of purpose, Park House, like other penitentiaries, could not survive the economic and other pressures of the inter-war years. By 1928 the House was seriously in debt. The number of residents had decreased, owing to the Home Office policy of sending girls for only short periods of 'correction', and so income had declined. When War came the nuns decided to close at the end of August 1940. The fall of France brought forward the closure.[96] The Sisters and some of the girls were distributed among other Clewer houses, but most of the girls were found jobs. The garden of Park House became wartime allotments.

After the War The Penitentiary and its immediate grounds were sold to the Council, by a conveyance dated 31 December 1945[97], and the remaining house properties auctioned. Park House became a casualty of the municipal housing programme, but its demolition allowed five and a half acres of land to be released for the provision of much needed accommodation for hundreds of local families.

Joan Schwitzer

1. *Victoria County History of Middlesex*, vol. vi (Oxford University Press, 1980), p.139

2. Hornsey Enclosure Map, 1816

3. Professor Hoskins maintained that writing the history of a landscape "requires a combination of documentary research and of fieldwork, of laborious scrambling on foot wherever the trail may lead. The result is a new kind of history ..." W.G. Hoskins, *The Making of the English landscape* (first published 1955, Pelican 1970, re-printed 1974), p. 15. See also his *Local history in England* (first pub. 1959, third ed. 1984), *passim*.

4. Roy Allen, "The Hampstead and Highgate Citadel. Defence plans against Napoleon ", *Camden History Review* No. 10 (1982), p. 7. This paragraph is based on this article and Roy Allen's "Napoleon's first invasion threat. The proposed northern line of defence round the capital" *CHR* No. 12 (1984)

5. William McBeath Marcham & Frank Marcham, *Court Rolls of the Bishop of London's Manor of Hornsey 1603-1701* (1929), p. 146

6. Marcham, pp.165, 171,189,190,199, 207, 209(2), 213, 231,187

7. Daniel Lysons, *The Environs of London*. vol. ii, p.431. An example of a Civil War fort is that discovered in Plymouth, built in 1643 as part of the defences against the Royalists; report and picture in *The Times*, 18 April 1992.

8. *VCH*, vol. vi, p. 125

9. Marcham, p. 53

10. *VCH*, vol. vi, pp. 124,151

11. Marcham, p. 146

12. LMAS *Transactions*, vol. 23, part 2, 1971-72, p. 171

13. LMAS Trans., vol. 23, part 2, p. 165

14. S.J. Madge, *The Early Records of Harringay alias Hornsey* (1938), p. 23

15. Marcham, p. 153

16. Marcham, p. 106

17. Marcham, p. 153

18. Marcham, pp. 148,152,162

19. Marcham, p. 172

20. Marcham, p. 209

21. Marcham, p. 200

22. Marcham, pp.175, 178,185, 200

23. Marcham, p. 250

24. Joan Schwitzer, " The tunnels on the Highgate Bulwarks – a discovery", *HHS Bulletin No. 26* (1985)

25. It is tempting to suppose the barn to have been the makeshift theatre for strolling players where one of the actresses was Harriet Mellon, later to become the wife of Coutts the banker and to settle in Highgate. But it would be incorrect. The theatre barn was further south, standing on Highgate School land, once Chapel Field. See Joan Schwitzer, "Highgate School estate tenants, 1817", *HHS Bulletin* No. 32 (1991), p.40

26. *Highgate School Register*, 4th ed., 1938

27. Indenture 12 May 1732; MDR 1732/1/350; GLRO

28. John Rocque's *Survey of . . . London . . . and . . . Ten Miles Round* (1746)

29. Indenture 7 Nov. 1749; Acc. 600, GLRO

30. Indenture 6 July 1752; GLRO

31. Indenture 20 Sept. 1752; GLRO

32. Copy of Will of John Southcote 15 April 1775; Gdl. MS 18559. See also recognition of new owner, Thomas Southcote, 23 May 1778, after John Southcote's death; Gdl. MS 10465/93

143

33. John Richardson, *Highgate. Its History since the fifteenth century* (1983), p. 155

34. Richardson, p. 227

35. The Citadel of Le Palais, Belle Isle, Western Brittany, re-fortified by Vauban in 1687.

36. Add. MS 18540; Gdl.

37. J.H. Lloyd, *The History of Highgate* (1888)

38. Add. MS 18540; Gdl.

39. Add. MS 18542; Gdl.

40. Potter Collection of North London Topography, vol. xiv, p. 77; BM

41. Gdl. MSS 10465/124 and 125

42. Lease for 21 years, dated 29 July 1814, to John Cooper from Bishop of London; Gdl. MS 12385

43. Reference in Admission of Tenants by Frankpledge in 1825; Gdl. MS 18540

44. Burke's *Landed Gentry* (1848)

45. Highgate Assembly Book; HLSI

46. *Highgate School Register*, 6th ed., p. 55

47. Managers' Minutes; St Michael's C.of E. Primary School, N6

48. Highgate Book Society minutes; HLSI

49. Letter from Mr Cooper of Park House, *Labourers' Friend Magazine*, New Series, 1835; BL

50. *Labourers' Friend Magazine*, June 1836

51. John Bateman, *The Great Landowners of Great Britain and Ireland* (4th edition, 1883, re-printed 1971), p. 104

52. Document signed by Thomas Dickens, Steward to the Bishop of London's Manor of Hornsey, 16 June 1830; Gdl. MS18540. For position of the buildings see sketch map dated 6 March 1861 (fig. 38) and almost identical map provided with Indenture of Enfranchisement dated 18 Nov. 1862 (Gdl. MS 18540)

53. Hornsey Enclosure Map, 1816

54. O.S., 25 inches to 1 mile, 1st ed., 1865

55. Will of W.D.C. Cooper, 23 Aug. 1855; copy in HLSI

56. Kelly's *Directory of Middlesex*, 1845

57. *LIN*, 31 March 1849. For Reed's life, see DNB

58. Samson Low's *Charities of London* (1850), pp. 56-57

59. *The Athenaeum*, 9 August 1873; cutting in Potter Coll., xiv, 22

60. *London Illustrated News*, 31 March 1849

61. Enumerators' Returns, Census of Hornsey 1851; H.0.107/1702; PRO

62. *First Report of the London Female Penitentiary*, 1808; Gdl.

63. *Report of the London Female Penitentiary*, 1815; Gdl.

64. 18th Report of the L.F.P., 1825; Gdl.

65. F.K.Prochaska, *Women and Philanthropy in nineteenth century England* (O.U.P., 1980), pp.187-188

66. Catalogue of MSS; Gdl.

67. *Second Annual Report of the London Diocesan Penitentiary*, 1856/7; HI/ST/ L654; GLRO

68. Crockford's *Clerical Directory*, 1898 ed.

69. *Letters of Charles Dickens* (Pilgrim ed.), vol. v (1981), pp. 541-542

70. *Penitentiary Work in the Church of England. Papers prepared for discussion at the anniversary meeting ofthe Church Penitentiary Association 1873 at the request of the Council* (London, 1873); BL

71. *St. Michael's Church, Highgate, Parish Magazine*, October 1865; HLSI

72. *St. Michael's Mag.*, January, 1864; HLSI

73. Census of Hornsey, 1871

74. Census of Hornsey, 1881

75. Jan Morris, *The Pre-Raphaelite Sisterhood* (Quartet Books, 1985), p. 185

76. Georgina Battiscombe, *Christina Rosetti. A divided life* (Constable, 1981), p. 194

77. *St. Michael's Parish Magazine*, January, 1864. For a plan of the first floor showing the cubicles (each just over 5 feet wide) see Gdl. MS 18559

78. Gdl. MSS 18540 and 12385

79. Conveyance, 13 March 1863; Gdl. MS 18544. The extent of the estate is shown on the map attached to the Abstract of Title of the Trustees to the Property in 1946; private collection.

80. Gdl. MS 18544

81. *VCH*, vol. vi, p. 167. For a plan of the offices *c.* 1905, see Gdl. MS 18559

82. Bloomfield Road was originally called after Bishop Blomfield and was still officially so called in 1891 (see a legal agreement of 19 February 1891; Gdl. MS 18559) but in the same year Philip's *Handy-Volume Atlas of London* indexes the road as Bloomfield. By the mid 1890s the apparently more popular form of Bloomfield seems to have prevailed over the earlier spelling.

83. Paper by Sir James Brown; HLSI

84. Gdl. MS 18546 (Agreement of 26 April 1870)

85. *VCH*, vol. vi, p. 131

86. Abstract of Title, 1946

87. Potter Collection, vol. 14, p. 22; BM

88. *St. Michael's Parish Magazine*, October, 1865;

89. Gdl. MS 18544

90. Abstract of Title, 1946. J.P. Cory-Wright's offer to buy was dated 11 May 1896 and the Penitentiary's acceptance 15 May; Gdl. MS 18561

91. Information from Miss Dorothy King, Miss Doris Pritchard and Mrs Margaret Serner

92. Alliance Fire Policy, 1921, No. 6025675; Gdl. MS 18599

93. *1st Report,* 1808

94. *18th Annual Report,* 1835

95. Appeal booklet "*The House of Mercy*", *c.* 1928; archives of All Saints' Church, Highgate

96. *HJ,* 19 July 1940

97. Gdl. MS 18644

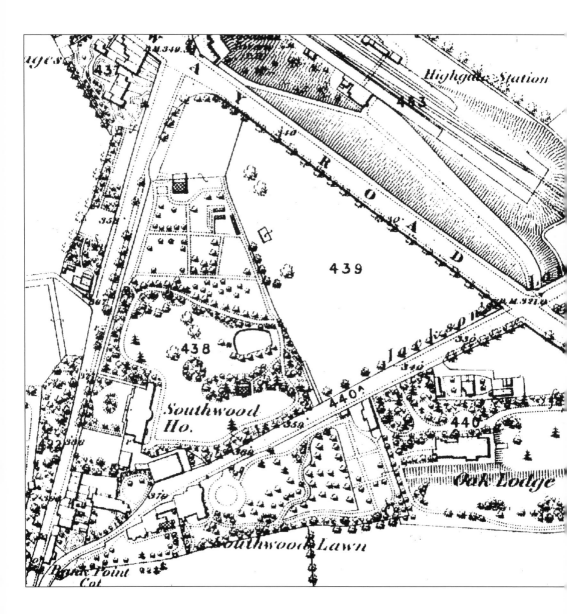

42. The Southwood House estate in 1870

A place of retirement:
Southwood House and the
estate's development

Southwood House was situated on Southwood Lane in Highgate a little way below the point where Southwood Lane meets Jacksons Lane. The estate, in the shape of a triangle, extended to the present day Archway Road, and possibly for a time beyond it.

In the Middle Ages Southwood Lane was used by pilgrims on their way from the Highgate hermitage of St Michael to the chapel of Our Lady at the Mosewelle (Muswell). Jacksons Lane led to Hornsey church and its burial ground. Even before the Norman Conquest the surrounding area appears to have been owned by the Bishop of London as part of his manor of Hornsey. Until the 1660s the Bishop retained hunting rights in Hornsey Park although actual hunting had ceased in the mid fourteenth century and deer were no longer stocked there. The boundary of the park was Southwood Lane and Highgate Common bordered it on the east. The Southwood House estate was taken out of the common.

According to the Hornsey Manor Court rolls, there was a building on the estate at least by 1736.[1] It is marked on John Rocque's map of 1746[2] as standing at right angles to Southwood Lane. There is however a small problem with this. In 1745 the property had been acquired by Field Marshal Wade who had immediately begun building Southwood House – *parallel* to Southwood Lane. Rocque probably intended to show the position of the old house, but he may have used guesswork to delineate the unfinished one.

The estate consisted of two acres of land and this would indeed be the size of the present triangle bounded by Southwood Lane, Jacksons Lane and Archway Road, albeit the latter was only built in 1813.

Marshal Wade and his house in Highgate
Marshal Wade's name is forever connected with the tremendous network of roads in Scotland with its forty stone bridges which he and his "highwaymen" as he called his soldiers had constructed between 1726 and 1737. This was part of the 'pacification' of the Highlands after the abortive Jacobite uprising of 1715. An obelisk on the road from Inverness to Inveraray celebrates his achievement:

Had you seen these roads before they were made
You would lift up your hands and bless General Wade.

George Wade was born in 1673 in Kiavally, West Meath in Ireland. As a soldier he served in Flanders, Spain, Minorca and with the Vigo Expedition. He rose to the rank of Field Marshal and became Commander-in-Chief of the British forces in Flanders in 1743. But by then he was seventy years old and age and gout obliged him to resign. He returned to England just when Charles Edward Stuart, the Young Pretender, launched the Scottish rebellion. Wade was the only senior officer who knew the highways and byways of Scotland and so George II appointed him Commander-in-Chief in England and ordered him to march northwards. Such was the nation's trust in him that a new verse was added to the National Anthem:

> God grant that Marshal Wade
> May by thy mighty aid
> Victory bring.
> May he sedition hush,
> And like a torrent rush
> Rebellious Scots to crush,
> God save the King.

In the event his campaign proved a disaster and he was relieved of his post. He returned home and until his death in 1748 he lived in Highgate, though retaining his Town house in Cork Street, Piccadilly.[3]

George Wade was a flamboyant character who loved wine, cards, women, comfort, good furniture and Art. He had friends in high places but gambled in low dives. He was good-humoured and established excellent labour relations with the civilian road workers and his troops. Once at the completion of yet another stretch of road the soldiers invited him to celebrate; afterwards he wrote, "Two or three days later I felt much better".[4] He was a Governor of the Academy of Music, and was from 1714 until his death a Member of Parliament. First he represented Hindon in Wiltshire and from 1722 Bath. It was the age of Sir Robert Walpole's governments, and in his only recorded speech in the House in 1733 he declared that he had supported the Whig administration almost invariably except over the South Sea Company. Here he had been one of only 55 MPs voting against the grandiose scheme of buying the Company's stock in exchange for the bulk of the National Debt, resulting in the South Sea 'Bubble' that burst, implicating Ministers and royal mistresses. The speech in which he referred to this, dealing with rules for courts martial, was the only other occasion when he disagreed with the government.[5]

Luckily for posterity, he was a vain man who liked to have his portrait painted, often in shining armour, and thus we know what the first inhabitant of Southwood House looked like – an impressive and handsome man. In this house he instructed the famous sculptor Louis Francois

The Honble George Wade Esqr

Lieutenant General and Commander in Chief

of all His Majties Forces, Castles, Forts and Barracks in North Britain, &c.

43. General George Wade, celebrated for road building in Scotland and commander of the British troops at the outset of the 1745 Jacobite uprising, had Southwood House built for his retirement.

Roubiliac (1705-1762) to design his monument for Westminster Abbey and to include a portrait bust medallion. He chose as his theme "Fame Prevents Time From Destroying The General's Trophies". (In the case of Southwood House, Fame did *not* succeed in preventing Time from destroying it.) The monument can still be found over the entrance to the cloisters in Westminster Abbey.[6] It is said that Roubiliac could often be seen standing beneath it with tears in his eyes – not because he was mourning Wade but because he considered his masterpiece to have been hung too high.

Retiring in 1745 to Highgate was not like moving into the wilderness. Within a stone's throw stood several substantial buildings belonging to prosperous people. In Jacksons Lane there were Hillside and Southwood Lawn, and, nearby, Southwood. In the High Street stood Hertford House and Bisham House. In South Grove were the Old Hall, formerly Arundel House, Ashhurst House (on the site of St Michael's church), and South Grove House. On Highgate Hill stood Winchester Hall, Cromwell House and Lauderdale House. Smaller houses were to be found in Southwood Lane, in the High Street and in South Grove. Numbers 1 to 6 in The Grove had been built as far back as 1688. There were also cottages, and workshops and stables and sheds. Highgate in 1745 was a flourishing little town, boasting many inns, including the Rose & Crown and the Angel in the High Street and the Mitre and the Bell & Horns in North Road.

The house Wade built was neither large nor architecturally outstanding but nevertheless was a landmark clearly visible from the north and west. It did not need to be particularly grand or spacious. Wade was a bachelor but had two sons and one daughter by one lady and another daughter by a second lady, all of whom he acknowledged but who do not seem to have lived with him.

Nikolaus Pevsner describes Southwood House as having "three bays with two lower bay wings, the porch later, C.18. The two centre windows above it are of Venetian type."[7] (This means they were in three sections, with an arch above the middle section.) From photographs and architectural drawings we can add to Pevsner that it was a flat-roofed brick building with stone window dressings with prominent keystones between rubbed bricks, protruding lintels and sills with rendered reveals. The rear had a semi-circular bay with three windows on every floor. Surprisingly, the lower part of the rear was only rough-rendered while the upper part was hung with tiles. The wings were set back from the front but continued the building line at the rear; they were two-storey structures with pitched roofs.

The architectural drawings prepared in the 1920s for the London Society[8] show the west elevation and a section through the house.It is not impossible that parts of the building extant in 1736 were incorporated into the larger house while in front an entirely new facade was created. Internally the dominant feature was an imposing staircase with wrought iron railings.

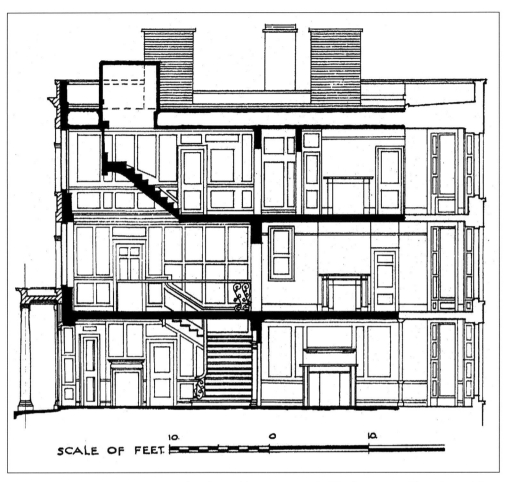

SCALE OF FEET

44. Architectural section through Southwood House, recorded in the 1930s. Elevations of the house and stables and studies of individual features were also made.

There were large fireplaces, and all the walls, at least on the ground floor, were wood-panelled. The sash windows went almost down to the floor. Old Highgate residents who had visited the house as children particularly remembered the staircase and the sombre panelled rooms. Sadly, neither drawings nor photographs of the interior have been located.

Who was the architect? Marshal Wade's much grander Town house in Piccadily had been designed by Lord Burlington, but his hand cannot be detected in Southwood House. Perhaps there was only a builder, though one versed in current architectural fashion and directed by his client. No other name based on work elsewhere has been advanced.

The photograph of the house (fig. 45) was first used to illustrate an article on "The Domestic Shell" in which Edwin Smith wrote that "By virtue of size a large house can indulge in considered details; for example a window

151

arched and curiously grouped, repeated in affection, as at Southwood House, Highgate."[9] Now the only reminder of the building are some foundations in the back garden of No. 94 Southwood Lane.

Southwood House after Marshal Wade

George Wade died only three years after acquiring the site, in March 1748 leaving well over £100,000 – a colossal sum at the time. His two sons inherited the estate. One was a serving Army officer, the other an official of the East India Company, and neither wanted to live in Highgate. They sold to one Robert Booth. He was neither famous nor notorious and no information about him has been found.

For a while the house was owned by Sir Richard Pepper Arden (1745-1804), who was elevated to the peerage as Baron Alvanley, a great friend of William Pitt the younger. He was M.P. successively for Newton, Aldborough, and Hastings, and, finally, like Wade, for Bath. He became Solicitor General and Lord Chief Justice. He was known for the elegance of his diction, and was an occasional, though unpublished, poet. His nickname was Little Peppy.[10]

By the end of the eighteenth century another M.P. had taken over the estate. George Longman was a paper manufacturer and wholesale stationer who in 1806 and 1807 was returned as the Member for the Kent borough of Maidstone. 1806 was the year when both Fox and Pitt died, and the 'Ministry of all the Talents' collapsed. After serving through the vicissitudes of the Napoleonic Wars, he lost his seat in 1812, but in 1818 he was again summoned to Westminster to represent Maidstone. That Parliament saw the Peterloo Massacre, and the House passed the notorious Six Acts, repressing the freedom of the Press and the right of public meeting. A mere eighteen months later Parliament was dissolved. Longman was not re-elected and died in November 1822.[11]

His daughters, Elizabeth and Judith, 'the Misses Longman of Southwood House', stayed on in Highgate, and Elizabeth lived until at least 1853. They were owners of land on Archway Road on either side of Jacksons Lane; the sites of the present Community Centre and the shopping parade to its right were both owned by Miss Longman. She and her sister were relatives of the publishers of the same name.

In 1853 the house was acquired by Robert Besley, a type founder, who owned the Fann Street Letter Foundry in London. Robert Besley & Co. were successors to the W. Thorowgood & Co. foundry, and their 1862 catalogue, a "General Specimen of Printing Types" with a supplement, has survived.

After Besley, from 1860, a solicitor called Walter Hughes owned the house. He died a few years later, but his widow remained there till about 1890. According to the Census of 1881,[12] she employed only two servants and a gardener – a very small establishment for such an estate.

45. The house *c.* 1940

Thomas Boney, formerly of Cholmeley Lodge, Highgate, acquired the estate after Mrs Hughes for £13,000. He was a cloth merchant who was also a director of the Prudential Mortgage Co. and Vice-Chairman of the Freehold & Leasehold Investment Co. When he died, at Southwood House, in 1909, he left estate valued at £35,527.1s.4d gross (£13,770.14s.6d net). He was then 81, another example of the longevity bestowed by Highgate's healthy air.

What was the property like in Victorian times? The house itself had been little altered since the eighteenth century. The porch, with its Ionic columns and heavy decorated roof was attractive in design, but was not a happy addition to the original building as it interfered with a view of the window above it and spoiled the overall proportions. By c. 1870 there was a wall running from the north end of the house to the outer wall shielding the plants in the circular driveway's centre-piece from cold winds. In the twentieth century these were locally renowned white holly and rhododendrons.

Along Southwood Lane and Jacksons Lane ran high walls, broken only in Southwood Lane to allow access to the house. A small section of the wall on Southwood Lane is still standing, terminating in a brick pier from which projects half of a large curved lamp bracket; here was the entrance. On the other side of the house was a pond and several winding paths flanked by trees, and the main garden. Below, by Southwood Lane, was the kitchen garden, with several greenhouses. Bordering Archway Road and the lower part of Jacksons Lane was a field edged with tall trees, presumably kept as grazing for the horses.

A number of outbuildings shown on the four editions of the large-scale Ordnance maps from 1870 to 1935 were drawn in detail for the London Society. One was the stables – a long low building by the upper part of Jacksons Lane. Quite near the big house stood a smaller square building which may well have housed the staff. By 1914 this was connected with Southwood House by a conservatory. No trace of any of these ancillary buildings has been found. Not so far seen on any maps were tall brick structures near Jacksons Lane still standing in 1957. They could have been remnants of demolished wartime buildings, or, more romantically, a folly.

The coming of Hillside Gardens and the end of Southwood House
It is not surprising that with the coming of the motor age and increasing traffic on Archway Road the field was sacrificed. Thomas Boney decided to develop the lower portion of the estate by building a new road between Southwood Lane and Jacksons Lane running parallel to the main road. This street was to be called Hillside Gardens, although the land had never been part of the "Hillside" grounds. The new road would curve at either end so as to meet the old lanes at right angles. There would be three openings from Hillside Gardens into the estate, one of which, paved with cobblestones, has recently been found when a garage was being enlarged.

In March 1896 Thomas Boney signed a contract with Harry Harper, a local builder, to construct 47 buildings in accordance with plans drawn up by W.H. Boney, a surveyor from 124 Chancery Lane, and most likely a relative of Boney. The area covered was the new street, both Southwood Lane and Jacksons Lane from Hillside Gardens to Archway Road, and the whole stretch of Archway Road between the two side roads except for the corner with Jacksons Lane where W.H. Boney was to build the Methodist church in 1905 (now the Jacksons Lane Community Centre). The project appears to have been completed within the two years stipulated in the contract. Some of it was terraced housing, some blocks of mansion flats, and in Archway Road shops and flats opposite Highgate station. All the buildings are still standing.

The Carrs were the last family to inhabit Southwood House. Thomas Boney was followed by Alfred Hollis Carr who was his son-in-law, having married Boney's daughter Alice. He was Carr of the Carr's biscuits family whose business was eventually taken over by Huntley & Palmer. There was also a family connection with Carr's bootblacking. Alfred Carr was a collector of coloured prints and it was he (or possibly his father-in-law) who established the exotic trees in the garden. Mrs Carr's brother, Arthur Boney, remained unmarried, and lived at Southwood House until his death in 1938.

The last Carrs were born at Southwood House, Matthew in 1889 and Alfred Risdale in 1894. Both were sent to Highgate School. Matthew Carr became a Brigadier and earned high military honours, also from the French and the Americans. Until 1947 he was Deputy Chief of the Allied Commission in Italy. Alfred Carr stayed at Southwood House at least until the outbreak of war in 1939. He died in 1959.[13]

Sometime during the 1939-1945 war the house was vacated. Thereafter the beautifully kept garden with its masses of rhododendrons ran wild. Vandals broke windows and removed doors and other timbers for firewood, the bust over the door disappeared, and soon the once proud house became derelict, a haunt of tramps and an eyesore. In 1951 Hornsey Council, by compulsory purchase order, bought the estate for £5,400. The Council had all sorts of building plans, including a welfare clinic, Council flats, police flats, and old people's housing, but they found all the schemes too expensive; by that time the Government had passed legislation about development charges which were a multiple of the cost price. Also, there was the question of the fast decaying house; to restore it would be unacceptably expensive, and indeed for what purpose? But pulling it down would cause an outcry from the good people of Highgate who had already seen too much of their architectural heritage disappear. Conveniently, during the night of 23 February 1953, someone solved the dilemma by burning the house down.[14]

New developments

With the building demolished, Hornsey Council gave up its own development plans and put the estate on the market. In 1956 they invited tenders for developing the estate, subject to a total of no more than 43 houses or maisonettes. (At this point, one feels, the Council, having acquired the land by c.p.o., should have offered it back to the last owners.) One of the tenders received was from a solicitor, Robert Potel, acting on behalf of a young and penniless group of architects: Andrews, Sherlock, Emmerson and Keable. Their scheme seemed too progressive for Hornsey Council, and, as it turned out, their tender was not the highest. They offered £30,000 for the land. To their credit, and to the amazement of Mr Potel, Hornsey Council accepted their bid and plans. At that time the Southwood House estate was the largest private development ever to be undertaken in Highgate.

The scheme envisaged a mixture of two- and three-storey houses with three or four bedrooms each. Those in Hillside Gardens and Southwood Lane were to be modified open plan dwellings, while the Jacksons Lane houses would be more traditional, at least internally. Every house was to get a small private garden and all the gardens were to lead into the middle of the estate where a communal garden would be landscaped with a central play area. All trees wherever possible were to be preserved. According to one authority, the tree planter *c.* 1900 "must have known a considerable amount about the decorative species that were available at that time, and also have had a rather cultivated taste." The majority of the trees were from North America, They included a cucumber tree (*Magnolia acuminata*), Indian bean tree (*Catalpa bignoninoides*), sycamore (*Acer pseudoplatanus*), false Acacia (locust tree or Robinia), Sumach (*Rhus typhina*), tulip tree (*Liriodendron tulipifera*), sweet chestnut (*Castanea sativa*), and, most majestic of all, the swamp cypress (bald cypress, *Taxodium distichum*). There may well have been other trees, apart from a large number of shrubs, but the above named survived and made the terraced communal garden a most attractive feature.

The plans met with considerable public criticism: kitchens faced the street; there were flat roofs; the housefronts smacked of brutalism; the texture and the colour of the bricks was crude; and the blue of the dustbin recesses and the panelling below the kitchen windows jarred with the staid 1896/8 houses opposite, with their Dutch gables. Today, the rear elevation, facing the communal garden, with large slatted windows and timbered patios, is seen as a unity and is much admired by groups of visiting architectural students.

By 1957 the plans were ready and building permits granted. The estate agents, Folkard & Hayward, agreed to act, without much enthusiasm. Building societies shook their heads when faced with such 'modern' or 'contemporary' dwellings which they feared would prove unsaleable. The price for the Hillside Gardens new houses was £5,050, which was considered

156

outrageously high, plus £40 per annum ground rent. To everyone's surprise, however, these 'chicken coops' as a local estate agent called them, with their double height dining rooms and staircase exposed in the middle of the living area, sold immediately.

Several of the original buyers are still living on the former Southwood House estate, and two generations of children have played where Marshal Wade used to walk.

Klaus Hinrichsen

References

1. *VCH*, vol .vi, p. 127

2. *...London ... and the Country Ten Miles Round*

3. *DNB*

4. J.B. Salmond, *Wade in Scotland* (1934)

5. *Parliamentary Debates*, 1734, p. 411

6. Thieme-Becker *Kuenstlerlexikon*

7. Nikolaus Pevsner, *The Buildings of England. London except the Cities of London and Westminister* (Penguin, 1952), p. 379

8. Formerly at the RIBA, now in the National Buildings Record of the Royal Commission on the Historical Monuments of England, Blandford Street, London W1.

9. *The Saturday Book* No.4 (1944)

10. Lloyd, *Highgate* (1888), p. 277

11. *Members of Parliament*

12. PRO or BCM

13. *Highgate School Register 1833-1964* (1965)

14. *Daily Telegraph*, 24 February 1953

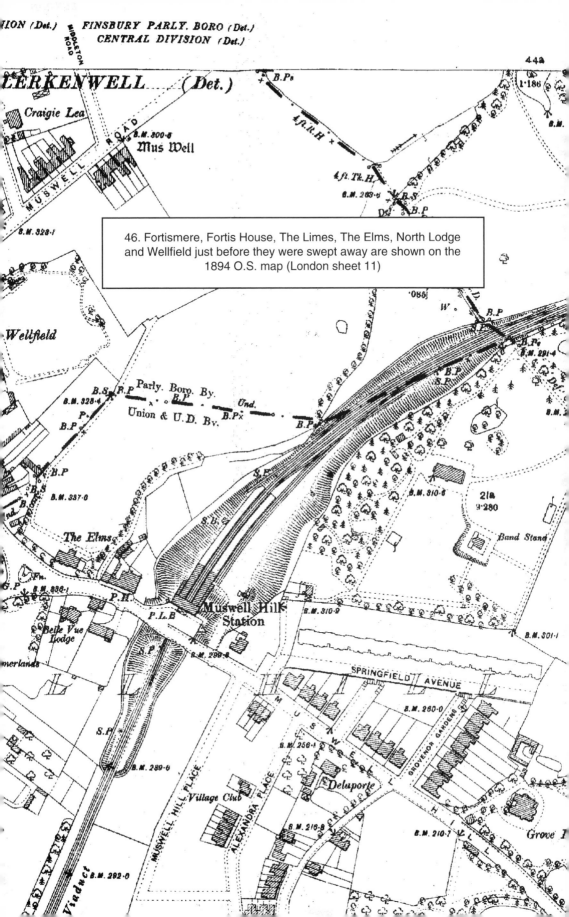

46. Fortismere, Fortis House, The Limes, The Elms, North Lodge and Wellfield just before they were swept away are shown on the 1894 O.S. map (London sheet 11)

Holding back the urban tide: The Limes and other Muswell Hill estates

The house known latterly as The Limes stood at the southern end of Colney Hatch Lane, at the junction with the road from Highgate. The 1894 Ordnance Survey map[1] shows it set well back from the corner, with a semi-circular drive. Two years later, in 1896, The Limes and Fortis House, nearby to the west, which together had stood in some 20 to 30 acres between Colney Hatch Lane and Fortis Green Road, were demolished. Across their estates James Edmondson of Highbury began to build the new urban suburb of Muswell Hill, laying out Queens Avenue and Princes Avenue over the green spaces and building tall shopping parades around the perimeter.

Till this time Muswell Hill's old estates had been almost inviolate, a place for private pleasures amidst rural charm. The only losses had been two ancient houses on Muswell Hill itself, Bath House and The Grove, both demolished so that the 1873 branch line to Alexandra Palace could be built. Despite the loss of these two houses and the coming of a railway to the village, it was not until the demolition of The Limes and Fortis House that the place was transformed. Next to go was Hillfield, a late Victorian villa south of The Limes, then The Elms at the top of the hill over which Dukes Avenue was laid out, then Wellfield and North Lodge in Colney Hatch Lane. All these fell to Edmondson. Another major developer, William Jefferies Collins built over the Fortismere and Firs estates on the west side of Fortis Green Road and developed Muswell Hill Road. Summerlands and Belle Vue Lodge, two properties on the south west corner of the hilltop were lost to other developers.

Origins

How old were the houses which disappeared, particularly The Limes? Cartographic evidence[2] shows that a house stood on the site of The Limes in 1725. Other evidence suggests that it might be a late 17th century establishment. Ownership of the land can be traced back to the early 17th century when in 1629 the estate passed by marriage into the Rowe or Roe family.[3] These were already prominent landowners in Muswell Hill for, from 1577, they owned the former nunnery land on the other (east) side of Colney Hatch Lane. This property, known as Muswell Hill Farm, had been established in the mid 12th century by a gift of manorial land from the Bishop of London, lord of the manor of Hornsey, to an Augustinian order of nuns established *circa* 1100 in Clerkenwell.[4] On this land was the holy well which was to give Muswell Hill its name and next to it the nuns built a chapel and farm buildings. With the Dissolution of religious houses by Henry

VIII the land passed in 1540 (with other estates belonging to the nunnery in five counties) into civil ownership. Much of the land in Muswell Hill (including the Limes estate) was held by copyhold tenure with transactions recorded in Hornsey Court Rolls, but jurisdiction over the 64.5 acres east of Colney Hatch Lane, was successfully claimed by the parish of St. James, Clerkenwell and until the year 1900 the land was known as Clerkenwell Detached.[5] Local landholdings were cited as being either in Hornsey or Clerkenwell.

The Rowe family were City gentry with aristocratic connections. Their lineage has been traced back to Roger de Rowe (1236) and a manor near Aylesford in Kent. Three of its members became lord mayors. One branch was to produce Sir Thomas Roe (1581-1644), a notable courtier, explorer and ambassador, serving Elizabeth I and her successors.[6] Court rolls and wills show that the Rowe family held several properties and houses at Muswell Hill. At first they held a mansion on the site of the nuns' chapel in Clerkenwell Detached. From 1601 they leased this to Bartholomew Matthewson and the house is referred to as Mattysons on a 1619 map[7] and was occupied by Sir Julius Caesar, Chancellor of the Exchequer to James I. In 1663 they gave up the Clerkenwell land to Sir George Benyon (who later sold it to Sir Paul Paynter) but kept the mansion. In 1677 Sir Thomas Rowe (1641-1696) demolished a mansion of 16 hearths and sold the materials; he may have retained the site, as buildings said to have been the grange of Rowes were apparently blown down in 1701.

Before he died, however, Sir Thomas Rowe had built a new Muswell Hill mansion, as is shown by his Will, proved 1697. This makes interesting reading:

"Whereas Muswell Hill is now double the value of what it once was when my father left it to me, and whereas I have bought one house of my sister Mary and built a new house on the common, whereby the copyhold estate is much increased. I do therefore order that my wife enjoy her joynture and that my son Thomas Rowe do have all the rest of the estate being about £220 a year. After decease of my wife I give him the whole estate at Muswell Hill hoping he will be a good husband and leave it to his [heir] as I with great [deal] of paine and care have preserved for him."[8]

Rowe's 'paine and care' would have anticipated his remand to the Fleet Prison for contempt of court during his probably fraudulent handling of the College of Infants in Clerkenwell, as a result of which he shot himself.[9] This 1697 Will gives ground for presuming that the site of Rowe's 'new house upon the common' was that of The Limes. The south side of the road from Highgate to Muswell Hill was Muswell Hill Common, not enclosed until 1816. 'Waste' or common land usually lay each side of medieval roads and it is likely that a strip of common land on the north side of this road was used by Thomas Rowe to build a mansion. This is unlikely to have been Bath House,

47. Bath House, located next to The Green Man, Muswell Hill, was owned in the eighteenth century by the Pulteney family, earls of Bath. It became Bath House Academy but was later divided into three houses before being sold for construction of the Great Northern Railway branch line to Alexandra Palace and of Muswell Hill station.

48. The Limes, viewed from the road junction at the top of Muswell Hill, with its surrounding wall carrying a Colney Hatch Lane nameplate

another Rowe mansion. Warburton's 1725 map shows The Limes, no house on Clerkenwell Detached and two other large houses on the north side of Muswell Hill which would be Bath House and The Grove. Bath House, just below The Green Man, was set some way back from the road so presumably not built upon the waste, where the gradient was steep. Bath House took its name from the Pulteney family, created Earls of Bath in the 18th century, later owners, and it was probably the house commented upon in the anonymous 1776 *Description of the County of Middlesex* which says that "Roe's noble mansion became the property of the Earl of Bath but was lately converted into a public house".[10] Rocque's 1754 map[11] shows a house on the site of The Limes and also depicts the well-laid out gardens surrounding The Grove, shortly to become the country residence of Topham Beauclerk, Earl of St. Albans,[12] with Bath House north of it. On Rocque's map another smaller property on the corner of the Hill is likely to have been the house called first Hilltop then The Elms. This was situated in some 11 acres just south of Clerkenwell Detached; a Victorian photograph shows it as Georgian.

Unfortunately no views have been traced picturing The Limes in earlier times. The one known photograph[13] dating from the end of the 19th century shows little of the house, which stands behind a low wall with railings, bearing a Colney Hatch Lane name-plate. It was remembered after demolition as "a fine old brick built house with stone ornamentations". "Station-parade is built on the kitchen garden which extended to the present Woodberry-crescent and, abutting on Colney Hatch Lane was a high garden wall upon which was grown on its southern side many espalier fruit trees."[14] Old houses are frequently remodelled, or demolished and rebuilt, and this photograph holds no firm clue to the age of the original building. Of interest is that Miss Mudie, who had lived at The Limes, told local historian Dr. F.W.M. Draper that "the house was built by a Spaniard and in the foreign style – that is with rooms opening into one another all round the house, at any rate on the upper floors".[15] A Spanish merchant lived at The Limes 1812-1825 but her description of the interior layout would as well fit a 17th or 18th century house; it was only by the early 19th century that corridors were being built on to older houses to save people from having to go from room to room. So the core of The Limes, demolished in 1896, could well have been late 17th century.

The branch of the Rowe family holding land at Muswell Hill petered out in the early 18th century and the estate, by then heavily encumbered, was sold under the will of Henry Guy who had acquired the rights of the co-heirs.[16] Guy was a wealthy MP, guardian to William Pulteney, and in 1726 it became Pulteney's property from whom it descended to Henrietta Laura Pulteney, countess of Bath, who on her death was adjudged the richest woman in England.[17] Henrietta died childless in 1808 and the Muswell Hill estate passed to William Harry Vane, earl of Darlington and later duke of

Cleveland. In 1810 he sold the estate in seven lots; included were properties on the Hill: Bath House Academy (as Bath House then was) which went for £1,400 and The Green Man inn next to it which went for £1,000.[18]

Early 19th century owners

Purchaser of the lot on the corner of Muswell Hill was Abbott Kent (possibly a descendant of Joseph Kent, an earlier Muswell Hill property owner). Kent was admitted to the copyhold on 15 February 1810, acquiring a capital mansion house, coach house, stabling, lawn, pleasure grounds, yards and appurtenances situate on the north side of Muswell Hill, together with meadow land by Red House Lane (an early name for present day Pages Lane[19]) paying the earl of Darlington "£5,500 of lawful money". The Court Roll entry, as well as detailing the mansion house surroundings, defines the areas of the estate as being bounded on the north west by Red House Lane, on the north east by the road to Colney Hatch, on the west side by lands belonging to the Quakers' Charity, on the south side by the road from Muswell Hill to Finchley Common (today's Fortis Green Road) and by the copyhold premises of George Maynard, and on the south east by the road from Highgate to Muswell Hill. The purchase also included a "Bowling Green (formerly waste)". This is described as being separated only from the said capital mansion on the north east side thereof by the road leading from Highgate to Muswell Hill, and on the remaining three sides by Muswell Hill Common. The Bowling Green is referred to in the 1663 Court Rolls[20] as being granted to Thomas Rowe: "a parcel of the waste now enclosed for the recreation and accommodation of all the tenants of the said manor, and of the gentlemen who shall contribute to the work and expense of a Bowling Green being made at a rent of 4d p.a." This Bowling Green is mentioned again in 1695 when Sir Thomas Rowe's property passed to his son.[21] Its site would have been the land between Summerland Gardens and the hilltop.

Abbott Kent lived only a few weeks after acquiring the property. By his Will of 19 April 1810 his executors sold the property to José Cayetano de Bernales, who was admitted to copyhold ownership on 2 March 1812. It is de Bernales's name which is on the 1816 Hornsey Enclosure map.[22] The index to this shows that de Bernales held all the plots between Pages Lane, Colney Hatch Lane, Muswell Hill Broadway and Fortis Green Road, except for plots on the western side of Colney Hatch Lane and the eastern side of Fortis Green Road. (The latter was owned by George Maynard and the 1816 map shows a house built on it.) The Limes is shown with an avenue of trees stretching from the mansion towards the north west, similar to the 1865 O.S. map. The index also shows that de Bernales held the site of the Bowling Green (plot 29), and that he also had purchased the northern portion of Muswell Hill Common (plot 166), paying £490 for four acres, 3 roods and 25 perches. Purchase was possible because the three commissioners responsible for dividing, allotting and enclosing the Hornsey commons and waste had power to sell land 'to cover their expenses'. About a fourth of the common land was sold in this way, bringing in £7,248.[23]

Contemporary reports show that Muswell Hill at the end of the Napoleonic wars was a very pleasant place in which to live. Situated some five miles from London, it was rural, with extensive woodlands still existing towards Highgate and towards Finchley.

"Leaving the delightful scenery around Southgate, we rise a considerable hill and at the distance of two miles reach Muswell Hill", wrote John Hassell in 1817, and "here again, is another little paradise: the succession of enchanting scenery with the abundance of rising hills, all clothed with the richest verdure, and encircled with a redundance of wood will captivate and delight the admirers of landscape scenery".[24]

Brewer, writing about the same time, is almost unctuous: "from this elevation are commanded beautiful and varied prospects; and to the credit of modern taste, there are here constructed numerous detached villas, in every respect calculated to embellish a spot so rich in natural circumstances. These are, in general, of modest through spacious proportions and are provided with ample grounds".[25]

It is no wonder that such an area was sought after by merchants and professional people for a second residence close to the capital. José (or Joseph) Cayetano de Bernales was a merchant with a house at 28 Finsbury Place in the City. A native of Lempias, near Biscay, on the coast of Spain, born 1751, he had obtained Letters Patent of Denization[26], in 1806, four years before buying The Limes. Possibly this was at the time of his marriage to Elizabeth, born 1791, forty years younger than himself. An 1822 letter from Elizabeth survives, written from Finsbury Place, to John Northcote RA (1736-1831) making an appointment to have her portrait painted, delayed because she had been extremely ill.[27] Elizabeth died in September 1823,[28] aged 32. Despite efforts to trace the painting, no portrait of her by Northcote has been found.

De Bernales went downhill after the death of his wife. In 1824 the 72-year-old merchant became bankrupt and entered the Debtors' prison. His case was heard on 28 July 1825[29] when he was discharged under Acts for the relief of insolvent debtors. This was contingent upon the sale of his property, the effects having been assigned to Henry Dance of Lincolns Inn Fields for disposal, "except the wearing apparel and other necessaries of the said insolvent and family, not exceeding in the whole the value of £20."[30] On 16 October 1825 De Bernales died, aged 74. Buried in old St. Pancras churchyard, his tombstone says he was "generally regretted for his generous and benevolent disposition and upright character." His property was put up for sale in 14 lots by auctioneer Charles Lancelot Hoggart.

Purchasers were William Brodie Gurney, who was the largest buyer and took the house, John Gibson of Stratford, Essex, chemist and Thomas Bird and George Maynard, both of Muswell Hill.[31] Thomas Bird already owned land north of Pages Lane and at the top of Muswell Hill and in 1826 he also purchased former nunnery land on Clerkenwell Detached.[32] Here he leased Wellfield to Thomas Rhodes of adjacent Tottenham Wood farm. (This house does not appear on either 18th century or early 19th century maps and presumably was built around 1830; it appears on an 1846 map and is called Wellfield on the 1865 Ordnance Survey map).[33] George Maynard, who owned land and a house on the east side of Fortis Green Road, bordering The Limes estate, took the opportunity to extend eastwards. From this time two estates, known as Fortis House and The Limes, occupied the area between Fortis Green Road and Colney Hatch Lane. Later in the 19th century they would again come under single ownership.

William Brodie Gurney (1777-1855), the new owner of The Limes, was the grandson of Thomas Gurney (b.1705) of Woburn, Bedfordshire, who took over an early form of shorthand, developed in 1672 by William Mason, and evolved his own Gurney system under the title of 'Brachygraphy' or 'Swift Writing'. (Today's more widely used Pitman shorthand was not devised until 1837, one of five 19th century systems). A clockmaker by trade, Thomas was employed as a shorthand writer at the Old Bailey from 1737 till his death in 1770, during which time he improved his system. Thomas Gurney's son Joseph Gurney (1744-1815) edited a ninth edition of the handbook and used it at parliamentary committees. William Brodie Gurney (Brodie was his mother's maiden name) was born at Stamford Hill and adopted the family profession, commencing practice in 1803, covering trials all over the United Kingdom.[34] Whether Gurney relished his name being included by Lord Byron in *Don Juan*, ill received at first when published 1819-24,[35] is open to question but it does underline the fact that Gurney was a nationally known name. Byron in his first canto relating Don Juan's amorous adventures wrote:

> *"And how Alfonso sued for a divorce*
> *Were in the English newspapers, of course.*
>
> *If you would like to see the whole proceedings,*
> *The depositions and the cause at full,*
> *The names of all the witnesses, the pleadings*
> *Of counsel to nonsuit, or to annul,*
> *There's more than one edition, and the readings*
> *Are various, but they none of them are dull;*
> *The best is that in short-hand ta'en by Gurney,*
> *Who to Madrid on purpose made a journey." (CLXXXIX)*

Gurney became president of the Sunday School Union and for 10 years helped to edit *The Youth* magazine. An anti-slavery advocate, he contributed to the rebuilding of chapels in Jamaica. In 1826, after the purchase of the Muswell Hill residence, Gurney invited the Rev. Eustace Carey to live with him and the house was licensed as a place of worship, with evening services held in the drawing room. (Gurney was a contemporary of the Norwich Quaker family of the same name, which included Elizabeth Fry and the banker Samuel Gurney, but was apparently not related).

In 1830 Gurney's wife, whom he had married in 1803, died at Muswell Hill. Within a year he had sold his Muswell Hill property and moved away. He died in March 1855 at Denmark Hill. Gurney sold the estate[36] in 1831 to Richard Marshall, a successful bookseller, for £4,540. The purchase included 'a capital copyhold mansion' situated on the north side of Muswell Hill with three acres containing a coach house, stabling, lawn, pleasure grounds, gardens and outhouses. In addition there was land adjoining the mansion of 11 acres 1 rood 7 perches plus meadow, pasture formerly the Bowling Green, and other parcels of land, including two cottages and a tenement erected by Gurney on the 11 acres.

Richard Marshall and mid-19th century Muswell Hill

49. Richard Marshall (1780-1863), partner in the Simpkin Marshall firm of book distributors, resident at The Limes

Richard Marshall (1789-1863) had entered the book trade through a near relation, Benjamin Crosby, who had set up a successful business selling stock, including bargain 'remainders' to London and provincial book-sellers.[37] The firm also published some books, including the Gurney shorthand manuals, and it would have been through this business acquaintanceship that Marshall bought Gurney's house. The firm of W. Simpkin and R. Marshall was formed in 1815 when Crosby died and Richard Marshall and William Simpkin became partners. They were aided by John Miles, a wealthy member of a book trade family whose most distinguished member had been Joseph Johnson (1730-1809)[38], whose business John Miles inherited, taking over a debt of about £15,000 owed to Johnson by Crosby and Co.[39] In 1828 John Miles bought out William Simpkin and became Richard Marshall's partner. In 1838 the firm became Simpkin, Marshall & Co. after the retirement of John Miles when his second son, also John Miles (1813-1886), succeeded him. The firm acted as a clearing house, providing books from different publishers against booksellers' orders, keeping large stocks. They continued trading from premises in Paternoster Row and Stationers Hall Court, with warehouses near St. Paul's cathedral, until in December 1940 they were demolished in the Blitz, when the firm lost three million books. The firm continued after the Second World War (it had become Simpkin Marshall Hamilton Kent & Co. in 1889 when it was merged with another Miles family firm) but was later purchased by Robert Maxwell and ended up in receivership.[40]

Work in Simpkin Marshall was very demanding. This was found by many including Daniel Macmillan, the future publisher, who when he reached London from Scotland in 1833 looked for a job in the book trade. Macmillan found that work at Simpkin Marshall involved very long hours, often right through the night, and so he did not take an offer of employment at £60 per year, living in, made to him by Richard Marshall, but took a job elsewhere.[41] Harsh employment conditions may have contributed to the suicide in 1831 of Richard Marshall's brother, Thomas, who hanged himself at Paternoster Row. Thomas was responsible for binding all the firm's books and his work had been criticised. A witness at the coroner's inquest said that a fortnight before his death Thomas had suffered a head injury after the phaeton he was driving collided with a coal waggon and he had "not been right in his mind since". The verdict was temporary insanity.[42] Richard Marshall, in charge of paper, print, publications and country accounts, "was a stern disciplinarian; untiring himself, and throwing all his energies into his daily work, he expected and he exacted the same assiduity from all the subordinates, and very largely succeeded in obtaining it. A common remark of his to an assistant was 'I expect you to have gumption, sir, without that you will be no good to me, nor to yourself either'. In keeping of stock and of all accounts therewith, there was the most marvellous precision".[43]

Richard Marshall married a Phoebe Fairbrother (1788-1863) and they had two sons and five daughters. His eldest son, Richard (Junior) became a partner in the firm but died early in 1840. The next son, Benjamin Crosby Marshall was a partner in the firm for a short time only. Sarah Marshall, the eldest daughter (1814-1908) married, in 1834 at St. Mary's Hornsey, John Miles's son Joseph Johnson Miles (1811-1884) and the couple went to live in Millfield Lane, Highgate. Two surviving water colours by the Irish artist Samuel Lover RHA, dating from 1835, include Sarah amongst the Miles family seen at John Miles's residence at West End Hall, Hampstead. Two daughters from this marriage were to marry into the Clay family of printers who lived in Avenue House on Muswell Hill (on the site of the Rookfield estate). Margaret Miles (1842-1923) married Richard Clay in 1863 and Edith Miles (1848-1913) married Arthur Lloyd Clay in 1873. The previous generation, Richard Marshall's daughters, had been known as the Belles of Muswell Hill,[44] and after Sarah Marshall's marriage her sister Emily married the Rev. Henry Rhodes of Swains Lane, Highgate (close to Millfield Lane) and her sister Margaret married Henry John Smith and was to live in North Lodge, Colney Hatch Lane, a property leased from The Limes. The Miles family continued to have a connection with The Limes, for four generations were to be associated with the firm founded by C.E. Mudie, who was to become the next occupant of the house after Marshall.

Richard Marshall was to occupy The Limes until his death in 1863, with his wife, his daughter-in-law Harriet (widow of his son Richard) and grand-daughter Catherine (who had been born at sea on the Bay of Biscay) and five servants.[45] The gross estimated rental for rating purposes was £160 for the house, £49 for the land and £18 for the two cottages plus £43. 15 shillings for an additional 12 acres and £14 for four acres, making it a substantial property.[46] By 1850 it was named as The Limes and described as "the seat of Richard Marshall, Esq.," by Keane in his *Beauties of Middlesex*, who wrote:

"This beautiful villa-residence is approached by a double carriage-drive and lawn. The two handsome lofty iron gates produce a very favourable impression of the interior. The carriage-road sweeps under a semi-circular grove of lime and other trees, from one gate around by the hall door and out by the other. We are the more particular describing this approach as it is the most convenient for setting down company, and gives a full flowing line and a finished appearance to the whole composition."

Keane is mainly concerned with landscape gardening and so, unfortunately, does not give any further information about the house. But he describes the garden and its setting lyrically:

"This verdant velvet lawn is divided into two rich landscape scenes by a long avenue of lime trees that approach, but do not reach, within fifty or sixty yards of the house . . . This long promenade and shady retreat is bounded on the west by a raised bed of roses, with a walk to the more distant scenes and to the lake that supplied Muswell Hill with water . . . The conservatory near the house, is sixty five feet long by sixteen wide . . . In the kitchen garden are some good wall trees and in the vinery was a good crop of grapes . . . The home grounds are retired, but by stepping a few yards across the high road from the neat and clean farm buildings and stables, a splendid prospect opens to view; it is a broad tract of country adorned with all that is necessary to constitute beautiful landscape scenery with the exception of that very useful element, water. Shooter's-hill is seen in the far distant horizon, with the more prominent and picturesque features of Highgate, St. Paul's Cathedral, Islington and Hackney".

In the thirty-two years that Richard Marshall occupied this pleasant estate Muswell Hill remained rural but saw some steady changes, with villas being built in Colney Hatch Lane (Nos. 3, 5 and 7 still survive), more cottages in St. James's Lane (where a village community developed) and St. James church built in 1842 to meet the needs of the gently rising population, saving a journey either to Hornsey or to Highgate for worship. With it came in 1850 St. James's National School for Infants, destined to survive on its Fortis Green site (where Clore House now stands) for 120 years. It was not until July 1863, the year Marshall died, that Alexandra Park was formally opened on Thomas Rhodes's farmlands, incorporating the empty Grove estate on Muswell Hill. Muswell Hill's population was mainly professional and trades people and their servants and craftsmen. This was the class that could afford 10 or 20 acres and a house in London's countryside after they had established themselves, but not wealthy enough to invest in larger estates further afield.[47]

One professional man whom Marshall might have met as a near neighbour was Dr. Protheroe Smith (b.1809), a West End physician who numbered Lord Palmerston (twice Prime Minister in the 1850s and 60s) among his patients, who made The Elms, at the top of Muswell Hill, his

50. The Elms, Muswell Hill. Residence of Dr Protheroe Smith, medical reformer. Rear view, with croquet lawn, from the 1880 sale catalogue.

country retreat. Before him it had apparently been used as a home for the mentally deficient.[48] Son of a Devon doctor,[49] Protheroe Smith studied at Barts Hospital and began to specialise in women's diseases, a neglected field of practice, and in 1842 he helped found the first women's hospital in the world in Red Lion Square, later in Soho Square, "for the treatment of those maladies which neither rank, wealth or character can avert from the female sex".[50] He was one of the pioneers in England for using chloroform during childbirth. His concern for hygiene caused him to have the Muswell Hill pond removed in 1858. (The pond was situated between The Limes on the north west corner of the road junction and The Elms on the south east, where Muswell Hill roundabout now is.) A local resident (Mr. Yorke, born 1851)[51] remembered that the pond and pump gave way to a tank and a tap in a wall, and that both The Elms and Wellfield had wells with pumps. (There was a thriving trade in Crouch End where a man sold buckets of water from the pump in the Broadway at a half-penny a time). When The Limes was sold in 1865 the conveyance included a clause obliging the owner to keep up and renew the pipe which supplied the well and pump at Muswell Hill.

Protheroe Smith lived in his freehold property for over 20 years. The 1880 sales catalogue[52] described it as a fine old family residence improved some years back by Cubitt, with grounds laid out by Sir Joseph Paxton. The 11 acres contained large elm trees, two rented outhouses and a cottage, detached stabling for four horses and a double coachhouse for four carriages, a six room gardener's cottage, cow houses and greenhouse. Accompanying photographs show a Georgian house with croquet being played on the lawn. The three-storeyed house had nine bedrooms and rooms for three servants. In 1880 it was proposed that a road be laid across the estate to allow development but this did not happen until 1900 when Edmondson laid out Dukes Avenue. (Muswell Hill Baptist church stands near the site of the house, as Edmondson pointed out when he gave the Baptists land from his new estate.[53])

Another Muswell Hill mansion, Bath House, had by 1860 been divided into three residences. The centre one was occupied by William Manson, a barrister known for his defence of the right of local parishioners to use the footpath from Colney Hatch Lane over the Rhodes farmlands to gain access to the ancient well in Clerkenwell Detached. (This route is now Muswell Road). His son Frederick Manson lived in and owned Wellfield and was also to own the empty Elms, when inhabited only by a gardener, and, reputedly, a ghost.[54] In 1867 Bath House was bought by the London, Highgate & Edgware railway company and demolished so that the branch line to Alexandra Palace could be built.

In January 1863 Richard Marshall's wife Phoebe died and he survived her only till November of that year. They are both buried in Highgate Cemetery, in a vault, now overgrown, belonging to the Miles family.[55] Interred there too are their son Benjamin Crosby Marshall, who died in 1888, and a Caroline Marshall, who also died in 1863, possibly Richard's sister. Reference to Richard's hard work, business intelligence and personal integrity, contributing to the pre-eminence of Simpkin Marshall was made in the trade press. A portrait shows him as a somewhat Gladstonian figure.[56]

At Marshall's death Muswell Hill still retained its sparse population even though the opening of Hornsey railway station in 1850 was to presage the gradual urbanisation of the rest of the parish, beginning in the late 1860s. An attempt to build on The Limes estate was now made for it was purchased in 1864 by The London and County Land and Building Company for £10,000 from the Marshall estate trustees, *i.e.* Benjamin Crosby Marshall, Joseph Johnson Miles and others. Purchase was subject to leasing North Lodge in Colney Hatch Lane to Henry John Smith for seven years, to perpetuate a lease of 1838 made when Smith married Margaret Marshall. At the same time the company purchased Clerkenwell Detached land north of Wellfield[57] where roads including Muswell Road and Muswell Avenue, began to be laid out from 1879, and plots were slowly taken up for building. This was the first urbanisation of the rural area. But the project to build on The Limes estate was still-born due to neighbouring landowners. When the estate was put up for auction in lots in 1865 they purchased it.[58] These landowners were Joseph and Samuel Somes who for £10,000 bought 10 acres with the mansion and other properties "known as The Limes, late in the occupation of Richard Marshall, Esq., deceased but now untenanted". "The capital messuage abuts on the south east of the public road leading from Highgate to Hornsey called or known as Muswell Hill Road" (earlier this had been called Southwood Lane Road), "on the north east by Colney Hatch Lane and on the north west by land and premises belonging to the said Joseph Somes and on the south west by land and premises belonging to James Hall Renton".

The Somes or Soames family lived across Fortis Green Road in an estate called Fortismere by 1865[59]. A house and tree-encircled estate here are already shown on the 1816 Enclosure Map; the mansion would have been located about a third of the way down present day Fortismere Avenue. South of it in 1816 was another house on land owned by Thomas Tatham, named by 1865 as The Firs. The Soames were a ship-owning family,[60] and in 1861 Fortismere was occupied by Samuel Soames, his sister and his widowed mother. By 1871 he described himself as a commission merchant and by 1881 as a merchant banker. He married one of Dr. Protheroe Smith's daughters and was a J.P. The presumption must be that he used the family wealth to ensure the continued rural charm of his Muswell Hill estate. This human factor delayed urbanisation here and elsewhere in the country.

The Soames's attitude is likely to have been shared by James Hall Renton who lived in Fortis House, the estate to the west of The Limes which

51. Fortismere, residence of Samuel Somes, JP, purchased in 1895 by W. J. Collins who was to demolish the house shortly afterwards and build over the estate

had been acquired by George Maynard in 1825, from whom Renton had probably purchased it. Fortis House stood on the site of 124-148 Fortis Green Road, built in 1900 by Edmondson as Grand Parade; the coach house which abutted it on the east side still stands at 38 Princes Avenue. This rare Muswell Hill survival is in mid-19th century style, but possibly it was added to a much earlier house. Renton, who was eventually to become the owner of The Limes estate as well, was a Stock Exchange member born 1821 in Scotland. He shared occupancy of Fortis House with his wife, five children, governess and servants.[61] Renton became successful enough to have a house in Park Lane and to develop his Muswell Hill property as a stud farm for horses.[62] His son, Leslie Alexander Renton (1868-1947) was educated at Harrow and Sandhurst, fought in the South African and First World Wars and was to be Liberal MP for Gainsborough 1906-1910.[63]

Charles Edward Mudie and late 19th century Muswell Hill

The next occupant of The Limes after the Marshalls, and probably the most well-known, was Charles Edward Mudie (1818-1890) to whom Joseph and Samuel Soames granted a lease[64] in 1867 for 21 years (from March 1866) for £540 annual rent, comprising the mansion and some ten acres. Here Mudie

173

52. Charles Edward Mudie (1818-1890),
founder of the Select circulating book library,
resident at The Limes

was to live with his family until 1887. Born in Cheyne Walk, Chelsea, the youngest of several sons of Scottish parents, Mudie emulated his father in 1840 by opening a newspaper and stationery business. Mudie was of an enquiring mind and within two years was lending books and also publishing in a small way, including the first volume in England of the American poet, James Lowell. Lending books at the low charge, compared with rivals, of one guinea a year, Mudie developed his successful Select Library, at first in Southampton Row, then from 1852 in larger premises at the corner of New Oxford Street and Museum Street. His careful selection of books, excluding some for 'moral' reasons, gave the Victorian public confidence.

New books became immediately available. Between 1853 and 1862 Mudie added almost 960,000 volumes to his library, nearly half being fiction, notably three-decker novels. Branches were established in Manchester, Birmingham and the City of London and loans made as far afield as China. Boxes with books bearing Mudie's distinctive yellow label (copies are still to be found in second-hand bookshops) were to be seen in houses, clubs, trains and steamships. A choice of foreign literature was added following the absorption of Hookham's English and Foreign Library. By the end of the century the library had 7 1/2 million books.[65]

In 1871 Mudie's eldest son, Charles Henry, then 21, entered the firm, destined to carry on his father's business. By this date Mudie and his wife Mary had two sons, Charles and Arthur (16), and five daughters, Mary (22), Christabelle (14), Constance (13), Beatrice (11) and Ethel (7) living with them at The Limes along with nephew Herbert Pawling (17). Mrs. Mudie's father, the Rev. Henry Pawling, and her mother had also lived at The Limes but had died in 1869 and 1870 respectively. The household included gardener, page, coachman and wife, grooms and other servants including a butler, some living in other properties on The Limes estate.[66] Charles Mudie fell in love with Rabie Lermitte, daughter of a family who lived nearby in the Thatched House in

Colney Hatch Lane, and in due course the newly weds went to live in an adjacent villa, Melford Lodge. (The site of both houses is now occupied by Barrington Court, erected c. 1936). Mudie's other son Arthur married another Colney Hatch Lane neighbour, the daughter of Henry Smith of North Lodge.

Sadly Charles was to die on 13th January 1879, thirteen days before his 29th birthday[67]. An active young man who belonged to East Finchley Congregational Chapel, served on the committee for the enlargement of St. James's, indulged in amateur acting and visited the Continent, he had tried to take some of the weight of business care from his father's shoulders. In December 1877, for example, he had got up early and walked over the open snow-covered fields before dawn to catch the 7.20 am. train from Wood Green, a distance of some twenty-five minutes from The Limes. (Transport to or from Muswell Hill other than by private coach or horse was very limited at this time). Charles's death left his father grief-stricken and he never recovered from the loss. From then he took progressively less interest in his business and in 1884 he relinquished all active duties to Arthur and others. By 1894 the business had passed its peak but it continued to be carried on, from the 1920s in smaller Kingsway premises, until in 1937 its stock was bought by Harrods for its own lending library. The famous New Oxford Street premises were destroyed in the Second World War.

Ill fortune is the theme of a legend Miss Mudie told, that a willow by the pond in The Limes estate had been grown from a cutting taken from a tree in St. Helena beside Napoleon's grave. This willow was said to flourish or fade with the fortunes of the Bonapartes. When Napoleon III was defeated at Sedan the willow almost died, leaving only a small shoot; when the Prince Imperial was killed in South Africa, the shoot died.[68]

A glimpse of The Limes at this time is given in the trade press[69] which in 1885 described Mudie as

"a sociable man . . . in the habit of giving high entertainments at his garden parties in the comfortable house on the top of Muswell Hill where he had a fine collection of photographs, the result of foreign travel, to which at one time he was much addicted . . . There are interesting associations connected with the Muswell Hill house, which is still a fine country residence though there is now a railway station near, and bricks and mortar are filling the vacant green slopes which have been so dear to many generations of Londoners . . . . In the grounds of Mr. Mudie's house there is an arbour in which Robert Hall, the illustrious pulpit orator of a past generation was wont to smoke his pipe, when smoking was not quite so fashionable as it is today . . . . It is a lovely spot, but even there sickness intrudes and Mr. Mudie, to the regret of his friends, may now be described as a permanent invalid. One great calamity he has experienced there by the death of his eldest son".

As well as being an effective businessman Mudie was deeply religious, a nonconformist preacher and dedicated social reformer who had served on the London School Board along with his rival, the second W.H. Smith, who had also established a successful lending library. Each was an enemy of illiteracy and of trashy literature.[70] Mudie had poetry published and was also a hymn writer; it was reported after his death that the beautiful avenue of limes was a favourite walk of Mr. Mudie's to a summer house near the spot where on his former lands Muswell Hill Congregational church was to be built, and "there is reason to believe Mr. Mudie wrote there the hymn 'I left my heart to the Saviour Divine'".

The end of The Limes and rural Muswell Hill

The next occupant of The Limes after the Mudie family was William Robert Lake, a consulting engineer who by 1891 lived there with his wife and nine children, ranging in age from 29 to three.[71] Lake had been granted a lease at £250 a year in August 1889 for seven years, expiring September 1896. This was for The Limes and just over seven acres.[72] The lease was granted by James Hall Renton who must by then have purchased The Limes from Soames, so making the land between Fortis Green Road and Colney Hatch Lane again one property. Lake remained at The Limes[73] in 1895 but changes were taking place in Muswell Hill. More houses were being built on Clerkenwell Detached and a row of three-storey houses had been built by 1894 on the corner field opposite St. James's church[74]. (Two of these remain in Muswell Hill Road; the others which had long gardens were demolished in 1936 to make way for the Odeon cinema and car park). In 1895 Samuel Soames sold his Fortismere estate to the future developer William Jefferies Collins (1856-1939), the contents having been auctioned in August 1895[75]. In 1896 Collins bought The Firs, south west of Fortismere from John Tatham's widow.[76]

1896 was also the year that the long history of The Limes as a private estate and mansion came to an end. The purchaser was the developer James Edmondson (1858-1931), whose Highbury-based firm had the previous year built Topsfield Parade in Crouch End on the corner of Middle and Tottenham Lanes. "It was while out for a spin on his cycle that the natural beauties of Muswell Hill, and its advantages as a prospective suburb, first impressed him". "The first development towards building a town was made by Edmondson in 1896 when he purchased The Limes and Fortis House, two fine mansions. These two properties were in the possession of a Mr. Renton, a wealthy gentleman who used his extensive grounds, which . . . covered about 23 acres, as a stud farm".[77] "The Limes were just coming on to the market and James Edmondson bought the 17½ acres for £23,000, a tremendous price in those days".[78]

The contents of The Limes were auctioned on the premises on 28 July 1896.[79] By September 1896 Hornsey Urban District Council was already examining plans for 19 dwelling houses and shops with stabling at the rear for Queens Parade, Muswell Hill Road, the first buildings to be erected (now 91-211 Muswell Hill Broadway) and for 14 dwelling houses and shops with rear stabling at Station Parade, Colney Hatch Lane (now 225-333 Muswell Hill Broadway) all on the 'Muswell Hill Estate'. Plans were approved in October 1896, subject to land being given up for road widening, including part of Tetherdown to where The Limes estate extended.[80] Edmondson was a man of nonconformist religious beliefs, worshipping at the Highbury Congregational church and he expressed these by donating the sites of both Muswell Hill Baptist and Congregational churches and selling the site for the Presbyterian church at half its actual cost.[81] He also built the Athenaeum and gave sites for a library and a fire station, the latter near the site of The Limes mansion in Queens Avenue.

For the residents of the time, though, Edmondson destroyed a village of rural charm. "Messrs Edmondson & Son are already engaged in the work of destruction prior to that of creation in some thirty acres which they have acquired. The late residence of Mr. Mudie, of the well-known library . . . stands on part of the land and Fortis House and grounds occupy the remainder . . . Yes, even Muswell Hill will within a few years be covered with commodious villa residences which yield so much delight to the owner of ground rents. Will the Alexandra Park be saved?"[82] In the following year Mrs. Emily Rhodes, daughter of Richard Marshall, wrote a letter to a friend:

"We have not heard anything particular about the building horrors at Muswell Hill. Do you refer to The Limes and are they going to demolish the poor old house to build their horrid shops? . . . the building craze respects nothing and it makes me quite sad (savage, I was going to say) to see houses and streets where fields and trees and woods used to gladden our eyes . . ."[83]

The irony is that, for our own times, the 'horrid shops' are now in a Conservation Area, protected for their period charm in a unique Edwardian suburb.

The Limes thus passed away. Embedded in the front garden walls of some of the large houses which Edmondson built in his generously wide Queens Avenue are to be seen carved pieces of stone from the house. In 1899 it was reported that 'a row of young lime trees have been planted either side of Queens Avenue'. These (and possibly some protected trees in Queens Avenue gardens) are the only indications that a house called The Limes once stood where Queens Avenue joins Muswell Hill Broadway.

Ken Gay

References

1. London sheet 11, 1:2500; Godfrey edition

2. John Warburton's map of Middlesex; C29 f.6, BL (Map Room)

3. Deed of Covenant dated 15 December 1825, Acc. 549/Bundle 33 (GLRO) tracing ownership back to Henry Guy, 1707; *VCH*, vol. vi, p.147, tracing ownership from Guy back to Rowe family.

4. *VCH*, vol. vi, p.144 for history of nuns' Muswell Hill property; *VCH*, vol. i, pp. 170-174 for Clerkenwell priory

5. 1873 O.S. 6 in. map gives 64.542 acres

6. Michael Strachan, *Sir Thomas Roe 1581: 1644 – A Life* (Michael Russell Pub. 1989)

7. William Robinson, *History of Tottenham* (1840), vol. i, map of 1619 made for Earl of Dorset

8. Reproduced in J.F. Connolly and J. Harvey Bloom, *An Island of Clerkenwell* (1933)

9. Dr. F.W.M. Draper in *Muswell Hill Record*, 15 April 1938

10. Quoted by Draper in *Muswell Hill Record*, 15 April 1938

11. John Rocque's map of Middlesex; 175.t.1 (2), BL (Map Room)

12. See Joan Schwitzer on The Grove in *Lost Houses of Haringey* (1986), p.46

13. North Middlesex Photographic Society, No. 632; H. Lib.

14. Recollections of Mr. Henry T. Nobbs in *Muswell Hill Record*, 18 December 1936

15. Draper; *Muswell Hill Record*, 25 March 1938

16. *VCH*, vol. vi, p. 147

17. Information kindly supplied by Dr. Michael Rowe of Bath who is researching the history of the Pulteney family.

18. Hornsey Manor Court Rolls 10465/125; Gdl.

19. *VCH*, vol. vi, p. 105

20. Marcham, p.157

21. Marcham, p. 234

22. MR/DE HOR/1,2,3; GLRO. A copy is also in BCM and Gdl.

23. See J.H. Lloyd, ... *Highgate* (1888) p. 173

24. J. Hassell, *Rides and Walks*, vol I, p. 194

25. J. Norris Brewer, *The Beauties of England and Wales* (1816), vol. iv, p. 211

26. Acc 549/Bundle 35 (Schedule to 1865 Conveyance); GLRO

27. Add. MS. 42524. f.8; BL (Manuscripts)

28. F.T. Cansick, *Epitaphs of Middlesex (Old St. Pancras)* (1869), p. 113

29. Certificates of Conformity, B6/66 Town Register No. 3; PRO

30. Acc. 549/Bundle 33: Indenture dated lst June 1825; GLRO

31. Acc. 549/Bundle 33: Covenant dated 15th December 1825; GLRO

32. Connolly and Bloom, p. 11

33. See *Ordnance Surveyors' Drawings of the London Area 1799-1808* (London Topographical Society Publication No. 144, 1991); *Plan of the Parish of Clerkenwell* by Thomas Hornor (1808) which shows Clerkenwell Detached (Islington Libraries); *Plan of Holborn and Finchley Sewers – Northern District* by Richard Spencer (1846) in BL (Map Room) Crace Collection; and *O.S. map 1865*

34. *DNB* (separate entries for the 3 Gurneys)

35. *Oxford Companion to English Literature*, ed. Margaret Drabble (1985), p. 282

36. Hornsey Court Rolls 10465/146; Gdl.

37. *The Bookseller*, 4 June 1886; Obituary of John Miles (1813-1886)

38. *Times Literary Supplement* 2.12.1994; "Publisher in Prison" by Claire Tomalin

39. Information from Mr. and Mrs. Marley, descendants of the Miles family to whom the author is indebted for many references and sources for Marshall and Mudie.

40. Tom Bower: *Maxwell The Outsider* (Aurum Press, 1988; Mandarin, 1991)

41. Charles Morgan, *The House of Macmillan (1843-1943)* (Macmillan, 1943)

42. *John Bull*, 12 September 1831

43. Obituary of John Miles in *The Bookseller*, 4.6.1886

44. Draper, *Literary Associations of Hornsey* (1948), p. 25

45. Census returns 1851 and 1861; PRO

46. Hornsey rate books; BCM

47. See F.M.L. Thompson: *English Landed Society in the 19th century* (Routledge, Kegan Paul, 1983) for a discussion on changing land ownership patterns

48. *Muswell Hill Record*, 29 June 1923

49. Draper, Muswell Hill Record, 3 February 1939. See also Jules Kosky: *Mutual Friends: Charles Dickens and Great Ormond Street Children's Hospital* (Weidenfeld & Nicolson, 1989)

50. John Richardson, *London and Its People* (Barrie & Jenkins, 1995), p. 197

51. *Muswell Hill Record*, 29.6.1923

52. 137 all (3); BL (Map Room)

53. *HJ*, 6 July 1901

54. Draper, *Muswell Hill Record*, 24.9.1943

55. Plot No. 11807

56. *The Publishers Circular*, 24.9.1863

57. Connolly & Bloom, p. 12; Wellfield house and grounds survived south of Muswell Road until demolition by Edmondson c. 1902; *cf.* 1894 O.S map.

58. Acc. 549/35; Conveyance, 2.10.1865; GLRO

59. OS map 1865; Census returns 1861

60. Draper, *Muswell Hill Record*, 24.9.1943

61. Census returns for 1871; PRO

62. *Muswell Hill Record*, 27 August 1920

63. *Who Was Who 1941-1950*

64. Acc. 549/35: Lease 30.1.1867; GLRO

65. Guinevere L. Griest, *Mudie's Circulating Library and the Victorian Novel* (David & Charles, 1970)

66. Census Returns 1871 and 1881; PRO

67. *Charles Henry Mudie – A Memorial Sketch by One of his Sisters* (1879). Memorial volume by his sister Mary in H.Lib

68. Draper, *Muswell Hill Past and Present* (1935), p. 22

69. *The Booksellers' Circular*, 9 April 1885

70. Charles Wilson, *First with the News: The History of W.H. Smith 1792-1972* (Jonathan Cape, 1983); see also *DNB*

71. Census Returns 1891; PRO

72. Acc. 549/35; Lease 26.8.1889; GLRO

73. *Kelly's Directory of Hornsey* 1895

74. O.S. map, 1894

75. *HJ*, 10 August 1895 (advertisement)

76. Hornsey manorial rolls 10465/211; Gdl.

77. *Muswell Hill Record*, 12 June 1931

78. *Muswell Hill Record*, 5 October 1934

79. *HJ*, 25 July 1896 (advertisement).

80. Minutes of HUDC, 1896; H. Lib.

81. *Muswell Hill Record*, 12 June 1931

82. *HJ*, 17 October 1896

83. Letter in possession of Mr. and Mrs. Marley.

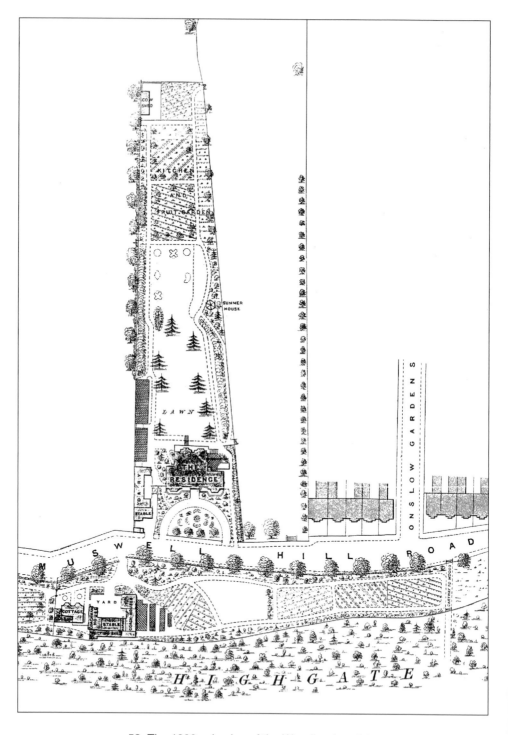

53. The 1890 sale plan of the Woodlands estate

180

Woodlands, a footnote to Victorian literary history

The Woodlands estate stood astride both sides of what is now Muswell Hill Road, but was then still known as Southwood Lane. Woodland Rise and Woodland Gardens were built on the site of the house and its large garden. Across Southwood Lane was a long narrow strip bordering Highgate Wood, roughly covering the same ground as that now occupied by the row of houses and shops which stretch towards the corner of Woodside Avenue. On this strip of land were the Woodlands kitchen gardens, the gardener's cottage, beehives, a pigsty, a pasture for the cow, its shed and other working structures.[1]

Woodlands was probably built around 1850. For some fifteen years from 1861 it was the country residence of Frederick and Nina Lehmann. The Lehmanns knew many literary and artistic celebrities, including Charles Dickens, Wilkie Collins, Robert Browning, George Eliot, Arthur Sullivan, Edwin Landseer, Lord Leighton, Joseph Joachim, Sir Charles Hallé and many other famous figures whom they entertained at both their London home and Woodlands. The house attracted much praise for its delightful unspoilt situation and for its beautiful garden. Among Nina Lehmann's closest friends was Anne Proctor, the wife of "Barry Cornwall" the poet and intimate of nearly every English writer from Charles Lamb to the Brownings. In the August of 1872, when Barry Cornwall was 85 and his wife 73, they were staying at the Vicarage, Highgate. The Lehmanns were away in Scotland and Germany. Anne wrote to Nina:

"Yesterday I walked to Woodlands and sat for nearly two hours in that lovely garden . . . It seemed to me as I sat there that life could offer nothing better than to live there . . . Your garden is a blaze of colour . . . Martin [the Woodlands butler] was most polite and showed me round the Kitchen Garden. We looked at the Bees and the Pigs. It is a great treat to us to sit in your garden and we shall go there very often."[2]

Nina Lehmann had loved Woodlands ever since she first rented it for her health's sake from its owner Mr Cameron in 1861. It very soon became her "dear, dear, dearest Woodlands." The house had three floors with attics. To the left of the circular drive, screened by bushes, was the coach-house; behind that was a large dovecote overlooking the rear lawn. A photograph of the front, taken in 1890, shows it heavily covered with ivy. An earlier photograph shows the back of the house in the 1860s. A balcony stretched across most of the first floor. To one side of the balcony was a conservatory.

54. Woodlands from the garden in the early 1860s

The balcony was supported on pillars which, positioned before the french windows on the ground floor, formed a kind of verandah. Here were placed garden tables and chairs giving a view across the long lawn with its tall deodar cedar trees bearing large barrel-shaped cones. Under the trees lay a small fish-pond which on occasion supplied small perch for dinner. At the bottom of the lawn was a fruit garden and orchard, giving on to more vegetable beds. What gave Nina intense pleasure was the view from her room across the trees to the white houses and the old tower of Hornsey church. Across the fields, dotted with horses, cows and sheep all peacefully grazing, on a clear day the Essex hills formed a distant background. A viewing platform in the centre of the rear roof extended the horizon.[3]

Nina was particularly struck during her first year at Woodlands by the invigorating purity of the air, which seemed to her to have almost the refreshing qualities that a glass of pure sparkling water would have to someone dying of thirst. The contrast with the London atmosphere was such that she "began to tremble at the chances of my ever being able to live contently in town again." Frederick and Nina had moved two years before into their first London house at 139 Westbourne Terrace. At Woodlands Nina delighted in the flourishing flower beds crammed with the heavy blooms of late summer: dahlias, asters, canariensis, nasturtiums, the still gorgeous roses, and a great leander bush with its pink and purple flowers.[4]

Nina and Frederick determined to buy Woodlands, and the next year Mr Cameron was persuaded to sell. Nina embarked on an orgy of decorating and refurnishing. Over the next few years extensive alterations to the house itself were carried out. The architect in charge was an F.G. Widdows, whose nephew remembered driving to Woodlands with his uncle to look over the work being carried out by the builder, Mr Colls. Frederick showed them all over the house, apologising for omitting one room where Wilkie Collins was writing. On the top landing, the builder Colls was unable to work the newly installed fire-escape. Widdows' nephew remembered Colls desperately struggling to make the ladder drop, while Frederick straightfaced shouted out in mock solemnity, "The flames are roaring and raging around us! Great Heaven, this is death!" It was irresistibly funny.[5] Anne Proctor wrote to Nina in 1866 asking if the Highgate house was finished.[6]

Frederick Lehmann came from a German artistic family. His brothers, Henri and Rudolf were painters of international repute. Henri, a pupil of Ingres and a friend of Liszt, mainly worked in Paris; Rudolf, taught by his brother and by Ingres, was equally successful in Rome, much in demand as a portrait painter. Frederick was very musical but only a gifted amateur on the violin. He remained constantly divided between his love of music, art and literature, and his determination to achieve business success. His sister's husband, Ernst Benzon, was a principal in the engineering firm of Naylor Vickers and he made Frederick a partner. For the rest of his life Frederick travelled all over the world on their business, especially to the manufacturers of America. In 1869-70 he journeyed round the world, visiting Japan and India.[7]

Nina was the daughter of Robert Chambers, the Edinburgh publisher and first editor of *Chambers' Encyclopedia* and many other well-known books of reference. Nina and Frederick had married in 1852, settling in Sheffield after a long combined business and honeymoon journey to America. Nina's sister Amelia married Frederick's brother Rudolf in 1861 and went with him to Rome until he finally settled for good in London at Campden Hill five years later. It

55. Frederick and Nina Lehmann, soon after their marriage in 1852

was their family and business connections and friendships which led to Frederick and Nina becoming acquainted with the whole strata of Victorian literary and artistic life. Their artistic gifts were handed down through their son Rudolph, Member of Parliament, an authority on rowing, and writer for *Punch*, to their grandchildren: Rosamond Lehmann, the novelist; Beatrix Lehmann, the actress; and John Lehmann, poet, editor, publisher and friend of Virginia Woolf. Liza Lehmann. the daughter of Rudolf the artist, was a famous singer and composer of *In a Persian Garden.*

It is not always possible to separate Frederick and Nina Lehmann's activities as hosts at Woodlands from their hospitality at their homes in Town, first at Westbourne Terrace, then at Bolton Street, and finally Berkeley Square. A letter from Sir George Grove, of musical dictionary fame and director of the Royal College of Music, describes a Sunday spent with the Lehmanns in 1863. After lunch at Westbourne Terrace, the company went by carriage or horseback to see Woodlands. "A very pretty neighbourhood and a very pretty new house – everything regardless of expense, but in very good taste." Then all returned to Westbourne Terrace for dinner, when Robert Browning and others joined them.[8] A year later George Eliot wrote to Nina: "I should be much easier if you would not send the carriage but would simply leave us to find the way to you for ourselves; and if I am able to come to you allow the carriage to bring us home. But I do mean to be at Highgate tomorrow if I can . . . Mr Lewes is sure – so far as one can be sure – of presenting himself to you between five and six."[9]

Perhaps for the modern reader the most interesting literary friendship the Lehmanns formed was with Charles Dickens, Frederick became quite an intimate figure in Dickens's life[10] but is rather neglected by nearly all the biographers. This is strange because of the strong links that existed formed both by friendship and marriage. Nina's Aunt Janet married William Henry Wills who assisted Dickens in editing *Household Words* and then *All The Year Round* in which he owned a quarter share. He was Dickens's confidant and righthand man, He looked after Ellen Ternan when Dickens was away, especially during Dickens's lecture tour in America in 1867. It was through Aunt Janet and Uncle Harry (as Nina called Wills) that the Lehmanns had first met Dickens, when he gave a reading at Sheffield in 1858.[11] Uncle Harry was very fond of Nina.[12] The Lehmanns must therefore have been more aware than most of Dickens's clandestine relations with the young actress he had fallen in love with, forcing his wife Catherine out of their home in 1858 after 22 years of marriage and bearing him ten children. Nina once told her nephew C.E.S. Chambers that Dickens "had actually lived for some twelve years with a well-known actress", adding in token respect of Wills's confidences about Ellen Ternan, "I forget the name."[13] Nina's son, Rudolph C. Lehmann edited the correspondence between Dickens and Wills in *Charles Dickens as Editor.*

Frederick and Nina were invited to the wedding of Dickens's daughter Katie to Charles Collins in 1860. Charles was the younger artist brother of Wilkie Collins, the novelist. Wilkie was Dickens's "dearest and most valued friend",[14] according to Forster, and he also looked upon the Lehmanns as his closest friends. Like Wilkie, Frederick (and sometimes Nina) accompanied Dickens to Paris.[15] Frederick on one of his American business trips brought back as a present for Dickens a great lovable Newfoundland dog.[16] Don, as he was called mated with Dickens's other dog Linda, of St Bernard descent, siring two huge puppies. During Dickens's last years he was generally accompanied by the four great dogs, Don, Linda and their two sons, an escort almost as formidable as a mounted picket of Household Cavalry, and a constant reminder to Dickens of his friends, the Lehmanns.[17]

Nina was seeking to improve her health at Shanklin during July 1860.[18] Frederick missed the special train laid on for Katie's wedding. Arriving at Higham station, he was told by the stationmaster that the wedding party had already passed on its way to church. Frederick decided to walk straight on to Gad's Hill, Dickens's house. He was overtaken by the returning wedding party, which included Nina's sister as one of the bridesmaids and, of course, Aunt Janet and Uncle Harry. The invitation of the Lehmanns to Katie's wedding indicates that they were, according to Forster, among "the faces that were most familiar at Gad's Hill in these later years."[19] Frederick and Nina were also included among the few very close friends who were summoned to Gad's Hill to Dickens's deathbed after his stroke in June 1870.[20]

Did Dickens ever visit Woodlands? I believe that he did, and more than once.[21] There seems to be no obvious documentary evidence as there is for his dining at the other Lehmann homes *e.g.* a letter from Grove describing Dickens as a dinner guest at Westbourne Terrace in the early summer of 1863.[22] Georgina Hogarth, Dickens's sister-in-law, Robert Chambers, Robert Browning, Sullivan, Dannreuther, Chorley, the artists E.M. Ward and Holman Hunt and many others were there the same evening, which included a musical soirée. Dickens's eldest daughter Mamie was a good friend of Nina, visiting Woodlands and accompanying her on holidays to Worthing and elsewhere.[23] It is hard to believe that her father, who had so many mutual friends with the Lehmanns, those friends to whom at this period he largely confined his ventures into society, did not, like nearly all of their circle, visit Woodlands and look at the view of Hornsey Church with its sad memories of his sister Fanny, a view which he describes in *David Copperfield*. There is, I am glad to discover, an oral tradition of Dickens being at Woodlands. The local historian F.W. Draper, who read a paper in 1947 to the Hornsey Literary Circle, said he "was actually told of his [Dickens] visits by the old inhabitant [of Hornsey] who first drew my attention to the Lehmanns." So it can be safely assumed that Dickens more than once rode up Southwood Lane between the woods and enjoyed the Lehmanns' lavish hospitality and music.

Frederick and Nina shared with Dickens concern and support for the Great Ormond Street Hospital for Sick Children. Nina's sister Ella married Dr. William Priestley (later Sir William). Dr Charles West, Great Ormond Street's founder, was a good friend of Priestley. He persuaded Mrs Priestley to join his group of devoted "Lady Visitors" who gave voluntary service to his hospital. In Great Ormond Street's archives can be found the confidential reports written by some of the Lady Visitors on conditions and nursing care in the wards; Mrs Priestley's are among the most interesting. In 1869 Great Ormond Street opened Cromwell House, Highgate, as its Country and Convalescent Branch. Frederick and Nina had been regular donors and subscribers to Great Ormond Street and a year or so after Cromwell House was opened as a children's hospital, they increased their donations considerably. Frederick donated £50 and Nina increased her annual subscription to five guineas, quite large amounts for those days. No doubt it was the opening of a a branch in Highgate which had called forth their generosity, but possibly there was another and more personal reason. Dickens had died in the summer of 1870. Perhaps the Lehmanns increased their support for Great Ormond Street as a tribute to their friend's association with the children's hospital he had loved and done so much for. They would not be alone: for the three years after Dickens's death, annual donations of £5 were made to the hospital "In Memoriam, Charles Dickens". The donor's initials "H.F.C." hide the identity of Henry Fothergill Chorley, friend of the Lehmanns and of Dickens who was very fond of him. Chorley's *In Memoriam* donations ended only with his own death in 1872.[24]

The lovable and eccentric Chorley, music critic and reviewer in *The Athenaeum* for many years, was often at Woodlands. He accompanied Frederick on many European journeys, meeting Pauline Viardot, Frederick's artist brother Henri, Gounod, Meyerbeer, and Turgenev.[25] He had long admired Nina's sister Amelia: but in the end she married Rudolf, Frederick's other artist brother. This left Chorley a rather lonely man. He consoled himself by giving elaborate dinner parties and accepting the frequent invitations of his friends. With the years, however, he indulged rather too freely in the wine bottle, becoming more eccentric than ever, but still retaining his not inconsiderable charm and good nature. Once, staying at Woodlands, during dinner he became convinced that he was in his own home, and acted the host, ringing the bell, addressing Martin the Lehmann's butler as Drury, the name of Chorley's own man. The next day a neighbour of the Lehmanns, a Mr Bockett from The Firs (the large house up the road, nearer to Muswell Hill) was invited to dinner. Chorley's delusion that he was at his own house returned. He of course, knew all the other guests, Wilkie Collins, Charles Reade, Anne Proctor and the rest, but he had never met

Bockett and was considerably puzzled by his presence. But he was greatly taken with him, pressing all the dishes upon him and plying him with champagne, much to the amusement of Nina and her guests. After the meal, Chorley said he would certainly ask Mr. Bockett to dine again as he was very nice![26]

Nina was very fond of Chorley and remembered him with affection. When Wilkie Collins died in 1889, and Woodlands had long been given up, she wrote to Frederick: "Wilkie was almost the very last link left that bound us to the glory of departed days. Dickens, Lytton, Houghton, Wilkie, Charles Collins, poor old Chorley – it seems like a former life, not on this earth at all."[27]

It was Wilkie Collins who, as John Lehmann writes, "became the most attached, the most closely enmeshed" in Nina and Frederick's lives.[28] He was their most frequent guest at Woodlands and elsewhere. He became their children's favourite grown-up, taking them to the pantomime, helping the boys with their homework for Highgate School, and telling them exciting stories and memories of the great prize fighter Tom Sayers and Tom's marathon contest with the American Jack Heenan for the first world championship.[29] Frederick, with Augustus Egg, Henry Buller, Edward Ward and Holman Hunt, was one of the small select male gathering at Wilkie's Harley Street rooms, who celebrated the immense success of *The Woman in White*.[30]

56. Woodlands from the road in the late 1880s

Nine years after, in 1869, Wilkie stayed at Woodlands while writing the greater part of his novel *Man and Wife*. The Lehmanns gave him a quiet secluded room, a bedroom and meals in company or in solitude as he required. The family adjusted their day around him, making sure he had quiet and peace to work (everyone was told to walk softly past his room when he was writing), and society in the evening or at other times when he wanted amusement and diversion. Wilkie worked away at his novel at Woodlands at intervals until 1870.[31] Its completion coincided with very sad news. Wilkie wrote "I finished *Man and Wife* yesterday – fell asleep from sheer fatigue – and was awakened to hear the news of Dickens's death."[32] *Man and Wife* was dedicated to the Lehmanns.

Over the years Wilkie and the Lehmanns had been much together. Frederick was asked for advice on Wilkie's sometimes involved finances and offered him help. He was well aware of Wilkie's secrets, of his dependence on opium. When they were together in Switzerland, Frederick had to go to four chemists in turn to get legally the large dose of Laudanum that Wilkie needed – he suffered agonies from gout and rheumatism. Futhermore, Frederick knew of Wilkie's two mistresses, Caroline Graves and Martha Rudd. It is possible that Nina also knew of them, and may have, despite the strict social code preventing wives from visiting the women of irregular liaisons, actually called on Martha Rudd. She was broadminded, she knew of Dickens's supposedly secret affair with Ellen Ternan, and she was very friendly with George Eliot and G.H. Lewes, another famous literary unmarried couple. Wilkie wrote numerous letters to Nina, whom he addressed as "Padrona". When Frederick was away on business all over the world, Wilkie would write him news of Nina. One of his very last letters to Frederick ended, "My grateful love to the best and dearest of Padronas." His last unfinished novel, *Blind Love*, was based on a true story told to him by a friend of the Lehmanns.[33]

It would be far beyond the confines of this chapter to relate stories about all of the Lehmanns' other famous friends, many of whom visited Woodlands. Their names would form an honours roll of literature, art and music. One was Arthur Sullivan who set Adelaide Proctor's *The Lost Chord* to music; another was Bulwer Lytton who was much taken with the Lehmmans' little daughter. Sir Edwin Landseer, the painter of *The Stag at Bay*, was once driven to Woodlands in the Lord Chief Justice's carriage, and quarrelled bitterly with him over Shakespeare's accuracy in describing a stag weeping "big round tears" in *As You Like It*; the Lord Chief Justice, enraged by this slur on the genius of Shakespeare, refused to take Landseer back to town, so the eminent painter had to beg an uncomfortable journey home in a fellow guest's overcrowded conveyance; it was a Sunday and no cab could be ordered.[34] Frederick vainly tried to make peace after this absurd quarrel between two of his eminent guests.

Robert Browning was one of the Lehmanns' most steadfast friends and a most welcome guest. They first became acquainted a year or two after Browning returned to London following Elizabeth Barrett Browning's death. He took a house in Warwick Avenue, not much more than ten minutes' walk from the Lehmanns in Westbourne Terrace. Frederick and Nina were among the very first friends that Browning made after the secluded period of his widowerhood. He was much struck by the Lehmann family having originated in Hamburg, the native town of his maternal grandmother, Mrs Wiedemann.[35] Like Wilkie Collins, Browning soon became very fond of Nina and her two little boys. In June 1863 he offered the eldest boy, Rudolph, the Italian pony belonging to his own son, Pen. But Rudolph was only seven, half Pen's age, far too young to ride a spirited Sardinian pony much larger than the usual Shetland or New Forest ponies. Browning and Rudolph developed a special friendship. Rudolph recalled nearly a half a century later how the great poet "had the happy knack of making a small boy feel that it gave him real pleasure to shake that small boy by the hand or to pat him on the back and talk to him about the little interests of his life." Frederick became, according to Browning, "Pen's very earliest patron" when he bought one of Pen's first paintings. Rosamond Lehmann remembered vividly the enormous canvas of an elderly French curé enjoying his liqueurs and coffee dominating her father Rudolph's house at Bourne End.[36]

Again like Wilkie Collins, Browning wrote many letters to Frederick and Nina. One addressed to her in July 1867 refers to his unpunctuality in arriving at Woodlands. It ends "Thank you for your beautiful flowers – I can give nothing in return – unless you bear with a photograph? Yes, you will, and here it shall be. Goodbye over again, dear friend. I am ever – so believe it – in all affection, yours."[37] Frederick bought an early wax cylinder gramophone. In April 1889 Browning was persuaded to record his *How They Brought the Good News from Ghent to Aix*. The cylinder still exists, a wonderful human link with the poet, whose memory broke down after the first few lines and can still be heard expressing his amazement at forgetting his own verses.[38] Frederick's brother Rudolf drew and painted Robert and Elizabeth Browning several times. His last portrait of Browning was made in 1883 and eventually given to the National Portrait Gallery.[39]

The long enduring friendship between Browning and the Lehmann family owed not a little to a mutual love of music. Browning attended every concert of importance when he was in London.[40] Music was very important to him. In some of his best known poems he celebrates the power and complexity of music.

"What? Those lesser thirds so plaintive, sixths diminished, sigh on sigh . . .
Hark, the dominant's persistence till it must be answered to!
So, an octave struck the answer . . . "[41]

Frederick, who had the ability to become a concert violinist, and Nina, who had a remarkable gift for the piano, played much chamber music with their talented friends, both amateurs and professionals, including the great violinist Joachim. George Eliot was quite a good pianist;[42] one year Frederick went every Monday evening to her house off Regent's Park, and played with her all the violin and piano sonatas of Mozart and Beethoven.[43] Browning certainly heard much Beethoven played by the Lehmanns and their friends at Woodlands and elsewhere. His greatest poem *The Ring and the Book* was published in 1868-69. Was he thinking of the Lehmanns and their musical evenings at Woodlands, when after over 21,000 lines of blank verse, he made the final dozen or so lines begin

"So note by note, bring music from your mind,
Deeper than ever e'en Beethoven dived"?

The Lehmanns probably remained at Woodlands until about 1875. (The Great Ormond Street subscription list amended their address from "Woodlands" to 15 Berkeley Square around this time.[44]) The rebuilt Alexandra Palace and the railway line from Highgate were reopened that year,[45] – a warning that Woodlands would no longer be a secluded and peaceful rural retreat. The Woodlands estate was sold in 1890, and developed by a Mr R. Metherell. By 1905 he was advertising houses in Woodland Rise for sale from £550 or for rent from £55 a year.[46]

When Frederick died in 1891, the great singer Pauline Viardot wrote from France: "My darling Nina, is it not dreadful to lose one's true and only real companion of life? Oh, I know that so well, I have felt it . . . I send you all the love and sympathy of a faithful heart."[47] Nina decided to build a new house in Portobello, near Edinburgh her childhood home. Despite her poor health, she lived on into the new century, dying at her son's house at Bourne End.[48]

At sunset or in the early mornings she so loved, her memory comes easily to mind in Highgate and Queen's Woods, where the paths and groves retain something of the atmosphere of what the Woodlands grounds and gardens must have been like in their glory.

Jules Kosky

Sources:
Rudolph C. Lehmann, *Memories of Half a Century, A Record of Friendship* (1908); John F. Lehmann, *Ancestors and Friends* (1962); Rudolf Lehmann, *An Artist's Reminiscences* (1894) and William M. Clarke, *The Secret Life of Wilkie Collins* (1988), have been my main sources, supplemented by the standard lives of Charles Dickens and of Robert Browning. I have also drawn upon records and papers at the Great Ormond Street Hospital for Children and at Dickens House, Doughty Street.

For local Hornsey history and for details of the Woodlands Estate Sale with its unique 1890 plan of Woodlands, I am greatly indebted to Jack Whitehead, *The Growth of Muswell Hill* (1995), and David E.D. Freeman, *Looking at Muswell Hill* (1984). Dr Joan Schwitzer also made several valuable suggestions.

References

1. Jack Whitehead, pp. 97-100

2. R.C. Lehmann, pp. 172-73

3. John Lehmann, pp. 160, ill. opp. p. 177, pp. 226-228

4. *Ibid.*, pp. 226-228

5. R.C. Lehmann, pp. 106-8

6. *Ibid.*, p. 164

7. *Ibid.*, pp. 2-3; John Lehmann p.141 *et seq.*

8. John Lehmann, p. 216

9. R.C. Lehmann, p. 134

10. John Lehmann, p. 164

11. John Lehmann, p. 162; John Forster, *Life of Charles Dickens* (1911), vol. 2, p. 249

12. John Lehmann, p. 188

13. Letter of C.E.S. Chambers 21 Jan. 1934; Gladys Storey papers, Dickens House, Doughty Street, WC1

14. Forster, vol. 2, p. 82

15. John Lehmann, pp. 164 & 189

16. R.C. Lehmann, p. 102

17. Forster, vol. 2, p. 241

18. R.C. Lehmann, p. 193

19. Forster, vol. 2, p. 263

20. John Lehmann,p. 230; Peter Ackroyd, *Dickens* (1990), p. 1071

21. Fred Kaplan in his biography of Dickens, *Dickens, A biography* (1988), also thinks Dickens was often at Woodlands.

22. John Lehmann, p. 216

23. *Ibid.*, p. 167

24. Lady Eliza Priestley, *Story of a Lifetime* (1908); Jules Kosky, *Mutual Friends. Charles Dickens and Great Ormond Street Children's Hospital* (1989); various papers and records and Annual Reports for 1861-1927 held in the archives of Great Ormond Street Hospital for Children.

25. John Lehmann, p. 205

26. R.C. Lehmann, pp. 232-34

27. John Lehmann, p. 233

28. *Ibid.*, p. 173

29. W.M. Clarke, pp. 124-5

30. *Ibid.*, pp. 99-100

31. *Ibid.*, pp. 124-5

32. *Ibid.*, p. 128

33. *Ibid.*, p. 176; R.C. Lehmann, p. 76

34. R.C. Lehmann, pp. 256-59

35. Rudolf Lehmann, p. 223

36. R.C. Lehmann,pp. 110-125; John Lehmann, pp. 168-9; Rosamond Lehmann, *The Swan in the Evening*

37. R.C. Lehmann, p. 119

38. Irvine & Honam, *The Ring, the Book and the Poet* (1975) p. 513

39. Rudolf Lehmann, p. 223

40. Maisie Ward, *The Two Robert Brownings* (1969), p. 163

41. Robert Browning, *A Toccata of Galuppi's*

42. F. Karl, *George Eliot* (1995), pp. 25 & 460

43. R.C. Lehmann, p. 132

44. Records and papers, Great Ormond Street Hospital

45. D.E.D. Freeman, p. 29

46. Whitehead, p. 101

47. John Lehmann, p. 233

48. *Ibid.*, p. 277

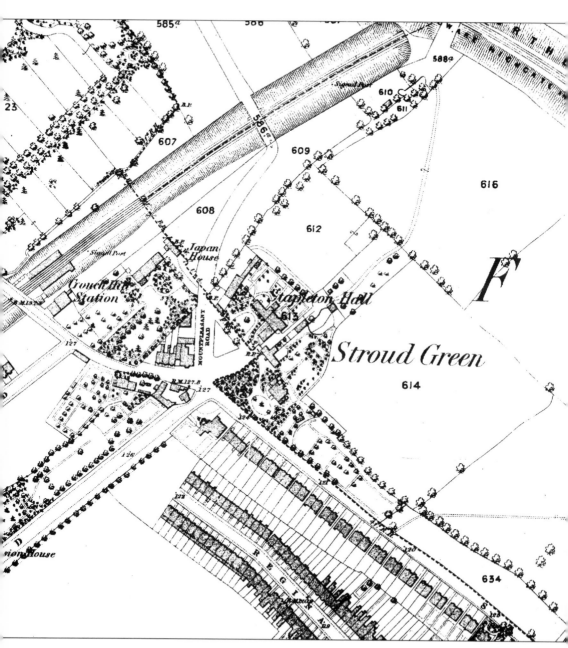

57. Stapleton Hall and the farmland, 1870.
Residential development was nearly all on the south-west (Islington) side.

Preserving a heritage:
The case of Stapleton Hall

Stapleton Hall, Stroud Green, situated in present day Stapleton Hall Road, and close to Hornsey's boundary with Islington, is one of the oldest buildings in Haringey. It is still in use after having existed in different guises over the centuries, and is not a "lost" house but more a disguised one. Its history reflects the history of the whole area.

The Stapleton Hall estate would appear to have been mentioned in Domesday Book:

"In Stanestaple the canons have four hides. The arable land is the two-plough lands, and so now; and there are seven villeins who hold this land under the canons, and two cottars. Pasture for the cattle of the vill. Wood to feed one hundred and fifty swine, and ten shillings rent. In total value it is worth 50s, when they received it the like. In the time of King Edward 60s. This land has formed and is now parcel of the demesne of the Church of St. Paul."[1]

In the Middle Ages a house called Stanestaple was the residence of the Steward of the Manor of Hornsey.[2] But we do not know enough about land-holding in this district to be able positively to identify "Stanestaple" with the later Stapleton Hall estate.

A house was mentioned on the site of Stapleton Hall in 1577. By 1609 it was re-built or extended by Sir Thomas Stapleton, whose initials and the date were carved on the datestone above the door and on the internal panelling.[3] The Stapletons were an old Oxfordshire family and like so many others with money to invest, when the New World was opened up became plantation owners in the West Indies.[4] The baronetcy was created in 1679 when Sir William Stapleton was appointed Governor of the Leeward Islands and became the first baronet.[5] The Stapletons were still in residence in 1735[6] but at some point during the next 30 years they ceased to live there. Who the estate owners were after their departure has so far not been discovered.

In 1765 the house was licensed as the Stapleton Hall Tavern,[7] and was also known as The Green Man.[8] For many years it had the inscription above the door: "Ye are welcome all / To Stapleton Hall". This was the heyday of the London pleasure gardens, and Stapleton Hall attracted many visitors to its grounds with their rural surroundings and the cakes and ale. It was an attractive place of entertainment for those on a day out from the capital. In London itself the taverns were doing a roaring trade as the headquarters of various clubs that were being founded by gentlemen in the

58. Enamel badge of the 'Corporation of Stroud Green', depicting St George and the dragon with the words "Justice, Truth and Friendship". The reverse is inscribed "The Right Worshipful Sir Thomas Legg, Knight of the Oak, Elected Mayor of the Corporation of Stroud Green on Monday, July 26th, 1773".

arts and professions. There were clubs to suit all tastes, from sporting to literary and satirical. One particular satirical club parodied the grand ceremonies and feasts of the City of London and styled itself The Ancient Corporation of Stroud Green.[9] It elected its officers and servants, who were given splendid badges of office.[10] What could be more amusing than to have such a band of officers to administer an obscure hamlet on the outskirts of London? During the winter they held their meetings in various taverns in the City and in Islington, and in the summer trooped out in a body to Stapleton Hall. Such a visit, on June 6th, 1769, is recorded thus:

On Monday last the Mayor, Aldermen, and Recorder of Stroud Green, assisted by the Sheriffs, held a Court of Conservancy, according to ancient custom, at the Green Man, on Stroud Green, known by the name of Stapleton Hall; where an elegant entertainment was provided by the Mayor, and many loyal toasts were drunk in honour of His Majesty's birthday. After dinner they returned to their Mansion House, The Crown, in the Lower Street, Islington; and the evening concluded with a ball, and every demonstration of joy suitable to the happy occasion.[11]

This club seems to have flourished between 1750 and 1780 after which it fades into memory.

By the late eighteenth century Stapleton Hall had become a private residence again. In 1796, a Mr Lucas held the western portion of the estate. He was succeeded by John Lucas in 1808 who was still the owner in 1822 but in 1823 William Lucas had taken over. John Lucas was one of the subscribers to Nelson's *History of Islington*, published in 1811, and his ownership of eighty acres of land is mentioned by the author. During the occupancy of William Lucas alterations were made to the house to make it a more suitable residence for a gentleman farmer:

59. Stapleton Hall and farmhouse, *c.* 1820

Mr William Lucas, a late occupant of the premises, converted it into two houses, one of which has a handsome stuccoed front, and wears quite a modern appearance. [12]

Stroud Green had always been a sparsely populated area round the lane dividing Islington and Hornsey, and the first urbanisation occurred on the Islington side. By the time of the 1841 Census, Stapleton Hall was still the only building standing between Stroud Green and Manor House, Seven Sisters Road. It comprised the original Hall and a seventeenth century barn being used as a stable, and Stapleton Hall farmhouse. The Lucases no longer lived there, but the estate was enfranchised (converted from copyhold to freehold tenure) in 1856 and owned by Joseph Lucas between 1861 and 1876.[13] (Joseph Lucas subsequently sold land in the vicinity of what was to become Stapleton Hall Road, Victoria Road and Mount Pleasant Road, to Charles Turner,[14] of whom more is to come.) In 1841, with the Lucases as owners, the occupant of Stapleton Hall was a merchant called Richard Williams, with his wife, two sons and a daughter and four servants. The farm side was occupied by John Wells, his wife, three grown up children and one servant. The stable, or probably the hayloft above, as was often the custom in farmhouses and outbuildings, was home to a farm hand called Breen Miller, his two sons and three other labourers. Ten years later, the Census lists only John Wells, his wife, one of his sons and a grand-daughter. The main part of Stapleton Hall was presumably unoccupied.

By 1861, with the advent of Charles Turner as the farmer, the internal arrangements at Stapleton Hall would seem to have changed, and the big house to be once more the home of the person running the estate – as in the seventeenth century with the Stapletons. The Census of 1861 lists Charles Turner as the occupant and describes him as a "Farmer of 226 acres employing 8 men and a boy". He lived with his wife Dinah, daughter Mary Ann and two servants, Sarah Jones from Wales and Sarah Reed from Edmonton. Thomas Wareham from Norton in Suffolk was employed as a carter. (Two other names are also listed: R.E. Robinson, described as a barrister and member of the Stock Exchange, and David Roughhy, a Russia broker. Who were they? Guests, lodgers or relatives?) "Next door' (i.e. in the former farmhouse) was only a middle aged couple consisting of a jeweller and his wife. By 1871 they had gone and a music publisher was living there. By 1881 the farmhouse was unoccupied and Lucas's new wing was surplus to requirements. Charles Turner had re-established single occupancy and reclaimed the Hall for a working farmer.[15]

Turner was born at Hornsey Lane Farm on 13th March 1815 and came from a family that had lived and worked in Hornsey for generations. His father James Turner (1759-1829) and his unusually long-lived mother Frances Turner (1774-1874) are both buried in Hornsey churchyard.[16] His wife Dinah, who was born in June 1809 at Leek in Staffordshire, and some of her ancestors feature in the novel *God and the wedding dress* by Marjorie Bowen.[17] Charles was an enterprising man and obtained extra farmland by renting part of Hornsey Wood and clearing and levelling it.[18] By 1871 it had been sold to form part of the new Finsbury Park, opened two years before, and the acreage of Stapleton Hall was down to 120 acres but as a dairy farmer Charles Turner still had employment for eight labourers.

He left his mark on the political life of Hornsey. He took part in many aspects of local politics, being first a member of the Highways Board and then the Hornsey Local Board from its foundation. As the Stapleton Hall estate became increasingly threatened by the march of bricks and mortar, Turner and his colleagues were struggling with an area that still possessed poor roads and primitive sanitation despite urbanisation. A perennial problem arose from the fact that the area round the farm straddled the border between Hornsey and Islington; agreement between neighbouring local authorities has always been notoriously difficult to achieve.

The Census of 1881 shows that Charles, now in his late sixties, had disposed of his cows, for he was described as a "hay dealer" and no longer as a farmer. His wife and a maid were the only other residents of Stapleton Hall, and he may have organised the hay-cutting by arrangement with a contractor. In 1886 nearby Womersley House on Mount Pleasant (built for the West End draper Peter Robinson) came on to the market. Charles and

Dinah left their old home and moved there with their daughter Mary Ann, her husband John Halsey and their children.

The open land south east of Stapleton Hall extending to Finsbury Park station (as shown on the 1873 Ordnance Survey map, surveyed 1862-9) was built over with terraced housing. In 1888 the old Hall, now surrounded by a new urban population, was leased to the local Conservative Party for use as a club. The adjoining barn and outbuildings appear to have been leased and rented separately to various people over the years, while the 'new' wing was demolished by c. 1893.[19] Charles was a lifelong Conservative, actively campaigning for the party well into old age. He was also Treasurer of the building fund and then the first churchwarden to be appointed at Holy Trinity church, Stroud Green. After he moved house he worshipped at St Mary's Church, Hornsey Rise.

Dinah Turner died in 1891 and "a vote of condolence was passed by the directors of the Stroud Green Conservative Club, and on the day of the funeral the blue ensign on the flag staff at Stapleton Hall was flying half mast."[20]

The following year Charles died, at Womersley House, and was buried in Highgate Cemetery. He was hailed as the "father of the district, and to a great extent as father of the [Conservative] party in the district."[21] He died a rich man. His executors and subsequent trustees of his property were his daughter Mary Ann Halsey, Alfred Thomas Tubbs – a fellow Conservative and churchwarden, and Edwin West. What was once Stapleton Hall Farm had now become:

My freehold estate situate in Stapleton Hall Road and Victoria Road and abutting on Mount Pleasant Road which I purchased some time since of a Mr. Joseph Lucas and Mr Hodson not including the house and premises now leased to Mr Tanner hereinafter otherwise disposed of but including the premises known as Stapleton Hall and the buildings, barns, sheds or outbuildings held therewith or belonging thereto and also the adjoining or out buildings now let or in the occupation of Mr Taylor, Mr Anderson and Mr Gurney.[22]

In 1896, Charles Turner, the last farmer of Stapleton Hall, and his wife were commemorated by a memorial window depicting Faith, Hope and Charity erected in St Mary's, Hornsey Rise.[23]

The Census of 1891 records the name of the Conservative Club steward, Samuel Dugall, and his wife and young family, at Stapleton Hall. A glimpse inside is given by a visitor who attended a garden party there in 1909:

In the old buildings the famous oak panelled room (in which are to be seen the initials of Sir Thomas Stapleton and his wife, together with the date '1609') is now the

60. Front view of Stapleton Hall when used as Stroud Green Conservative Club, *c.* 1911

club reading room, supplied with all the latest newspapers and periodicals, most comfortably furnished and excellently lighted.[24]

As the years went by the buildings became expensive to maintain and a photograph of 1911 shows them in a dilapidated state.[25] The outbuildings were even worse and in 1930 a Mrs Blinco who rented the barn applied for a rate reduction.

Mr Hinton on behalf of the owner, said the buildings were originally cow-sheds of Stapleton Hall and were about 300 years old. The cost of repairs was high, and last year £45 had been spent in this way.

There were also workshops and two garages on the site.[26] The exterior of the Hall was described in 1933 as:

An old-fashioned building, having a cement facing, entrance porch and a modern tiled roof . . . Near by the house is an ancient barn with a weather-beaten tiled roof, and in front a circular drive, studded with trees and bushes, and at the back is an extensive garden.[27]

By 1935 the barn was pronounced unsafe, its walls and roof being patched with corrugated iron, and Hornsey Borough Council ordered its demolition. The barn was being used by Mr T. Seed who owned the adjoining timber yard and was "intending to have a new steel structure erected in its place." In fact the barn's timbers were remarkably sound and the demolition was an instance of officially sanctioned vandalism. Many interesting features were destroyed. The roof tiles were all hand made and oak pegged. Old wallpaper was found between 300-year-old rafters. The local paper noticed that at one end of the barn stone cobbles showed that it had been used as a stable. There were wooden mangers and iron rings for halters in the walls . . . "Hornsey's oldest of the old has gone."[28] The use as a stable reflects the change that had taken place over the centuries, from mixed farming including corn crops for the storage of which the barn would have been built originally, to dairying and hay cropping which the barn was converted to serve.

In 1962 Stapleton Hall itself was in danger of demolition. It was owned by a Miss Tubbs who lived abroad. The lease on the Club had only two years left to run, and a planning application for demolition and redevelopment had been submitted to the Council. Fortunately the building was saved when the Club raised the money for its purchase.[29]

The latest episode in the Hall's history came in 1989 when it was acquired for redevelopment as modern apartments by Lovell Homes. It was converted into twenty-six properties in which original features were preserved;

In Stapleton Hall itself, the old staircase remains have been carefully renovated. Original fireplaces are featured in certain apartments, although with reproduction mantels and surrounds. The ancient timber framing, joists and beams are exposed and 17th century panelling has been saved as a unique reminder of the house's origins.[30]

Another relic of the past came when a letter dated 1853 was discovered during building work. It was from Martha Hazell to her ten year old son Walter; her husband Jonathan was a jeweller and the family were the tenants of Stapleton Hall farmhouse at that time.[31]

Stapleton Hall although greatly altered in function has been preserved. Its presence in a modern housing complex is a reminder of the enduring legacy of the rural past to the townscape of twentieth century North London.

Roy Hidson

References

1. Lloyd, *Highgate* (1888)

2. Ian Murray, *Haringey before our time* (HHS, 1993)

3. *VCH*, vol. vi, p.147

4. *HHS Bulletin* No. 34 (1993), p. 26

5. Debrett's *Illustrated Baronetage* (1990)

6. Terrier of Brownswood Manor, mentioning Sir William Stapleton's grounds; MS 20686, Gdl.

7. *VCH*, vol. vi, p. 147

8. L. Wagner, *More London inns and taverns* (1926)

9. *The North Londoner*, 13 August 1870

10. Victoria & Albert Museum

11. S. Lewis, *The history and topography of the parish of St. Mary, Islington* (1842)

12. *Ibid.*

13. *VCH*, vol. vi, p. 147

14. Will of Charles Turner; SH

15. The preceding two paragraphs are based on the Enumerators Returns, Census of Hornsey, 1841-1881; PRO

16. P. Dallman and others, "Monumental inscriptions . . . St Mary, Hornsey" (1987), unpublished ts., HHS archives

17. Published 1938. In Islington Local Studies Library

18. *HJ*, 25 January 1892

19. *Cf.* 25" O.S. maps, 1870 and 1894

20. *HJ*, 31 January 1891

21. *HJ*, 25 January 1892

22. Will of Charles Turner

23. Islington Local Studies Library

24. I*slington Daily Gazette*, 15 July 1909

25. In H.Lib.

26. *HJ*, 11 April 1930

27. *HJ*, 12 May 1933

28. *HJ*, 17 May 1935

29. *HJ*, 20 July and 23 November 1962

30. Lovell Homes brochure, 1989

31. *HJ*, 14 June 1990

Appendix

The document printed here, translated from the original Latin text, is a record of legal transactions concerning an estate studied in this book, Winchester Hall, Highgate. It is an example of an extensive series of such records in the Hornsey Manor Court Books, from the late seventeeth century onwards, to be found in the Guildhall Library, London EC2, and is included as representative of hitherto little used sources, at the Guildhall and elsewhere, that are available for the history of individual properties.

Note: The date is before the revision of the calendar in 1752 when New Year's Day was moved from March 25th to January 1st, so that '13th March 1709' was by modern reckoning 13 March 1710

Guildhall Library MS 10,465/25
Diocese of London Manors. Court Book for 1709-10

"*Haringey alias Harnsey*

The Court Baron of the Honourable and reverend Father in Christ for the time being, Henry, by Divine Permission Bishop of London., Lord of the aforesaid Manor, held at Highgate for the aforesaid Manor before William Sayle, Gentleman, Deputy Steward of Francis Dickens, Esquire, Chief Steward there, on the Thirteenth day of March in the Year of our Lord, 1709, and in the Ninth Year of the Reign of our Lady Anne, by the grace of God, Queen of Great Britain, France and Ireland, Defender of the faith etc.

Homage of the Lord there Francis Coverdale, John Bayes
　　　　　　　　　Thomas Monk, [?] Swain

The Fine, the Perquisite of this Court　　　0:10 0

Admission of Lewis

At this Court it is Found by the Homage, by the relation of the Deputy Steward aforesaid, that on the seventeenth day of August in the Year of our Lord 1709, and in the Eighth Year of the Reign of our Lady Anne, by the grace of God, Queen of Great Britain, France and Ireland, Defender of the faith etc. there came before William Sayle, Gentleman, Deputy Steward of Francis Dickens, Esquire, Chief Steward of the aforesaid Manor, Robert Bumpsted of Bishops Hall in the parish of Stepney, in the County of Middlesex, Gentleman, and Elizabeth, his wife (formerly Elizabeth Cooke And the same Elizabeth was first solely and secretly examined by the aforesaid Deputy Steward) and surrendered into the hands of the Lord of the aforesaid Manor, By the rod, By the hands and acceptance of the aforesaid Deputy Steward, according to the custom of the aforesaid Manor, All that Customary Messuage or Mansion House previously in the possession of Susanna Winch, widow, and now in the possession of Thomas Lewis of London, Merchant, and Six Acres of pasture to the same belonging and adjoining, together with outhouses, Stables, Barns, Gardens, Orchards and Appurtenances thereto belonging. Also all that Customary Messuage or Tenement previously in the possession of [name omitted] Merrall and now in the occupation of Peter Smith, Gardener, and also four Acres of pasture to the same belonging, with the Appurtenances, situate and being in Highgate, within the Manor aforesaid, together with all and singular the Appurtenances to the aforesaid premises belonging or in any otherwise Appertaining (all which premises the same Elizabeth, By the name of Elizabeth Cooke of London, widow, surrendered into the hands of the Lord of the aforesaid Manor to the use of George Lisons of Lincolnes Inn, in the County of Middlesex, Esquire, for Assurance of the payment of one Hundred and twenty pounds or thereabouts of lawful money, together with interest for the same. And also the same Elizabeth, By the aforesaid name surrendered the aforesaid premises to the use of Thomas Mulso of the Inner Temple, London, Esquire, for the payment of the sum of one Hundred pounds of like money, together with interest) With all the Right, estate, title, interest, Equity of redemption, Claim and Demand whatsoever of the same aforesaid Robert Bumpsted and Elizabeth, his wife, of, in and to the aforesaid premises or any parcel thereof To the use and behoof of the aforesaid Thomas Lewis, his heirs and Assigns for and during the term of the natural life of the same aforesaid Elizabeth, according to the Custom of the aforesaid Manor, Subject however to the payment of the separate sums of money abovementioned Whereupon there comes here into Court the aforesaid Thomas Lewis And he begs to be admitted to the aforesaid premises To whom the Lord, By his Deputy Steward aforesaid, Grants seisin thereof By the rod, To Have and to Hold the Messuages, Tenements and Hereditaments and all and singular the aforementioned premises, with all and singular their Appurtenances to the aforesaid Thomas Lewis, his heirs and Assigns, for and during the term of the natural life of the aforesaid Elizabeth Bumpsted, Subject however to the payment of the aforesaid money, of the Lord, By the rod, at the will of the Lord, according to the Custom of the Manor aforesaid By the rent and services previously owed and accustomed And for having such estate there in he Gives to the Lord for a fine as etc and he is thus Admitted Tenant. And he does fealty to the Lord.

[*Translator's Note:* In the margin, opposite to the lines containing the information regarding the rent, is written 0:18:8 and 0:14:8 which presumably are the rents of the two properties]

Lewis to Rogers

And immediately the aforesaid Thomas Lewis, in open Court, surrendered into the hands of the Lord of the aforesaid Manor, By the rod, By the hands and acceptance of the aforesaid Deputy Steward, according to the Custom of the aforesaid Manor, the Messuage or Mansion House aforesaid now in the possession of the same Thomas Lewis and Six Acres of pasture to the same belonging and adjoining, together with outhouses, Stables, Barns, Gardens, Orchards and Appurtenances thereto belonging. Also the aforesaid Customary Messuage or Tenement now in the occupation of Peter Smith, Gardener, and also the aforesaid four Acres of pasture to the same belonging, with the Appurtenances, situate and being in Highgate, within the aforesaid Manor, together with all and singular the Appurtenances to the aforesaid premises belonging or in any other wise Appurtaining With all the right, Estate, title, interest, Claim and Demand whatsoever of the same aforesaid Thomas Lewis of, in and to the aforesaid premises or any parcel thereof To the use and behoof of Thomas Rogers of the parish of St. James, Westminster, in the County of Middlesex, Innholder, his heirs and Assigns, for and during the term of the natural life of the aforesaid Elizabeth Bumpsted, Providing always and on condition that if the aforesaid Thomas Lewis, his heirs, Executor or Administrator, shall pay or cause to be paid to the aforesaid Thomas Rogers, his Executors, Administrators or Assigns, the full and just sum of two Hundred and fifteen pounds of lawful money of Great Britain in the manner and form following (that is to say, the sum of one Hundred and ten pounds, part thereof on the Twenty fourth day of December now next following And the sum of one Hundred and five pounds, the rest thereof, on the Twenty fourth day of December then next following And which will be in the Year of our Lord, 1711, without deceit or delay (the same sum of two Hundred and fifteen pounds being part and parcel of the money mentioned in the same Condition and Obligation bearing date the Seventeeth day of August now last past, in which the aforesaid Thomas Lewis stands Bound to the aforesaid Thomas Rogers in the penal Sum of Sixty pounds for the Payment of the money mentioned in the said Condition) Then the present Surrender shall be void and of no effect, otherwise it shall remain in full strength and face, according to the Custom of the aforesaid Manor"

Index:

Illustrations of persons and places are indicated by page numbers in italics